Reemployment Bonuses
in the
Unemployment Insurance System

Reemployment Bonuses in the Unemployment Insurance System

Evidence from Three Field Experiments

Philip K. Robins and Robert G. Spiegelman
Editors

2001

W.E. Upjohn Institute for Employment Research
Kalamazoo, Michigan

Library of Congress Cataloging-in-Publication Data

Reemployment bonuses in the unemployment insurance system : evidence from three
field experiments / Philip K. Robins and Robert G. Spiegelman, editors.
  p. cm.
  Includes bibliographical references and index.
  ISBN 0–88099–225–5 (pbk. : alk. paper)—ISBN 0–88099–226–3 (cloth : alk. paper)
    1. Insurance, Unemployment—United States—States—Case studies. 2. Welfare
  recipients—United States—States—Case studies. 3. Bonus system—United
  States—States—Case studies. 4. Insurance, Unemployment—Illinois. 5. Insurance,
  Unemployment—Pennsylvania. 6. Insurance, Unemployment—Washington (State).
  I. Robins, Philip K. II. Spiegelman, Robert G.

HD7096.U5 R35 2001
331.13'77—dc21

2001026848

The facts presented in this study and the observations and viewpoints expressed are
the sole responsibility of the authors. They do not necessarily represent positions of
the W.E. Upjohn Institute for Employment Research.

Cover design by J.R. Underhill.
Index prepared by Leoni Z. McVey.
Printed in the United States of America.

01 02 03 04 05 06 8 7 6 5 4 3 2 1

Contents

List of Figures

List of Tables

Acknowledgments

The three experiments that underlie the analytic content of this book were each conducted as trial programs within the state unemployment insurance (UI) systems. Therefore, considerable credit for the operational success of the experiments must be attributed to the staffs of the federal and state agencies who conducted the experimental programs and provided much of the data used in the analyses.

The Illinois experiment was funded and administered by the Illinois Department of Employment Security (IDES). Sally Ward, director of IDES, gave unstinting support to the effort. Mary Glusak directed the field operations and was responsible for its smooth functioning. The experiment was conducted in 22 Job Service offices, which could not have occurred without the support of the IDES regional managers, who authorized use of agency personnel to carry out the operational tasks. Special thanks also to the Job Service staff personnel who carried out the tasks of enrolling eligible claimants in the 22 offices and to the staff members who made it possible for us to obtain the IDES administrative data on which we relied. The research was carried out and funded by the W.E. Upjohn Institute for Employment Research, and the authors wish to give special thanks to Azman Abdullah, Jo Mayo, and Wei-Jang Huang for their work in assembling and maintaining the data and assisting with the data analysis.

The Pennsylvania experiment was funded by the U.S. Department of Labor (USDOL) and its operations conducted by the Pennsylvania Department of Labor and Industry. Special thanks is extended to William Coyne and Wayne Zajac, USDOL, who served sequentially as project officers, guiding the project through the design and implementation phases. Their work was carried out under Steve Wandner, who exercised overall responsibility for the conduct of the experiment and whose guidance and support was invaluable. At the state level, special thanks to Frances Curtin, who was responsible for the day-to-day coordination of the project, and to Robert Peebles, who developed and oversaw the state data processing effort.

Mathematica Policy Research designed the Pennsylvania experiment and conducted the research, funded by the USDOL. The authors want to extend special recognition to Stuart Kerachsky, MPR, who served with Walter Corson as principal investigator of the Pennsylvania experiment and was a co-author of the Pennsylvania Reemployment Bonus Demonstration final report. The success of the Pennsylvania project owes much to Shari Dunstan, MPR, who developed the operational design for the experiment and oversaw its implementation. Special recognition is also extended to Anne Ciemnecki, who developed and directed the survey used for analysis, and to Deborah Garvey, who provided programming support.

The Washington Reemployment Bonus Experiment (WREB) was a joint effort of the USDOL, the Washington State Employment Security Department (WSESD) and the W.E. Upjohn Institute. The USDOL effort was led by Steve Wandner, who provided continual guidance to the design and operational effort. Bill Coyne and then Wayne Zajac served as project officers. Douglas Scott deserves special mention for designing the innovative data management system under which the experiment operated. At the state level, the unstinting support of Jim Wolfe, UI assistant commissioner, was of critical importance. Project supervision was shared by Gary Bodeutsch and Kathy Countryman, who were deeply involved with the experiment. Patricia Remy was the WREB project coordinator. She and Kathy were critical to the experiment by assuring that the operational design was carried out in all 21 Job Service Centers in which the experiment was conducted. Other state staff members were also critical to the success of the operations and the acquisition of administrative data.

Financial support for the Upjohn Institute's research effort was obtained from the Alfred P. Sloan Foundation under the leadership of then president Albert Rees (since deceased). Special thanks are extended to Ken Kline, research associate at the Institute, for his outstanding management of the research data throughout the project. Thanks to Phyllis Molhoek for her administrative help in keeping the project on track for all three years of its existence. The WREB project benefited greatly from the guidance provided by an advisory committee composed of Orley Ashenfelter, Dale Mortensen, and David Card.

Finally, for this book, the authors wish to thank all the participants at the reemployment bonus conference held at the Princeton University retreat facility Dunwalke in June 1993. Their suggestions and constructive comments on an earlier draft of the book were critical to the quality of the final manuscript. The participants (in addition to the book's authors) were Orley Ashenfelter, Rebecca Blank, David Card, George Cave, Ronald Ehrenberg, and Robert LaLonde.

At the Upjohn Institute, critical to the quality of the manuscript was the typing and administrative support of Phyllis Molhoek and the manuscript editing of Robert Wathen. Comments from Kevin Hollenbeck, director of publications, and anonymous reviewers were also very helpful.

1

Introduction and Background of the Reemployment Bonus Experiments

Walter A. Corson and Robert G. Spiegelman

MOTIVATION FOR A BONUS OFFER PROGRAM: WORK INCENTIVES IN THE UNEMPLOYMENT INSURANCE SYSTEM

In the 1980s, the federal government sponsored several field experiments to evaluate alternative approaches to reducing voluntary unemployment and improving the functioning of the unemployment insurance (UI) system. Four of these experiments involved the offer of bonuses to encourage more rapid return to work by UI recipients. Other experiments to enhance work search and to encourage self-employment were also implemented. Some of these experiments emphasized the offer of "carrots" to encourage desired behavior, while other proffered "sticks." These two approaches are described more fully in later sections.

Theoretical and non-experimental empirical work had consistently found that the availability of unemployment benefits led to voluntary and unproductive reduction in work effort, thereby leading to unnecessarily high costs to the UI system. The three experiments that we describe in this study were designed to test whether offering bonuses to UI claimants would reduce voluntary unemployment. As we will show, the bonus experiments were successful in reducing the length of insured unemployment spells (see Chapter 4) and thus in reducing benefit payment costs to the UI system. They accomplished this reduction without any observed adverse effect on the quality of jobs obtained from job search (see Chapter 5), indicating that the bonus offer did not reduce effective job search activities.

The majority of the 11 alternative programs tested in the experiments, and all of the hypothetical programs using the combined data from the three experiments, generated positive net benefits to society (see Chapter 7). This result reflects the low costs of administering a bonus program, accompanied by the generally positive effects on claimants' earnings. However, only a few of the designs provided net benefits to government in general, or the UI system in particular, because the costs of paying bonuses usually exceeded the UI payment reductions. As discussed in Chapter 7, however, if one sector benefits from the program but other sectors do not, then the program can be implemented by transferring funds from the winners to the losers. For instance, if society benefits but the UI system does not, an option is to pay the bonuses out of general revenues.

These experiments were conducted over a decade ago. Why should we still be interested in them? The policy issue raised by the experiments, though temporarily in abeyance, is not a dead issue. The possibility of using bonuses or similar mechanisms (such as wage supplements) to encourage more active job search is still one under consideration. The Reemployment Act of 1994 (submitted by President Clinton, but not enacted by Congress) emphasized "UI flexibility" as an integral part of employment and training policy. The concept was that a series of interventions would include short-term compensation, reemployment services, self-employment assistance, and reemployment bonuses. The intent of the act was to turn the UI program toward reemployment assistance. When the Workforce Investment Act was passed by Congress five years later, the emphasis on UI flexibility was gone, but when the concept is again of political interest at some future time, consideration of bonuses can be expected to return.

This book also contains several features not often found in social policy research: 1) multiple experiments with very similar designs, enabling the comparison of results of experiments conducted in different locations and different social contexts; and 2) the transference from experiment to policy by considering impacts on nonparticipants and through explicit benefit-cost analysis.

The remainder of this chapter discusses the motivation for the experiments in more detail and their theoretical and historical underpinnings. An overview of the book is presented in the final section of this chapter.

THE UNEMPLOYMENT INSURANCE SYSTEM

As part of the Social Security Act of 1935, a national UI system was introduced to the country for the first time. After slowly building in the late 1930s and through the war period, the UI system reached its stride near the end of the 1940s, after the conversion from a wartime to a peacetime economy had taken place. By 1948, almost three-quarters of the unemployed were covered by UI, and total benefit outlays in that year were just under $800 million. By 1992, although benefit outlays had grown to $23 billion, coverage had declined to about one-third of the unemployed. In the remainder of the 1990s, outlays declined to about $20 billion per year, or even less, and coverage remained about one-third of the unemployed.[1]

As in any insurance program, UI has a mechanism to fund future obligations, a mechanism to determine entitlement, and a procedure for making payments. Administrative costs are mostly covered by the federal government, while benefit payments are made out of a trust fund, which is administered by the U.S. Treasury but funded through taxes on employers. Each state has an independently administered trust fund. If payments exceed the funds available in the trust, the state must borrow from the Treasury and repay with interest. Total state reserves were a comfortable $8 billion in 1948, representing 8 percent of total payroll. Reserves rose to $38 billion in 1990 but represented less than 2 percent of payrolls in that relatively prosperous year. After falling to $26 billion in 1992, reserves recovered to $48 billion in 1998, but that represented only 1.5 percent of payroll.[2] In 1948, the average employer paid UI taxes amounting to 1.2 percent of taxable wages. By 1992, that percentage had increased to 2.2 percent, about where it has remained to date. Interestingly, however, because of declining coverage, benefit outlays were 0.8 percent of taxable wages in 1948 and only slightly higher in 1992. By 1998, that percent had declined to only 0.6 percent. For detailed discussions of UI financing, see Vroman (1990) and Blaustein (1993).

A worker who is in a firm covered by the UI system and becomes unemployed because of lack of work (not because of voluntarily quitting, or being fired for committing acts detrimental to the employer) is entitled to receive unemployment compensation. Entitlement to compensation, however, is conditional on the worker having sufficient earnings in the *base period*, usually the first four of the last five calendar quarters prior to filing for benefits. The dollar value of benefits payable in a week in which the UI beneficiary is fully unemployed is usually 50 percent of previous weekly wages, subject to a minimum and a maximum. Because of minimums and maximums, on the average, UI recipients receive about 40 percent of previous weekly earnings. The beneficiary is entitled to these payments for a certain number of weeks during the year after filing for benefits (called the *benefit year*). Twelve states (including Illinois) pay benefits for a fixed number of unemployed weeks, typically either 26 or 30. However, most states (including Washington and Pennsylvania) pay benefits for a variable number of weeks, depending upon the claimant's work history. A beneficiary is said to have "exhausted benefits" if the beneficiary remains unemployed after having received all the benefits to which he or she is entitled for the benefit year. In some recession years, when unemployment has remained high, the federal government has financed extended benefit programs and benefits have been provided for up to 52 weeks.

From the start, however, there has been some ambiguity as to whether the system is primarily designed to "alleviate the hardships that result from the loss of wage income during unemployment" (Blaustein 1993, p. 43) or "to insure workers against the risks of earnings loss from unemployment" (Burtless 1990, p. 75). The system today contains elements of both. For instance, the replacement rates are higher for low-wage workers. On the other hand, the insurance concept prevails in the requirement that the claimant must be involuntarily unemployed to collect benefits. No one collects fire insurance for burning down their own house; life insurance is not usually paid in cases of known suicide. Thus, the insurance principle is violated if the insurance is paid for strictly voluntary periods of unemployment. This principle drove the requirements that unemployment beneficiaries be "able and available" for work and be actively seeking employment. Furthermore, benefits cease to be paid if the beneficiary refuses the offer of "suitable" work. That the work must be "suitable" implies that simply minimizing the period of unemployment by requiring beneficiaries to take any job is not an objective of the program. Extending the search to find suitable work is acceptable and even encouraged—

through, for instance, the requirements that the Employment Service (ES) assist the beneficiary to find suitable work.

Legislation in the second half of the 1990s has dramatically changed the nature and functioning of the UI system. The emphasis overwhelmingly has become the return to work. This emphasis, however, has been coupled with a vast simplification in the handling of claims to reduce administrative costs, a process that may not be totally compatible with the back-to-work goal. Changes in the UI system are foreshadowed in the reform of the nation's welfare system. The Personal Responsibility and Work Opportunity Reconciliation Act (PRWORA) established a system of bloc grants from the federal government to the states, with the fundamental requirement that states have most recipients working within two years of first receiving assistance benefits. Today, all but four states have what is called *work-based welfare* as their modus operandi.

The Workforce Investment Act (WIA) signed into law in 1998 includes many of the characteristics of the PRWORA for the UI system. The emphasis is on speedy reemployment, with training provided only if necessary to obtain employment; the philosophy is that the best training is a job. The new federal system under WIA provides reemployment services under one roof—including payment of UI benefits, job placement, counseling, and job skill training—unless initial claims are taken by telephone, in which case there is no UI office as such.

Unemployment Insurance and the Duration of Unemployment

Starting in the early 1970s, Martin Feldstein, and then others, argued that UI has contributed to increased unemployment by reducing the incentive to become reemployed (see especially Feldstein 1973). This problem can arise in any insurance scheme because of "moral hazard," whereby agents who are being insured against a state (e.g., unemployment) do not take all measures to avoid that state (Burtless 1990, pp. 78–79; Bailey 1977). If a job seeker extends unemployment in order to obtain a better job, society may be better off. However, if the additional unemployment is not used for effective job search, then the additional unemployment may be considered voluntary and a net cost to the system.

It would be desirable to be able to determine the effect of UI on the amount of voluntary unemployment and clearly distinguish it from the involuntary kind. But, as Burgess and Kingston (1990, p. 138) pointed out, such a distinction is muddy. There is an involuntary element in all unemployment, in the sense that no one chooses bad luck over good; there is also a voluntary element in all unemployment, in the sense that however miserable one's current work options, one could always accept some job (p. 138). Thus, in the end, the UI question is empirical—how much does UI increase unemployment and what is the result of the increase in terms of job matches?

A large body of research has estimated the effects of UI benefits on the duration of unemployment. Decker (1997) summarized estimates of how the entitled duration of benefits and the rate of wage replacement[3] affect the length of joblessness. The studies showed that lengthening the entitled duration of benefits by 1 week lengthens joblessness by between 0.1 and 0.5 weeks, and a 10 percent increase in the wage replacement rate is estimated to increase joblessness by between 0.3 and 1.5 weeks.

However, these results might understate the effects on the population of particular interest for the bonus experiments (i.e., those claimants not expecting recall to their previous job). The work by Topel and Welch (1979) is informative on this issue. Separating UI claimants on temporary and permanent layoff, they found that UI effects on duration were greater for the latter group. A 10 percent rise in the benefit replacement rate extended the average unemployment spell of insured workers who change jobs by 1.2 weeks; the increase was much less for those temporarily laid off.

A third group of studies measured the effects of UI compensation on the wage rate of jobs accepted after receiving benefits. Several studies found substantive effects of changes in the UI replacement rate, especially on male wages, with smaller effects on female wages.[4] Other researchers, however, have failed to find any earning effects (see Classen 1979; Welch 1977). Welch doubts there is one, because if all unemployed are searching more, the wage can not be expected to rise (Burtless 1990, pp. 96–97). Overall, the evidence as to whether or not there is an effect of UI on the reemployment wage rate is weak.

As noted above, theory suggests, and the empirical work demonstrates, that UI increases the duration of unemployment. Both theory and empirical evidence, however, are imprecise in estimating the quantitative effects and are ambiguous as to the extent to which the additional unemployment leads to improved job matches. Thus, the stage is set to design and test programs with the goal of reducing voluntary unemployment without adversely affecting the quality of job matches.

Why a Bonus Offer Might Reduce Unemployment

The expectation that an offer of a bonus would lead to reduced unemployment has theoretic roots in contemporary job-search theory, which developed the concept of an optimal search strategy for unemployed workers.[5] McCall (1965) described an optimal search rule for job seekers as involving a sequential process in which the worker decides whether or not to continue searching after obtaining each wage offer. In this context, a bonus offer to find a job within a specified time raises the cost of rejecting a given job offer, thereby reducing the reservation wage and increasing the likelihood of accepting any particular job offer (see Davidson 1990, pp. 15–17). This theory, in conjunction with job-matching theory, would hold that reducing the reservation wage would not necessarily reduce the offered wage because the higher reservation wage was unrealistic in terms of job offers available. Thus, the critical questions to be answered for a potential bonus offer program are 1) will it reduce unemployment and 2) will the reduction affect job matches?

Before discussing the three bonus offer experiments that are the main focus of this book, it is of value to briefly describe other experimental approaches to unemployment reduction. Experimental research could take two alternative directions: 1) programs that increase the requirements for job search and job acceptance and/or impose penalties for failure to conduct active search (i.e., a "stick"), or 2) positive incentives to increase the intensity of job search or more rapid acceptance of job offers (i.e., a "carrot"). The bonus offer is obviously of the latter category.

THE "STICK": UI WORK TEST REQUIREMENTS

Work Test Requirements and Their Implementation

State UI programs contain various work-test requirements to ensure that UI benefits are paid only to claimants who show a continuing attachment to the labor market. In most states, the cornerstone of these requirements is a set of provisions that require claimants to search actively for work. These requirements are integrated with work-test rules pertaining to claimants' ability to work, availability for work, and refusal of suitable work. By requiring active work search, these rules are also intended to increase the level and intensity of search and hence to promote rapid reemployment.

Individual states have latitude in defining and applying work-search rules according to their specific policy concerns, political climates, and economic conditions. Consequently, work-search rules and their application vary considerably among the states (Corson, Hershey, and Kerachsky 1986). Although a few states do not impose search requirements, most do impose some work-search requirements on claimants, exempting those with definite recall dates and those who use union hiring halls to find jobs. These search requirements typically specify either the number of contacts to be made by claimants or a specific number of contacts according to the claimant's occupation and local labor-market conditions. Most states with search requirements ask claimants to list their job contacts on a biweekly claim form. These forms are usually checked to determine whether job contacts are filled in, but few states actually verify the contacts. States that perform verification tend to do so only for a sample of claimants.

All states also expose claimants to job openings by requiring that claimants register with the state Employment Service (ES). However, the degree to which states monitor compliance with ES registration varies. Some states require proof of registration before UI claims can be completed, while others do no more than schedule a time for registration. More recently, in states with initial claims processing by telephone, ES registration is completed electronically. Even when ES registration was carefully monitored, fewer than half of the claimants who registered received job referrals or reemployment services from the ES (Corson, Kerachsky, and Eliason-Kisker 1988).

Research by Burgess and Kingston (1987) indicated that many claimants did not fully comply with their state's work test rules, particularly those pertaining to active search. In a five-state study, Burgess and Kingston found that half of the dollars overpaid in each of the states were due to work-search violations. Fourteen percent of claimants required to actively search for work failed to do so, and verification procedures were unable to confirm 25 to 50 percent of the employer contacts.

Burgess and Kingston's recommendation that computerized screening profiles be used to target administrative resources on high-risk claimants has been widely implemented. Their recommendations for increased penalties for noncompliance—presently, the main, if not only, penalty is return of overpayments without added penalty—and increased noncompliance detection have received much less support.

In fact, the main result of these recommendations in the 1990s has been a reduction in work-search requirements in order to reduce error rates. One major change in processing UI claims in the 1990s, which many believe actually reduces the motivation of UI claimants to seek work, is the adoption by most states of telephone processing of subsequent weekly claims. Only the new initial claim is filed in person. Other recent innovations center on the use of modern technology to improve job search. Automated job matching is starting up in Washington and other states. However, it is not clear whether modern technology reduces or increases work-search accountability.

The "Stick": Recent Experimental Evidence

Alternative job search strategies were examined as part of experiments in South Carolina, New Jersey, and Washington.[6] Some of this work was instrumental in the enactment by the federal government of the Worker Profiling and Reemployment Services (WPRS) System in 1993.[7]

The two federally sponsored studies in Charleston, South Carolina, and Tacoma, Washington, provided particularly strong evidence that tightening work-search requirements can be effective in reducing claimants' duration on UI and promoting reemployment.[8] Charleston's

Claimant Placement and Work Test Demonstration, conducted in 1983 (Corson, Long, and Nicholson 1985), made registration with the ES mandatory for all treatment-assigned claimants who received a first UI payment (except for those filing through mass layoff procedures). Compliance with the registration requirement was carefully monitored through a computer matching process, and claimants who failed to register could no longer receive UI benefits until they could verify that they were indeed available for work. Claimants were assigned to one of three treatment groups that represented three different levels of service: 1) a basic placement interview, 2) a more intensive placement interview with a second call-in for services, or 3) a more intensive interview with a call-in for a short job-search workshop, as well as the second placement interview. A fourth group, the control group, was not required to register with the ES.

As expected, each of the treatments increased the use of the ES among UI claimants. The experimental treatments also reduced weeks of UI benefits by 0.5 week for the group that received the basic call-in and placement interview and 0.75 week for the group that received the additional call-ins for the job-search workshop and second placement interview. Overall, the treatments were cost-effective, with net savings in UI benefit payments (after deducting added administrative costs) ranging from $46 to $56 per claimant. No evidence was found, however, that the treatments increased employment or earnings.

The Washington Alternative Work Search Experiment was conducted in Tacoma, Washington, in 1986 and 1987 (Johnson and Klepinger 1991). This demonstration, unlike the others, focused directly on work-search requirements (as opposed to strengthening the link between UI and the ES). A control group was subjected to Washington's standard work-search requirement that claimants make three employer contacts per week. Control group members were also required to participate in both group and individual interviews to review work-search and UI eligibility issues. These sessions were held about 13 to 15 weeks after the claimant filed the initial claim. One treatment enhanced this approach with a customized approach to work-search requirements,[9] and another treatment used a more intensive approach that included a two-day job-search workshop. A final treatment—exception reporting—abandoned all work-search reporting requirements. This final treatment required only that claimants report when they became reemployed or changed their earnings; if no report was made, a benefit payment was mailed to the claimant.

The exception reporting approach was clearly a disaster; it led to an *increase* in UI benefit payments of 3.3 weeks, on average. No significant differences in UI receipt were found for the customized approach relative to the standard work-search policy of three contacts per week, but a reduction of about 0.5 week in UI benefits was found for the more intensive service approach (Johnson and Klepinger 1994). Interestingly, a hazard rate analysis indicated that the impact of this treatment appeared to occur at the point when claimants received the letter telling them to come to the workshop, not at the end of the workshop. This finding suggests that the effect was the result of the claimants perceiving the workshop as a "cost" of receiving UI payments and not as a benefit.

Not all experiments that tested increased work-search requirements provided support for this approach. In 1991, Ashenfelter, Ashmore, and Deschênes (1999) evaluated an experiment conducted in four states with two treatments. In one treatment, the subject was exposed to the so-called Benefits Rights Interview (BRI), wherein the claimant's responsibility to actively search for work is explained on the first visit to the UI office. The controls would receive the BRI on the second visit, as would normally be the case. In addition, the treatment group received an expanded initial eligibility questionnaire. For a second treatment group, an additional aspect of the treatment involved an actual verification that the claimant undertook job search. There were about 1,900 experimental subjects and the same number of controls in four states: Connecticut, Tennessee, Massachusetts, and Virginia. No results in the individual states achieved a 95 percent confidence level. In the pooled data, claimants in the overall treatment group did show a 5 percent decrease in the likelihood of qualifying for benefits in the first week; however, there were no statistically significant effects on benefit amounts or duration, once qualified. The authors concluded that the results of this experiment failed to confirm the benefits of stricter work-search enforcement. This finding may only apply to the specific treatments tested, and does not necessarily contradict other findings that stronger work-search requirements would be effective.

THE "CARROT"

Self-employment experiments fall into this category. Two were conducted in the UI systems of Massachusetts and Washington. Benus, Wood, and Grover (1994) summarized findings of these experiments. The findings led to a temporary five-year authorization of self-employment assistance (SEA) being included in the North American Free Trade Agreement (NFTA) Implementation Act.[10] The Massachusetts design was implemented, as it promised a neutral impact on the Unemployment Trust Fund. SEA programs currently operate in 10 states, with New York having the most participants. Vroman (1999) summarized state SEA practices.

The reemployment bonus experiments have not yet been authorized by any federal legislation. However, as discussed in the first section of this chapter, the Reemployment Act proposed by President Clinton to Congress in 1994 recommended permitting states to establish reemployment bonus programs. Three of the experiments—those in Illinois, Pennsylvania, and Washington—are described in detail in this book. A fourth experiment conducted in New Jersey had a bonus component, but it had design characteristics that made it unfeasible to compare its results with those of the other three experiments. We provide a summary description of the New Jersey experiment in the following section.

The New Jersey Unemployment Insurance Reemployment Demonstration Project[11]

In 1986 and 1987, an experiment was conducted in New Jersey in which almost 9,000 claimants were assigned to one of three treatment groups, defined as follows:

- Treatment 1 (referred to as Job Search Assistance [JSA]): a set of requirements and services that began with a notification letter sent to each enrolled claimant after they received their first UI payment, which occurred in about the third week after filing. The letter required the claimant to come to the ES office for services. The services included orientation and testing in the fifth week, followed a week later by a job-search workshop consisting of five half-day sessions, and then a one-on-one counseling/assessment session, which usually occurred in the seventh week. Of course, employment or termination of benefit receipt could terminate the sequence at any time. There were periodic follow-up contacts 2, 4, 8, 12, and 16 weeks following assessment.

- Treatment 2: JSA plus training or relocation available after assessment. Those assigned to treatment 2 were told about the availability of classroom and on-the-job training and encouraged to pursue training.

- Treatment 3: JSA plus a reemployment bonus, which was offered to claimants who were still unemployed after assessment. The bonus offer provided for one-half of the claimant's remaining UI entitlement at the time of assessment, declining after two weeks at a rate of 10 percent of the original amount per week unit it was no longer available. To qualify, the claimant had to obtain a permanent, full-time job, not with a relative or the immediately preceding employer. Sixty percent of the bonus was paid after 4 weeks of employment and the remainder if they remained employed for 12 weeks. The full bonus offer averaged $1,644, and the overall average of the two bonus payments was close to $1,300 for those who received payment.

The eligible claimant population was restricted to workers who were over 25 years of age and identified as being *dislocated*, which was defined as having been employed by the same employer for three years prior to filing and not being on standby or a member of a union that places its workers through a hiring hall. The demonstration sample of 11,060 UI beneficiaries was randomly selected from the population of eligible UI beneficiaries filing in 10 of New Jersey's 38 local UI offices.

All 8,675 participants assigned to one of the three treatments were offered job-search assistance. Of these, 77 percent attended the initial orientation, 50 percent completed a job-search workshop, and 56 percent attended an assessment/counseling interview. About 15 percent of the claimants who were offered training participated in training, most of which was classroom training. Nineteen percent of those offered the bonus received at least the first payment, and 84 percent of this group also received the second installment.

The JSA and training provided by the experimental treatments were not unique in that these services were also available to nonparticipants in various forms, such as through the Job Training Partnership Act (JTPA). There were, however, significant differences in the amount of such services received by participants and nonparticipants. The most easily identifiable part of JSA is the job-search workshop. Whereas almost half of claimants assigned treatment received the workshop, only 7 percent of controls did (see U.S. Department of Labor 1989, Table IV.II, p. 248). The authors estimate that the 15 percent attendance rate of training classes for participants in treatment 2 was about three to four times that of similar nonparticipants.

There were strong effects of the treatments on UI outcomes, namely benefits paid and weeks paid in the benefit year.[12] Job-search assistance was associated with an average decline in UI payments in the benefit year of $87 and a decline in number of weeks of benefit payments of almost 0.5 week. The bonus offer was associated with an additional decline of $83 in benefit payments in the benefit year and an additional reduction of 0.5 week of benefit payments. The training offer had no effect on benefit payments in the benefit year, which may not be surprising, since the initial impact must be to increase UI payments during the training period. Any positive effects of training may show up in the second year.

Although the bonus offer treatment in the New Jersey experiment had strong results, we do not believe that this experiment provided much guidance for policy, because the particular bonus-offer treatment was not replicable. In the New Jersey experiment, bonus offers were made only after seven weeks of insured unemployment, and the pending offer was unknown to the selected participants prior to that time. Such a situation could not be replicated in a real program, as knowledge of the pending offer would be available to all claimants from the start of their benefit year (and probably prior to that, an issue that will be explored further in Chapter 6). This knowledge can be expected to critically affect job-search behavior during the first seven weeks of the benefit year, as well as during the period in which the bonus was available.

A more replicable bonus offer experiment, in which the experimental subjects are informed of the bonus offer at the time they file for UI benefits, thereby not contaminating the search process, was needed to provide guidance to policy in this area. In fact, a bonus offer experiment with this characteristic was undertaken by the Department of Employment Security in Illinois. The experiment in Illinois was to be followed by similar experiments in Pennsylvania and Washington. In this book, we report on the Illinois, Pennsylvania, and Washington experiments, because the designs of the three experiments were sufficiently similar to make comparison of results among them, and combining of data for simulations, feasible. The New Jersey experiment could not be used in this manner.

BONUS OFFER EXPERIMENTS IN ILLINOIS, PENNSYLVANIA, AND WASHINGTON

Three bonus offer experiments conducted in Illinois in 1984–1985, in Pennsylvania in 1988–1990, and in Washington in 1988–1989 provide evidence of the efficacy of a bonus offer program in UI. These three experiments are the subject of the remainder of this book.

In May 1984, the Illinois Department of Employment Security contracted with the W.E. Upjohn Institute to conduct an experiment with bonus offers in Illinois. This experiment was funded by use of the governor's discretionary money under Title 7(b) of the Wagner-Peyser Act, which allows states to use funds "for exemplary models for the delivery of services." The initial interest of the state was in an experiment involving an offer of a bonus to employers for hiring UI claimants within a specified period of time. A second experimental treatment, called the Claimant Experiment, in which bonuses were offered directly to unemployed claimants with the same proviso, was added in order to compare the effects on unemployment of a labor "supply" and a labor "demand" incentive. Because of very low participation, the Employer Experiment had little effect on behavior, but the Claimant Experiment was very successful in reducing UI benefit payments (see Chapter 4). Its success, plus the encouraging results of the New Jersey experiment, led the U. S. Department of Labor (more specifically, the Employment and Training Administration, Unemployment Insurance Service) to undertake two more bonus experiments, with offers made to claimants.

In 1987, the Department of Labor selected Washington and later that year selected Pennsylvania to be experimental states. The Department of Labor asked the W.E. Upjohn Institute to undertake the design and evaluation of the Washington experiment, which became known as the Washington Reemployment Bonus Demonstration[13] (henceforth referred to simply as the "Washington experiment"). The Upjohn Institute obtained a matching grant from the Alfred P. Sloan Foundation to fund the design and evaluation of the experiment. Institute staff worked with the Washington State Employment Security Department to design the Washington experiment.

In 1988, the Department of Labor selected Mathematica Policy Research, Inc., to design and evaluate the Pennsylvania Reemployment Bonus Demonstration (referred to in this volume as the "Pennsylvania experiment"). Washington was to be a pure test of the bonus offer, with several treatments providing a sufficient range of alternative bonus offers to permit mapping of the feasible alternative policy options. Pennsylvania was similarly to provide a range of bonus offers, some of which would also provide enhanced job-search assistance.

As this book unfolds, it will become clear that the bonus offer clearly reduced the weeks of benefit receipt and generally sped reemployment of UI recipients into fully satisfactory jobs. However, the net benefit analysis is not as strong. In general, the bonus offer appears to be of positive net benefit to society as a whole, but the benefits are usually not positive for the UI system, meaning that only if money is transferred into the system to pay the bonuses is it a benefit to the UI system. Such transfer, however, is well within a feasible policy set and may be undertaken for programs that are overall beneficial, even if not to the implementing agency. We believe, in addition, the results do provide important information as to the existence of voluntary unemployment by those receiving UI benefits. Secondly, we believe that this book provides important guidance to researchers and policymakers alike who want to understand how to use field experiments to design or improve social policy.

OVERVIEW OF THE BOOK

Chapter 2 starts by formally presenting the four elements that comprise an experimental design: 1) who will participate, 2) what are the experimental treatments, 3) how many subjects will be in the experiment and how will they be allocated, and 4) where will the experiment take place and under what conditions. The chapter next grapples with the essential feature of any experiment, i.e., random assignment, discussing the process and its success in this case and looking at the characteristics of the control populations across experiments. The chapter concludes with the description of experimental operations. The bonus experiments were unusually "clean" experiments in that they did not suffer from selection bias, contamination of treatments, difficult operational environments, or inconsistent treatments.[14]

Chapter 3 describes the participants and rules of participation, and it presents results on the rate of participation and the characteristics of participants and nonparticipants. In this chapter, the authors provide an estimate of the extent to which UI claimants assigned to the experiment failed to collect bonuses for which they appeared to be eligible. A large proportion of bonus money was "left on the table" so to speak, and this has important implications for estimates of the cost and benefits of a program that would be modeled after the experiments (discussed more fully in Chapters 6 and 7).

Chapter 4 presents the most critical results of the experiments, namely, the effects directly on the UI system. The impact of the experiment on two variables—namely, the dollar value of UI benefits paid out to claimants and the number of weeks (duration) of insured unemployment—are estimated. The chapter concentrates on the difference between experimental and control parameters over the benefit year. The results are presented utilizing different statistical methods, starting with a simple comparison of means that, because of random assignment, can provide unbiased estimates of the treatment impacts. The chapter then presents results that have been adjusted to account for accidental differences in the characteristics of treatment and control groups. Results are also presented to show how the bonus offers affect the timing of leaving unemployment and to show how the outcomes respond to sequential increases in the amount of the bonus offer and the length of the qualification period. Overall, the bonus offer tended to reduce the length of insured unemployment, and there were differences in impacts by size of the bonus offer and length of the qualification period.

Chapter 5 proceeds to discuss some other important results, primarily the impact of the treatments on the earnings of claimants, the nature and quality of jobs, and employer attachment (i.e., did it affect the tendency for UI claimants to return to their previous employer?). Earning impacts are investigated by comparing the earnings in the year starting with the quarter in which benefits are filed—thereby combining the direct impact of the offer on the timing of reemployment and any differences in wage rates in the post-filing job that might be due to the experimental treatment. The latter is directly addressed by comparing experimental and control differences in earnings after termination of UI benefits. The impact on the degree to which UI claimants returned to the pre-filing employer was deemed important because of employer concern that the bonus offer—not payable if the claimant is recalled to the previous job—might loosen employer attachment. No support for this concern was found.

Chapter 6 provides the bridge from experiment to program by discussing the various issues needed to translate experimental results into programs. It is both the most unique and in many ways most important chapter in the book; it reflects the need to consider how a policymaker is to make use of experimental results. Experimental results are confined to a subset of the total population who are exposed to the experimental treatment, but they provide no estimate of the experimental impact on subsets of persons in the total population who are not exposed to the treatment. In the case of the bonus experiment, all UI claimants are in the exposed group, leaving all unemployed workers who are not UI claimants outside of the experimental realm. In a full program, UI-eligible nonclaimants can enter the program realm by claiming benefits, while those ineligible for benefits might be affected by the program even if they do not participate in it. Chapter 6 attempts to measure these effects. This chapter discusses, and attempts to quantify, the effects of a bonus offer in a full program on the "entry effect" (i.e., the tendency to increase filing for UI benefits) and on "displacement" or crowding out (i.e., the tendency for participants to increase job acquisition at the expense of nonparticipants). The format and approach of Chapter 6, by necessity, differs from that of the proceeding three chapters. To measure entry and displacement effects in the economy at large, it is necessary to reach out to models of employment equilibrium. Thus, these results must be considered more speculative than those that are derived directly from experimental results.

Chapter 7 presents the results of a benefit-cost analysis that shows the net benefits that can be potentially derived from a bonus offer program from the perspective of society, government, the UI system, and claimants. Although recognizing that many benefits and costs cannot be captured in this analysis, it is suggestive of the net benefits to be derived from such a program from the perspective of different constituents. In the last section of this chapter, we attempt to show the impact on net benefits from the programmatic effects discussed in Chapter 6. Basically, the low administrative costs make a bonus offer an appealing program from society's perspective. Although only the high bonus program generated net benefits from the government's perspective, the treatment simulations, using combined data from the three experiments, demonstrated positive benefits from all three perspectives— society, government, and the UI system—from a relatively small ($500) bonus.

Chapter 8 presents an overview of what we have learned and the policy implications. The expected effects of a bonus offer program on work effort and the UI system are described, as is why an experimental approach to answering the questions seems warranted. The features of the experiments and the essential findings are reviewed. The average effects of the treatments in each of the three experiments are summarized in Table 8.1. The summary demonstrates that the treatments significantly reduced the number of claimants receiving benefits but that the bonus offer program appears to have been cost-effective only in Illinois. In assessing the experiments, Professor Robins, the author of this chapter, concludes that, from the standpoint of standards for social policy research, the experiments were quite successful. However, the experiments were not successful in pinpointing statistically significant differences across treatments, and Robins attempts to answer why this is the case. Most of the remainder of the chapter discusses alternative policies that could be employed to accomplish the goals of a bonus offer program to cost-effectively reduce insured unemployment. Four alternatives are discussed: earnings supplement, stricter sanctioning of work-search requirements, worker profiling, and Unemployment Insurance Savings Accounts.

Notes

1. U.S. Department of Labor, *Unemployment Insurance Financial Data*, ET Handbook 394, 1948–1998, and U.S. Department of Labor, Bureau of Labor Statistics, Labor Force Statistics from the Current Population Survey, 1948–1998.
2. U.S. Department of Labor, ET Handbook 394.
3. The replacement rate is the proportion of previous weekly earnings that is replaced by UI benefits; specifically, it is the ratio of the weekly benefit amount to the net pre-UI weekly wage.
4. Ehrenberg and Oaxaca (1976) estimated that a 10 percentage point rise in the UI replacement rate (40 percent to 50 percent) would increase a male's reemployment wage by 7.0 percent and a female's wage by 1.5 percent. Burgess and Kingston (1976) and Holen (1977) found similar results.
5. The origins of job-search theory are found in the work of George Stigler (1961, 1962).
6. For evaluations of South Carolina, see Corson, Long, and Nicholson (1985); for New Jersey, see Corson et al. (1989) and further discussion in the section below; for Washington, see Johnson and Klepinger (1991, 1994).
7. The unemployment compensation amendments of 1993 (Public Law 103-153) revised extended benefit rules and also required states to implement a system to identify UI claimants most likely to need job-search assistance to avoid long-term unemployment. The system for identification became know as the Worker Profiling and Reemployment Services system.
8. Later work-search demonstrations in Nevada and Minnesota (see Meyer [1995]) confirmed the positive effects of work-search requirements on duration of UI benefits.
9. Different work-search requirements were developed for different groups of workers, depending on their job prospects. In addition, search requirements were strengthened as the unemployment spell increased.
10. The NAFTA Implementation Act (Public Law 103-182) gave states the option of continuing UI benefits for claimants who elect to start their own business. Permanent authorization was granted by federal legislation in 1998 for states to provide self-employment assistance with UI trust fund money.
11. The design, operation, and evaluation of this experiment is described in detail by Corson et al. (1989).
12. A goal of the experiment and its most likely outcome is a reduction in UI utilization. These also happen to be outcomes that are readily measured, since receipt of unemployment benefits and weeks of benefits paid are data available directly from the UI record system. Thus, for the New Jersey experiment, as well as for the three experiments that occupy most of this book, a principal measure of experimental impact is the average difference in the dollars of benefits received and in

the number of weeks benefits were paid between those assigned to bonus offer treatments and those in the control group.

13. While Department of Labor refers to the Washington and Pennsylvania experiments as "demonstrations," we use the term "experiment" to make it clear that random assignment to treatment and control groups was used to permit unbiased estimates of program effects. Demonstrations do not involve random assignment and are most useful in testing workability of alternative administrative procedures.

14. See Nathan (1988) for discussion of what makes good demonstration research.

References

Ashenfelter, Orley, David Ashmore, and Olivier Deschênes. 1999. "Do Unemployment Insurance Recipients Actively Seek Work? Randomized Trials in Four U.S. States." Working paper no. 6982, National Bureau of Economic Research, Cambridge, Massachusetts, February.

Bailey, Martin N. 1977. "Unemployment Insurance as Insurance for Workers." *Industrial and Labor Relations Review* 30(July): 495–504.

Benus, Jacob, Michelle Wood, and Neelima Grover. 1994. *Self-Employment as a Reemployment Option: Demonstration Results and National Legislation.* Unemployment Insurance Occasional Paper 94-3, U.S. Department of Labor, Employment and Training Administration, Washington, D.C.

Blaustein, Saul. 1993. *Unemployment Insurance in the United States: The First Half Century.* Kalamazoo, Michigan: W.E. Upjohn Institute for Employment Research.

Burtless, Gary. 1990. "Unemployment Insurance and Labor Supply: A Survey." In *Unemployment Insurance: The Second Half-Century,* W. Lee Hansen and James F. Byers, eds. Madison: University of Wisconsin Press, pp. 69–107.

Burgess, Paul L., and Jerry L. Kingston. 1976. "The Impact of Unemployment Insurance Benefits on Reemployment Success." *Industrial and Labor Relations Review* 30(October): 25–31.

_____. 1987. *An Incentives Approach to Improving the Unemployment Compensation System.* Kalamazoo, Michigan: W.E. Upjohn Institute for Employment Research.

_____. 1990. "Monitoring Claimant Compliance with Unemployment Compensation Eligibility Criteria." In *Unemployment Insurance: The Second Half-Century,* W. Lee Hansen and James F. Byers, eds. Madison: University of Wisconsin Press, p. 138.

Classen, Kathleen P. 1979. "Unemployment Insurance and Job Search." In *Studies in the Economics of Search*, S.A. Lippman and John J. McCall, eds. Amsterdam: North Holland.

Corson, Walter, David Long, and Walter Nicholson. 1985. *Evaluation of the Charleston Claimant Placement and Work Test Demonstration*. Unemployment Insurance Occasional Paper 85-2, U.S. Department of Labor, Employment and Training Administration, Washington, D.C.

Corson, Walter, Alan Hershey, and Stuart Kerachsky. 1986. *Nonmonetary Eligibility in State Unemployment Insurance Programs: Law and Practice*. Kalamazoo, Michigan: W.E. Upjohn Institute for Employment Research.

Corson, Walter, Stuart Kerachsky, and Ellen Eliason-Kisker. 1988. *Work Search among Unemployment Insurance Claimants: An Investigation of Some Effects of State Rules and Enforcement*. Unemployment Insurance Occasional Paper 88-1, U.S. Department of Labor, Employment and Training Administration, Washington, D.C.

Corson, Walter, Paul T. Decker, Shari Miller Dunstan, and Anne R. Gordon, with Patricia Anderson and John Homrighausen. 1989. *The New Jersey Unemployment Insurance Reemployment Demonstration Project: Final Evaluation Report*. Unemployment Insurance Occasional Paper 89-3, U.S. Department of Labor, Employment and Training Administration, Washington, D.C.

Decker, Paul T. 1997. "Work Incentives and Disincentives." In *Unemployment Insurance in the United States: Analysis of Policy Issues*, Christopher J. O'Leary and Stephen A. Wandner, eds. Kalamazoo, Michigan: W.E. Upjohn Institute for Employment Research, pp. 285–320.

Davidson, Carl. 1990. *Recent Development in the Theory of Involuntary Unemployment*. Kalamazoo, Michigan: W.E. Upjohn Institute for Employment Research.

Ehrenberg, Ronald G., and Ronald L. Oaxaca. 1976. "Unemployment Insurance, Duration of Unemployment, and Subsequent Wage Gain." *American Economic Review* 66(December): 754–766.

Feldstein, Martin. 1973. "Unemployment Insurance: Adverse Incentives and Distributional Anomalies." *National Tax Journal* 27(June): 231–244.

Holen, Arlene. 1977. "Effects of Unemployment Insurance Entitlement on Duration and Job Search Outcome." *Industrial and Labor Relations Review* 30(July): 445–450.

Johnson, Terry R., and Daniel H. Klepinger. 1991. *Evaluation of the Impacts of the Washington Alternative Work Experiment*. Unemployment Insurance Occasional Paper 91-4, U.S. Department of Labor, Employment and Training Administration, Washington, D.C.

_____. 1994. "Experimental Evidence on Unemployment Insurance Work-Search Policies." *Journal of Human Resources* 29(3): 695.

McCall, J.J. 1965. "The Economics of Information and Optimal Stopping Rules." *Journal of Business* 38: 300–317.

Meyer, Bruce D. 1995. "Lessons from the U.S. Unemployment Insurance Experiments." *Journal of Economic Literature* 33(1): 91–131.

Nathan, Richard. 1988. *Social Science in Government: Uses and Misuses.* New York: Basic Books, Inc.

Stigler, George. 1961. "The Economics of Information." *Journal of Political Economy* 69: 213–225.

_____. 1962. "Information in the Labor Market." *Journal of Political Economy* 70: 94–104.

Topel, Robert, and Finis Welch. 1979. "Unemployment Insurance: What the Theory Predicts and What the Numbers (May) Show, Survey and Extensions." Photocopy, University of California at Los Angeles.

U.S. Department of Labor, Employment and Training Administration. 1989. *New Jersey Unemployment Insurance Reemployment Demonstration Project.* Unemployment Insurance Occasional Paper 89-3, U.S. Department of Labor, Employment and Training Administration, Washington, D.C.

Vroman, Wayne. 1990. *Unemployment Insurance Trust Fund Adequacy.* Kalamazoo, Michigan: W.E. Upjohn Institute for Employment Research.

Vroman, Wayne. 1999. *Self-Employment Assistance (SEA) Program: Report to Congress.* Unemployment Insurance Occasional Paper 99-5, U.S. Department of Labor, Unemployment Insurance Service, Employment and Training Administration, Washington, D.C.

Welch, Finis. 1977. "What Have We Learned from Empirical Studies of Unemployment Insurance?" *Industrial and Labor Relations Review* 30(July): 451–461.

2

Design of Three Field Experiments

Walter A. Corson and Robert G. Spiegelman

INTRODUCTION: WHAT MAKES AN EXPERIMENT AN EXPERIMENT?

The modern concept of experimental design is primarily a result of the work of R.A. Fisher, who developed the concept in the 1920s while conducting agricultural field experiments in England (see Fisher 1960; Fisher 1968). Fisher's approach had several statistical features and relied on randomization as the key to providing estimates of response variability. According to Charles Hicks (1982, p. 1): "A *true experiment* may be defined as a study in which certain independent variables are manipulated, . . . and the levels of these independent variables are assigned at random to the experimental units in the study." In essence, an experiment is a process of manipulation and randomization for the purpose of measuring the underlying responses to treatments. Its value over observational studies lies in the increased ability to elucidate cause-and-effect relationships (Fisher 1968, p. 246).

Despite the history of controlled experiments in the laboratory and the agricultural fields, the idea of such an approach did not enter the realm of social science until Heather Ross, a candidate for a Ph.D. in economics at Massachusetts Institute of Technology, presented such a plan to experiment with the negative income tax in a 1966 paper (Ross 1966, cited in Kershaw and Fair 1977). Until that time, the concept of manipulating human beings in the same manner as fertilizer or wheat varieties was not considered. However, the Office of Economic Opportunity (OEO) was eagerly searching for new ways to evaluate alternative negative income tax proposals and the academic community was eager to apply newly developed econometric and data handling techniques. The result was the New Jersey Income Maintenance Experiment, which was soon followed by income maintenance experiments in Seattle, Denver, Gary, and two rural areas. Experiments with housing vouchers, health insurance, and residential electricity pricing followed. New at the time was the idea that it was reasonable to establish a control group that represented a null treatment only in the sense that the particular intervention being tested was withheld. In every other sense, the control group represented the status quo—affected by all the programs, policies, and economic perturbations that existed in the general population. As we will see, experimentation in general and randomization in particular is often not as clean in practice as it is in principle.

Randomization is the process of selecting individuals from a specified population and placing them into one or more groups by a blind process that, in principle, assures that on average the characteristics of the members of the groups are the same.[1] This goal can be accomplished using a random number generator or the last four digits of an individual's social security number to make the assignment. If the process is done correctly and the samples are sufficiently large, then the members of each group will differ, on average, only due to experimental interventions. Basically, there will be two groups: a "treatment" group that receives the experimental intervention and a "control" group that receives no treatment. The number of experimental groups can be expanded, with each group receiving a different treatment. There will invariably be a control group to represents the status quo because a comparison between the treatment and control groups tells the evaluators what can be expected if the treatment is imposed in the then-current environment.

In this chapter, the design of each of the three bonus experiments is presented and the three are compared. The next section examines eligibility requirements for participation in the experiments. The experimental design is then described, comparing the nature of the treatments among the three states and pointing out their differences and their more pervasive similarities. We then discuss the number and allocation of participants in the experiment, followed by a discussion of the decisions as to the location and number of experimental sites. The environment within which each experiment was conducted, including the relevant economic characteristics of the states during the periods in which the experiments were conducted and the characteristics of the group of claimants selected to serve as a control group, is then described. We next evaluate the randomization process, whose object was to create treatment and control groups that had essentially the same characteristics, and then we describe the operation of the experiments, pointing out the overriding similarities as well as the few differences in operational designs. The final section briefly discusses an unplanned experiment generated by the Federal Supplemental Compensation program in Illinois.

ELIGIBILITY FOR PARTICIPATION IN THE EXPERIMENTS

General Issues

Participation in an experiment should be guided by the expected decision as to who would be eligible to participate in a program modeled on the experiment. Additional considerations that might further limit experimental eligibility are the likelihood of participation in the program and a desire to increase the homogeneity of the sample, thereby reducing the sample size required to achieve a given level of statistical reliability.

Although decisions regarding the characteristics of those eligible to participate in an experiment should reflect the purposes of the experimental program, limiting the sample also limits the information obtained from the experiment. For instance, in an experimental employment program that had the goal of increasing the employability of displaced workers, limiting enrollment to only displaced workers would result in an experiment that provides no information on the relative effects of the program on displaced and nondisplaced workers. Furthermore, a change in the definition of displacement would reduce the usefulness of the results of an experiment that enrolled only displaced workers under the old definition. It is, however, a waste of resources to include persons whose behavior is of no interest in reaching the policy decisions. If the resulting program has the reduction of unemployment insurance (UI) costs as a major goal, then it would seem to be unnecessary to include in the experiment persons not eligible for UI benefits, unless UI eligibility is affected by the experimental program.

Such an effect can arise because of the potential for an experimental program to generate unwanted increases in program participation (e.g., additional filing for UI benefits). This so-called "entry effect" is usually undetected in an experimental evaluation (see Moffit 1992).[2] In the UI bonus experiments (henceforth referred to simply as the "bonus experiments"), entry effects could only be determined if both employed and unemployed workers (including those not filing for benefits) were enrolled. This was not the case in any of the bonus experiments, thereby precluding any experimental measurement of entry effects. This issue is discussed more completely in Chapter 6 with regard to the bonus experiments.

Eliminating from a sample some persons who would be eligible to participate in the ensuing program is done primarily to reduce costs. For example, if relatively young and relatively old workers respond to programs differently than those in the age group 25 to 55, concentrating on the middle age group would reduce the sample size needed for any given degree of reliability. Of course, the results fail to inform the policymaker about the effects of the program on the excluded age groups.

Who responds to the treatment is relevant to the determination of net benefits, because of the potential for *windfall gains*, which are gains that accrue to participants in an experiment who receive the treatment benefits (such as a bonus payment) without any change in behavior. An example would be a program to pay moving expenses to unemployed workers who take jobs outside their area of current residence; windfall gain will be the payments to those who would have moved without the reimbursement. Net benefits will be larger as the proportion of payments made to such nonresponders gets smaller. However, windfall gain cannot be reduced to zero for two reasons: 1) equity considerations require a relatively comprehensive definition of eligibility (e.g., if black workers don't respond to the treatment, you cannot design a program that makes payments only to white workers), and 2) behavioral response is measured indirectly by a comparison of group behaviors; individual response is only inferred on a probabilistic basis.

Windfall gain is minimized by excluding from eligibility groups whose members have a low probability of responding to the treatment and whose exclusion does not involve substantial equity issues. For instance, in the bonus experiments, not paying bonuses to claimants who returned to their previous jobs helped reduce windfall gain.

Eligibility to Participate in the Bonus Offer Experiments

All three experiments started from the premise that a major experimental objective was to reduce costs to the UI trust funds by reducing the length of insured unemployment. Offering a bonus to unemployed workers who were not eligible to receive UI benefits would not contribute to achieving this goal because no change in the behavior of ineligible claimants could reduce UI benefit payments. With an exception of a few cases in Washington, all three experiments required that UI eligibility be established.[3] The criteria of UI eligibility meant that the claimant must have been monetarily eligible to receive benefits payable out of the host state's trust fund. Thus, veterans receiving benefits under the UCX (unemployment compensation for ex-service members) program, claimants with only interstate claims, and ex-federal employees under the UCFE (unemployment compensation for federal employees) program were all excluded because their benefits would not be paid out of the state trust funds. As shown in Table 2.1, these conditions were uniform across the three experiments; other conditions were not. The eligibility conditions in Table 2.1 are described in the sections that follow.

New benefit year

All three experiments required that the claimant be filing to establish a new benefit year. (See the Glossary on p. 275 for definitions of "benefit year" and other UI terms.) This requirement was imposed for two reasons: 1) it was felt that, in a steady state, the bonus offer would be made at the start of a benefit year and not sometime in its midst and thus the requirement would replicate that expected in a real program; and 2) it created a valuable homogeneity characteristic in that all experimental subjects would start with the same unemployment history (at least with regard to the current spell). In Washington, but not in Illinois or Pennsylvania, claimants filing "transitional" claims were eligi-

Table 2.1 Eligibility Conditions for Participation in the Experiments[a]

Eligibility conditions	Illinois	Pennsylvania	Washington
To participate			
New benefit year	Y	Y	Y
Monetarily eligible for UI	Y	Y	Y
Monetarily eligible for UI at time of filing	N	N	Y
No separation issues	Y	Y	N
Not totally interstate, UCFE, or UCX	Y	Y	Y
Not on standby or a referral union member	N	Y	N
Register with job service	Y	N	N
Backdated claims more than two weeks disallowed	N	Y	N
To receive a bonus			
Terminate benefits, become employed for 4 months	Y	Y	Y
Not be recalled, placed by union	N	Y	Y
Nonmonetarily eligible to receive benefits	Y	Y	Y

[a] Y: yes, it is a condition; N: no, it is not a condition.

ble to participate.   In a real program, it is doubtful that a claimant who received an offer in the initial benefit year would receive a repeat offer in a transitional year.

Monetary eligibility

As mentioned above, the programmatic goal of reducing UI system costs led all three experiments to require monetary eligibility for UI as a condition for participation in the experiments. In Pennsylvania and Illinois, a monetarily valid claim had to be established at the time the claimant filed for the first compensable week and/or the waiting week.

The requirements for monetary eligibility were more stringent in Washington. Only a claimant who had a monetarily valid claim at the time of initial filing was enrolled in the experiment. Thus, certain categories of claimants, particularly laid-off state employees whose wage histories would not be in the file at the time of filing and whose monetary eligibility would not be established until after filing, were excluded from the Washington experiment. This made administration of the experiment easier and permitted fixed dollar offers to be made at the time of enrollment. It is likely that the more equitable approach used in Illinois and Pennsylvania would be followed in a real program.

Nonmonetary eligibility

Claimants who were nonmonetarily ineligible for the duration of their claim were also not eligible to receive a bonus in any of the three experiments. Duration exclusions usually occurred because of "separation" issues; i.e., the claimant had been fired for cause or had voluntarily quit (does not include "good cause" quits, such as for sexual harassment). Nonduration issues, such as not being available for work, did not preclude eligibility for any of the experiments because these conditions were removable by the decision to search actively for work, an event regarded as positive for the experiment.

Nonmonetary ineligibility was handled somewhat differently in each of the three experiments. In all experiments, bonus offers were made to all who were monetarily eligible. However, in Washington and Illinois, an offer letter (officially making the offer) would not be sent until all nonmonetary duration stops had been removed for at least one week. If the stops were removed during the qualification period, then a bonus offer was made and a bonus could be collected. In Pennsylvania, nonmonetary eligibility was checked when the bonus was claimed. Individuals who had been disqualified for the duration of their unemployment were not eligible to receive the bonus, but individuals disqualified for shorter periods could receive the bonus.

Not totally interstate, UCFE or UCX

Interstate claims are filed by claimants whose wage credits were accumulated in another state; that state is then charged with the costs of benefit payments for the interstate claimant. UCFE is the code for federal employees and UCX is the code for veterans who have been recently discharged from the service. In both of these cases, the benefits are paid under special programs by the federal government. All three experiments eliminated these groups, because UI payments for these claims were not made out of the state UI trust funds, therefore there was no potential saving to the state UI systems for these groups. A universal system would probably include these groups.

Recall status or referral union member

In an effort to reduce windfall gain, groups of individuals whose *ex ante* identification could be used for screening and whose length of unemployment was primarily determined by someone other than themselves were excluded from the Pennsylvania experiment. One such group was UI claimants on standby awaiting recall to a prior job. A second group was members of full referral unions (i.e., unions that operate hiring halls and take full responsibility for placing their members). Claimants on standby with specific recall dates within 60 days and claimants who were members of full referral unions were exempt from UI work-search requirements in all three states.

The three experiments had different rules regarding participation of UI claimants on standby or of members of full referral unions, but the effects were not that different. These claimants were not eligible to participate in the Pennsylvania experiment as stated above, did not generally participate in the Illinois experiment, and were fully eligible to participate in the Washington experiment. In both Pennsylvania and Washington, however, claimants who were in fact recalled to their previous job were ineligible to receive bonuses, even if they had been enrolled in the experiment. In Washington (but not in Pennsylvania), the same was true for claimants who had been placed on their first post-unemployment jobs through union hiring halls. In Illinois, there was no prohibition against paying bonuses to recalled workers or to workers placed on jobs through a union hiring hall. However, workers expecting recall with firm recall dates or expecting to be placed by the union were not required to register with the ES and generally did not do so. If they did not show up the ES office, they would not have been enrolled in the experiment. Thus, most of such UI claimants were de facto excluded from the Illinois experiment.

For the Washington experiment, the rationale ran as follows: even an individual on standby or a member of a full referral union can seek, and obtain, other employment. Thus, the claimant's behavior can be influenced by a bonus offer, and he or she should have the opportunity to change behavior. However, there is no reason to pay a bonus to someone who is in fact recalled to his or her previous job or placed through the union hiring hall since the bonus offer could not have influenced that decision.[4] If the claimant could demonstrate that the job with the previous employer was a "new" job, then bonus payment would not be withheld. It was not desirable for the bonus offer to discourage workers who had been laid off from one job in a company from taking an entirely different job in the same company.[5]

In the design stage, several union representatives objected to this provision but went along with it as an experiment, although they stated that they would oppose this provision if the bonus offer were to become a regular UI program. Table 2.2 summarizes the recall requirements in the bonus experiments.

Although these rules were somewhat different among the states, the end results were similar in that recalled workers did not receive bonuses in Pennsylvania and Washington, and most of such workers had not registered with the ES in Illinois and thus were ineligible for the bonus.

Backdated claims

Backdating refers to the process of starting a benefit year at a date prior to the Sunday of the filing week. A one-week backdating to cover the waiting week often occurs if there is good reason for the claimant

Table 2.2 UI and Bonus Eligibility for Workers Expecting Recall[a]

Bonus receipt / Enrollment	Recalled worker can receive bonus	Recalled worker cannot receive bonus
Worker on standby can enroll in experiment	Illinois (only if worker registers with ES)	Washington
Worker on standby cannot enroll in experiment		Pennsylvania Illinois (if worker does not register with ES)

[a] Definitions of recall: Washington, return to same job with layoff employer; Pennsylvania, have recall date with layoff employer.

not filing in the first unemployment week. More extensive backdating occasionally occurs for a variety of reasons (e.g., claimant was ill). In the Pennsylvania experiment, a claim backdated more than two weeks made the claimant ineligible to participate in Pennsylvania. There were no such restrictions in Washington or Illinois.[6]

Register with the Job Service

Registration for job search was an explicit requirement for participation only in the Illinois experiment. In Illinois, enrollment took place in the ES office at the time the claimant registered for job search. Such registration was required of all claimants not explicitly exempted from job search.[7]

NATURE OF THE EXPERIMENTAL TREATMENTS

General Issues

A *treatment* is a particular program configuration that participants are offered or required to accept. A treatment may be a single well-defined program element (e.g., the offer of a $500 reemployment bonus) or it may be a combination of several program elements. For example, a treatment may combine an offer of a reemployment bonus with job-search assistance. If this is the only treatment, then the experimental results will be valid only for that particular combination of program elements. To determine the contribution of any one program component, it is necessary to have more than one treatment that properly nests the program components: for example, one treatment with bonus offer only, a second treatment with job-search assistance and work search requirements only, and a third that combines the two. The third treatment is necessary only if you believe that all the components together will have a different effect than the sum of the effects of the separate components (i.e., a strong interactive effect among the program components). If this is not the case, then either treatment 2 or 3 could be dropped.

In most social program experiments, those eligible members of the population assigned to the experiments are free to accept or reject participation in the program.[8] For instance, UI claimants assigned to receive bonus offers were not required to either change job-search behavior or file for a bonus if they met the conditions for payment. As long as all individuals *assigned* to the treatment group are considered members for evaluative purposes, no harm is done to experimental integrity by having acceptance of the program voluntary.

Variation in the level or quantity of the program elements is necessary if an experimental objective is to evaluate more than one level of a program or, more aggressively, to determine an optimum level for a program. If a program has more than one level (e.g., different support levels for an income maintenance program or different bonus offers for a reemployment bonus program), then interpolation between two treatments in the experiment can be used to estimate the effects of programs levels that have not been tested but that lie between the two tested levels. This, of course, is "modeling" in the strict sense, but the necessary assumptions are sufficiently weak as to not cause undue concern. Of course, if three levels are tested, then the linearity assumption can be more strongly evaluated.

Elements of the Bonus Treatment

The three bonus offer experiments all had the same three basic components: 1) the bonus amount—the dollar value of the bonus offer, 2) the qualification period—the length of time from the date of enrollment into the experiment to the last date on which the claimant must start a qualifying job, and 3) the reemployment period—the length of time after starting a qualifying job that the claimant must remain fully employed in order to collect the bonus.[9] The first two components varied among the three experiments, but the third did not. The reemployment period was set at four months in all experiments (16 weeks in Pennsylvania). The variations in bonus amount offered and qualification period among the three experiments are shown in Table 2.3.

The value of the bonus offer

Recognizing that acceptance of a bonus offer is intended to generate a change in job-seeking or job-accepting behavior, there is an implicit trade-off facing the claimant between the bonus and the UI benefits that will be foregone by taking a job sooner than would have

Table 2.3 Bonus and Qualification Period Structure of the Three Bonus Experiments

Treatment designation	Bonus offer ($)	Qualification period (weeks)	Average bonus[a] ($)	Average qualification period (weeks)
Illinois				
All bonus offers	500	11	500	11
Pennsylvania				
Short-low bonus offers	3 × WBA[b]	6	500	6
Short-high bonus offers	6 × WBA	6	1,003	6
Long-low bonus offers	3 × WBA	12	498	12
Long-high bonus offers	6 × WBA	12	989	12
Washington				
Short-low bonus offers	2 × WBA	(0.2 × UI duration) + 1	302	5.7
Short-medium bonus offers	4 × WBA	(0.2 × UI duration) + 1	610	5.8
Short-high bonus offers	6 × WBA	(0.2 × UI duration) + 1	917	5.7
Long-low bonus offers	2 × WBA	(0.4 × UI duration) + 1	303	11.0
Long-medium bonus 52 offers	4 × WBA	(0.4 × UI duration) + 1	612	11.0
Long-high bonus offers	6 × WBA	(0.4 × UI duration) + 1	924	11.1

[a] All dollar values are in nominal dollars. See Chapter 8, note 2, for information on use of the CPI to adjust the values for inflation.
[b] WBA: weekly benefit amount.

been the case without the bonus offer. The value of a week's worth of UI benefits is represented by the weekly benefit amount (WBA). Thus, a fixed dollar offer is worth more to a claimant with a low WBA than to a claimant with a high WBA because each week's reduction in benefit payments is more costly to the latter. With this view of the bonus offer, the Pennsylvania and Washington experiments both priced the bonus offer in multiples of the WBA. For example, a bonus offer equal to 3 × WBA implies that all claimants are offered a bonus equal to three weeks of UI benefits.

A second issue facing the designers of the experiment involved the range of bonus amounts—what should be the smallest and largest WBA multiplier and how many different multipliers should be used? The objective was to have a sufficient range and number of bonus offers to enable evaluators to determine how response is affected by the size of the bonus offer, thus permitting policymakers to select the most cost-effective bonus offer. The determination of the range and number of options was partly determined by decisions on a likely policy range, what differences would be large enough to elicit significant differences in response, how many treatments would be necessary to properly map the response surface, and finally, cost.

Two bonus offers, one at the minimum and one at the maximum of the feasible range, would be sufficient to provide a basis for estimating the effects over a full range of options. However, interpolations are constrained to an assumption of linear differences in effects. Thus, if one treatment is at $2 \times WBA$ and another is at $6 \times WBA$, then it must be assumed that a treatment at $4 \times WBA$ has an effect halfway between that of the two observed treatments. More than two bonus offer levels would permit validation of this linear effect hypothesis or some estimation of a nonlinear response surface. The three experiments differed in regard to ranges of offers. The $500 bonus offer in the Illinois experiment provided unplanned variations in the bonus/WBA ratio that ranged from $3 \times WBA$ to $10 \times WBA$.[10] However, the natural differences in this ratio may correlate with other variables that affect behavior and therefore do not provide as a good a basis for decision making as planned variations. Pennsylvania had two and Washington had three planned levels of bonus/WBA offers.[11]

Although the treatments in Washington and Pennsylvania were specified in terms of multiples of the claimant's WBA, the actual offer was for a fixed number of dollars. Thus, a claimant who had a WBA of $175 and an assigned treatment of $6 \times WBA$ received a bonus offer of $1,050. The claimant was not made aware of the algorithm used to calculate the bonus offer. The actual dollar offers varied over a fairly wide range, as follows:

Washington: the minimum bonus offer was $110 ($2 \times$ the minimum WBA of $55) and the maximum offer was for $1,254 ($6 \times$ the maximum WBA of $209). At the mean WBA of $153, a mid-range offer of 4 × WBA would have a value of $612.

Pennsylvania: the offers ranged from a minimum of $105 (3 × the minimum WBA of $35) to a maximum offer of $1,596 (6 × the maximum WBA of $266, increased from $252 in 1989).

Qualification period

The second component of the bonus offer is the qualification period, i.e., the maximum duration of the initial spell of insured unemployment that the participant could experience and still qualify for the bonus. The length of the qualification period is important because it may influence the cost-effectiveness of the prospective program. A long qualification period will permit more eligible claimants to be affected by the offer, while at the same time it increases the opportunity for persons who do not alter their job seeking behavior to collect a bonus. These contradictory behavioral outcomes imply that the net effect of differing qualification periods would need to be determined empirically. As a result, both the Washington and Pennsylvania experiments varied the length of the qualification period.

As noted above, earlier acceptance of a job to earn a bonus imposes a cost to the participant equivalent to the amount of UI benefit payments foregone. The qualification period should be considered in this context. A 12-week qualification period is 46 percent of the entitled duration of 26 weeks in Pennsylvania or Illinois.[12] However, in Washington, where the entitled duration ranges from 10 to 30 weeks, a 12-week qualification period may be as low as 40 percent of entitled duration to more than 100 percent. If claimant job-search behavior is related to the length of entitlement, then a qualification period as a fixed proportion of benefit duration rather than a fixed number of weeks represents a more homogeneous treatment in a state with variable benefit durations.

Thus, the Washington experiment design had two qualification periods, one at 20 percent of the time that the individual claimant could draw full benefits (i.e., the compensable duration) plus one week to account for the waiting week, and a second set of treatments at 40 percent of compensable duration plus one week. If the algorithm resulted in a qualification period having a fraction of a week, the qualification period was rounded to the next highest whole number of weeks. Since the duration of entitlement could run from 10 to 30 weeks, the short-qualification-period treatments ranged from a minimum of three weeks ($0.2 \times 10 + 1$ week) to a maximum of seven weeks ($0.2 \times 30 + 1$ week). The long-qualification period ranged from five weeks ($0.4 \times 10 + 1$ week) to a maximum of 13 weeks ($0.4 \times 30 + 1$ week).

In Pennsylvania, the 6-week qualification period was 22 percent of the 26-week entitlement faced by most claimants (i.e., 6/27ths of the period, including the waiting week), and the 12-week qualification period was 44 percent of the 26-week entitlement. These proportions are similar to those of the short and long qualifications in Washington. In Illinois, the qualification period was fixed at 11 weeks, which was 40 percent of the 26-week fixed entitled duration of benefits in Illinois (plus the waiting week).

The reemployment period

The reemployment period is the length of time that the participating claimant needed to remain fully employed after terminating receipt of benefits in order to qualify for a bonus. Four months was the length of time selected for this parameter of the system in all of the experiments (16 weeks in Pennsylvania). Response was not expected to be sufficiently sensitive to variations in this parameter to warrant varying it experimentally.[13] The four-month interval was believed to be sufficiently long to avoid encouraging claimants to accept short-term employment simply to qualify for a bonus. It was also sufficiently long to avoid payment for employment on temporary seasonal jobs (e.g., harvesting in the summer, Christmas employment, or canning in the fishing season).

The reemployment period had to be served with the same employer in Illinois, whereas it was only necessary that the claimant remain fully employed in Pennsylvania and Washington, which was defined as taking not more than a week to change jobs and not filing for benefits during the transition period. Eighty to 85 percent of participants who obtained qualifying jobs met the reemployment period conditions. Surprisingly, there was little difference in this regard between Illinois and the other two experiments.

DETERMINING THE NUMBER AND
ALLOCATION OF PARTICIPANTS

General Issues

Determining the number of claimants to enroll in the experiment
and the number to enroll in each treatment and the control group are
critical decisions. Nothing is more frustrating than spending several
years and several million dollars on an experiment only to conclude
that the number of participants was too small to enable the evaluators
to draw statistically reliable conclusions about the results. In the discussion to follow, the term *sample size* is used to describe the number
of claimants selected to participate in the experiment. Despite its
importance, the subject of sample size is given little attention in books
on experimental or evaluation methodology. In a 500-page book by
Rossi and Freeman (1989), sampling is mentioned only once and does
not merit inclusion in the index. Hausman and Wise (1985) discussed
sampling as an issue of randomization and selection, not as an issue of
size and cost. Cohen's (1988) important book deals with the sample
size implications of statistical reliability, but not with cost and feasibil-
ity.

On the other hand, actual experiments must deal with the trade-off
between cost and reliability in determining sample size. In the early
income maintenance experiments, the question was posed as a mathematical programming problem in which the sample was allocated
among income and treatment cells to get the maximum information
about labor supply response from a given budget.[14] In this approach,
the question was never asked as to whether the response would be sufficient for policy purposes.

The correct approach is to provide answers to the following four
sequential questions. 1) What effect must the proposed experimental
program have in order to justify its implementation as a full program?
2) What sample size will be needed to generate a result such that, if the
true response is the expected response, the result will be statistically
significant? 3) How much will this experiment cost? 4) Is the answer
sufficiently important to justify the cost? Thus, the experimental
designers must be prepared to abort the process if it is determined that

the budget available for the experiment is insufficient to generate a usable response. Each of the four points, especially the first two, are described in more detail below.

Sample Design for the Bonus Experiments

The critical operational question for sample design was the number of claimants that would need to be enrolled into each treatment or control group at each site to meet specified design goals. The principal design goal was to generate experimental samples that would have the ability to detect specified changes in the parameters of interest, namely the length of insured unemployment and the amount of UI benefit payments.

In the first bonus experiment, the Illinois experiment, these questions were not asked explicitly because the experimenters had no guideline as to what changes to expect and no guidance from the state as to what changes were of policy interest. The approach in Illinois was to first establish a budget for payment of bonuses, i.e., $750,000 for the two experiments based upon the Wagner-Payser funds available to the state of Illinois for these purposes.[15] The next step was to determine how many claimants needed to be enrolled in order to pay 1,500 bonuses of $500 each.

In Washington, there was no predetermined budget at the point the sample size was being determined. The sample requirements were based on the sample sizes needed in each treatment cell to detect impacts on weeks of insured unemployment as large as those found in the Illinois experiment (1.15 weeks). Based on Washington budget estimates, a budget was established by the U.S. Department of Labor for the Pennsylvania experiment. The sample design task in Pennsylvania was then to allocate the budget to achieve an optimum amount of information and to assure that the experiment could provide reasonable results. In the following discussion, we present the sample design procedures first for Illinois, then for Washington, and then the more elaborate modeling that resulted in the Pennsylvania design.

Sample design in Illinois

In Illinois, there were two treatments and a control group to which assignments were to be made.[16] The decision was made to assign one-third of the eligible population to each of the three groups. This was to be accomplished by using the last two digits of the claimant's social security number, a number which had been randomly generated, thereby assuring random assignment of the eligible population.

The sample design task was to determine how many bonus offers to make in order to make bonus payments of $500 each to 1,500 participants in the two treatments (just sufficient to exhaust the $750,000 bonus budget). The following estimates were made using the data provided by the Illinois Department of Employment Security (DES) on the number of ES registrants filing new valid claims in the last available quarter in the 19 UI offices that had been selected for the experiment: 1) the expected number of filers in Fall 1984 (the anticipated enrollment period), 2) the proportion that would be expected to accept the offer to enroll in the program, 3) the proportion that would be expected to obtain jobs within the qualification period and retain them for at least four months, and 4) an added proportion that might be expected to meet these qualifications as a result of the bonus offer.

The investigators arbitrarily assumed a refusal rate of 10 percent (based generally on experience). The estimated job acquisition rate of 0.317 was equal to the proportion of claimants in the observed period who obtained employment within 10 weeks of filing (the experimental design called for 11 weeks, but the data were provided on a 1–10 and 11–15 week basis). Of those obtaining employment, about 80 percent were estimated to have retained their jobs for at least four months, reducing to 1,212 the number of enrolled claimants expected to earn a bonus without any impact on behavior. We then assumed that two-thirds of those who actually terminated benefits in the 11–15 week period would respond to the bonus and reduce their unemployment spell below 11 weeks. Based on data for the period between July and September 1983, this would add 294 bonus recipients, bringing to 1,506 the expected number of bonus payments.

This rather ad hoc method of estimation was designed to provide a benchmark for enrollment. Continuous monitoring of the enrollment process was used to provide real-time estimates of the number of claimants terminating benefits within the qualification period and filing a notice in that regard. This monitoring process permitted the state to modify enrollment rates and determine the length of the enrollment period based on actual experience.

In the end, however, only 570 bonuses were paid, leaving half of the bonus budget on the table. A major reason for the large overestimate was the failure of the model to consider that many claimants would meet all the conditions for bonus eligibility but not apply (see discussion of the "take-up" issue in Chapter 3). This was particularly true in the employer experiment. While the model predicted that 29 percent of assigned eligible claimants would collect bonuses, the employer experiment paid bonuses to only 3 percent of the employers of eligible claimants. The claimant experiment also fell short of its goal, but by a considerably smaller amount. Fourteen percent of assigned eligible claimants collected bonuses, against a predicted 29 percent. (The shortfall in bonus payments was somewhat mitigated by assigning an additional 2,900 eligible claimants.)

Sample design in Washington

In Washington, sample sizes were selected to enable measurement of changes in key parameters vis-à-vis the control group. In determining the sample, attention was focused on the duration of insured unemployment, and sample sizes in each treatment were set to detect an experimental effect as large as that found in the Illinois experiment, i.e., 1.15 weeks.

Statistical texts such as Cohen (1988) provide the information necessary to determine sample size requirements utilizing four pieces of information: the number of treatment and control groups in the experiment, the estimated (or desired) experimental effect for each treatment group, an estimate of the standard deviation of the population, and the desired statistical properties of the results.

The required sample size for an experimental cell is dictated by two policy criteria: 1) the policymaker wants to have a high degree of confidence that it does not implement an ineffective policy and 2) the policymaker also wants confidence that it does not reject an effective policy. To meet these dual objectives, two statistical tests are administered: 1) a test of statistical significance, which means that, if a program is judged to be effective, the level of statistical significance gives the probability that this judgment is wrong, and 2) the power evaluation, which gives the probability that if a program is effective, our test will reveal it to be so.

A statistical significance level of 5 percent and a power of 80 percent is a typical combination of standards used by many analysts. If a program is judged to have an effect using these standards, there is a 5 percent probability that there is no effect and there is an 80 percent chance of detecting an effect when there is one. A decision must also be made as to whether a one-tailed or two-tailed significance level is to be used. The two-tailed test is generally preferred, unless it is almost certain that policy interest is in only one direction.[17]

In Washington, we imposed a more stringent 1 percent statistical significance test but used only the one-tailed criteria.[18] The 0.01 significance test was used with a power of 0.8. A table from Cohen (1977, pp. 54–55), part of which is reproduced as Table 2.4, shows that each cell would need at least 2,000 observations to meet these conditions.

To apply the Cohen table, the appropriate effect size index must be determined. For the Washington experiment, the effect size index was determined to be 0.1, based on a desire to measure a 1.15-week impact on weeks of insured unemployment and the determination that the standard deviation of the distribution of weeks in the population was about 12 weeks. The effect size index is the estimated impact in standard deviation units (i.e., 1.15/12).[19] The data in the table show that the sample size is very sensitive to the power requirements.[20]

The sample size requirement relates to that of a single cell. The next step in determining total sample size is to set the number of cells (treatment and control groups) and the degree of variation among treat-

**Table 2.4 Sample Sizes for Treatment Group,
Significance Level (one-tailed) = 0.01**

Power	Effect size index = 0.1[a]	Effect size index = 0.2
0.5	1,083	272
0.6	1,332	334
0.7	1,627	408
0.8	2,009	503
0.9	2,605	652

SOURCE: Cohen (1977), Table 2.4.1, p. 55.
[a] See text for discussion and calculation of effect size index.

ments. In determining sample size, the same considerations hold in designing experiments to distinguish between the impact of two treatments as in measuring the impact of a treatment relative to a control group.[21] If the basic treatment is an offer of a $500 bonus (compared with zero), much larger samples would be needed to detect the difference in impact of a $600 bonus offer. In Washington, each treatment progressed in increments of $2 \times WBA$. Since the Illinois treatment was equivalent to about $4 \times WBA$, we should have considered larger sample sizes to detect differences in impact among the treatments.

For a comparison of treatments that represent different quantitative measures of the same variable, imposition of some modeling constraints can reduce the sample size requirement. In the Seattle/Denver Income Maintenance Experiment there were 11 treatments. However, much of the analysis was conducted using a labor supply model in which the differences across treatments in tax rates and support levels were reduced to a model with two variables, thereby substantially reducing the sample size requirements for estimating experimental effects (see Spiegelman, Robins, and West 1983). In the bonus experiments, the bonus values and qualification periods were redefined as continuous variables and estimated in a model with essentially two variables. The cost, of course, is the imposition of constraints on the relationship among the treatment variables.

To estimate the cost of a seven-cell experiment with an average sample size of 2,000 observations per cell, it was necessary to estimate the cost in bonus payments. This required prediction of the average value of the bonus payment and the take-up rate (i.e., the proportion of eligible claimants who collected bonuses). Since the experimental design called for bonus offers to be multiples of the individual WBA, it was no longer a fixed dollar amount as it had been in Illinois. The final sample design called for an unbalanced design underweighting the more expensive treatments: 20 percent of the sample would be controls; 15 percent in each of the four treatments with multipliers of $2 \times WBA$ or $4 \times WBA$; and 10 percent of the sample in each of the two treatments with a bonus multiplier of $6 \times WBA$. The average bonus offer was predicted to be $565 using the 1988 average WBA in the state of Washington of $148 and an average multiplier of 3.8.

The take-up rate was estimated to be 0.1875, leading to an expected bonus cost per eligible claimant of about $106. The take-up rate was loosely based on the Illinois experience of 0.14 and an expectation that improved information to claimants and more extensive follow-up procedures would increase take-up. This did out not turn out to be the case.

As a result of these estimates, the total sample of 12,000 treatment-assigned claimants yielded a final budget estimate of about $1,270,000 (see Spiegelman, O'Leary, and Kline 1992, p. 21). The U.S. Department of Labor allocated $1.2 million for bonus payments. Despite some differences in actual parameters (the bonuses paid were larger and the take-up rate lower than projected), careful online monitoring led to actual bonus payments within 1 percent of those projected.

Sample design in Pennsylvania

In Pennsylvania, two major design goals were established: 1) the ability to detect a UI cost saving of $150 (about one week of average UI benefits) from the high bonus offer and 2) the ability to detect a $150 cost saving of moving from a 12-week to a 6-week qualification period. A third, subsidiary goal was to detect a $150 cost saving from the removal of the workshop offer.[22] Saving of a week's worth of benefit payments was about the average saving in Illinois and in the New Jersey experiment (although the Illinois saving resulted from a bonus offer closer to $4 \times WBA$, rather than the $6 \times WBA$ in Pennsylvania). The sample sizes per treatment cell were those necessary to meet the measurement goals at a minimum of 80 percent power for a one-tailed test at the 5 percent significant level.

A formal sample allocation model was developed for Pennsylvania, based on the design objectives, on assumptions about the magnitude of the response to the bonus offer, on the cost of individual treatments, and on an overall budgetary constraint for the treatments.[23] The sample allocation obtained from the model provided for 3,000 control and 10,120 treatment group members allocated among the six treatments, with cell sizes ranging from 1,030 to 2,240. In the end, the high-bonus, long-qualification-period treatment, both with and without workshop, had 3,370 observations (see Corson et al. (1991), Table I.2, p. 12).

SELECTION OF EXPERIMENTAL SITES

General Issues

Determining where to conduct the experiment (site selection) is an often trivialized activity that in fact is as important as determining the number of individuals to enroll in the experiment. The number of sites has important experimental ramifications. As the number of sites increase, several things occur: 1) the effects on the results due to the idiosyncratic actions of specific site administrators are reduced; 2) the influence of external shocks that may occur during the experiment in specific sites (e.g., a major plant closing) is mitigated; 3) the experimental sample, and thus the results, become more representative of a larger population group (i.e., a state instead of a city); and 4) the administrative costs increase.[24]

Although the increased administrative costs of a large number of sites is usually small relative to the total cost of an experiment, control over experimental operations—which is important—is weakened in a multisite experiment. The staff of the organizational unit managing experimental operations is usually small, making it difficult to properly monitor operations occurring simultaneously in many sites.

A case may also be made for a small number of sites if there are effects of scale in the operations. This is of little consequence in a bonus offer program but is important in workfare-type programs, in which a whole office is mobilized to carry out the experimental program. It is also important in training programs, where the breadth of the offering is important, and in counseling programs, where the existence of a dedicated staff is important.

Site selection may not arise in experiments that are conducted statewide. The U.S. Department of Labor had a requirement that experimental populations should be representative of the state in which the experiment was conducted. In the Washington experiment, this was accomplished by conducting the experiment in almost all of the state's Job Service Centers.

When the number of sites is a small proportion of the total available, site selection should be viewed as the first stage in a two-stage sampling process and the principles of randomization should apply to both stages; that is, there should be random selection of sites and random selection of sample observations within selected sites. Metcalf and Kerachsky (1988) pointed out that failure to recognize that site differences contribute to the variance in the parameter estimates can lead to design errors.

Site Selection in the Bonus Experiments

With a total desired sample size determined, the next step is to determine where within each state to conduct the experiment. This decision is intimately tied to sample size considerations, as well as to determination of the length of the enrollment period. The total sample size, number of sites in which the experiment is conducted, rate of enrollment at each site, and length of the enrollment period are all tied together in a single equation. A decision with regard to any one of these variables affects the parameters of the others.

In Pennsylvania and Washington, UI offices for filing claims served as sites. Employment Service offices for registering claimants (and others) for job search were the sites in Illinois. In Washington, UI and ES offices were coterminous. In Pennsylvania, there are both coterminous and noncoterminous sites, but only the former were included in the experiment. Illinois also had both coterminous and noncoterminous sites, but both were included in the experiment. The decisions as to the number of sites, their location within the state, and the flow rate of enrollees were made on the basis of several complex considerations, including the following.

1) Reliance on local office staffs with no previous experience in administering a bonus offer program indicated that a large number of agency personnel should be involved in order to reduce the influence of any individual agents. On the other hand, the need to train agency personnel and monitor their performance put practical ceilings on the number of sites.

2) The sensitivity of the results to job-search success indicated the need to minimize the potential impact of specific labor market influences, such as adverse weather or a large plant closing.

3) The desire to be able to generalize the results dictated that the experimental sample be representative of the state or other large

populations (coupled with the U.S. Department of Labor requirements for Washington and Pennsylvania that the sample replicate the characteristics of the host state population).

4) Treatment consisted only of cash offers in Illinois and Washington, so there was no critical mass needed to conduct the experiment. Pennsylvania, with its job-search assistance component, did have the potential of enrollment rates being too low to maintain a program effort. Even in Illinois and Washington, however, there were minimums because of the need to train agency personnel to conduct enrollment interviews and the desire to keep a sufficient caseload to maintain staff interest and capability. There were no numbers attached to this requirement, but enrolling 16 percent of eligible new claimants in Washington was regarded as a minimum.

5) The previous four considerations all deal with establishing minimum sample sizes. There were also some issues that would tend to set maximum sample size. During the four-month enrollment period in Illinois, all eligible claimants were offered the opportunity to enroll. The operational burden on the counseling staff was not a consideration because it was a time that caseloads were falling and counselors were easily able to handle the additional workload. In Washington and Pennsylvania, however, there were practical limits to the enrollment rate, because hiring new personnel was not considered and the ability to add caseloads to the existing staff was limited. The desire to reduce the possibility of displacement of control group members also supported the decision not to enroll all eligible participants at a single site. In Washington, 16 percent of eligibles were enrolled at 20 of the 21 sites, and 32 percent enrolled at the remaining site. In Pennsylvania, 26 percent of eligible UI claimants were enrolled. These percentages are large enough to raise the spector of displacement, an issue discussed in Chapter 6.

Site selection in Illinois

In Illinois, 22 Employment Service offices (also referred to as Job Service Centers) were used as experimental sites. Enrollment into the experiment was carried out by Employment Service counselors.

Although job-search services are often provided by the Employment Service and UI offices under a single roof, only 10 of the 22 Employment Service offices in which the experiment was conducted had coterminous Employment Service and UI offices, and almost all of these were outside of Chicago.[25]

Offices south of Springfield were eliminated to reduce administrative costs and to make the sample more representative of the industrial base; employment in the south of the state was more heavily in agriculture and mining. The central and northern areas were divided into four regions: Chicago (eight sites), Metro-outlying (four), Central (four), and Northwest (five) areas of the state. The largest offices in each area were selected with a view of acquiring the necessary caseload in four or fewer months and balancing the caseload among the four areas.

Site selection in Washington

Site selection decisions emanated easily from the basic decision to have the experimental sample replicate the characteristics of the state's population. The decision was simply to eliminate as few sites as possible and carry out the experiment in the rest of the Job Service Centers (all joint UI/ES offices.) In the end, 10 of the state's 31 Job Service Centers were eliminated: seven were too small and remote, two were part of other state experimental programs that could have contaminated the results, and one (Vancouver) was part of the Portland, Oregon, metropolitan area. The 21 offices included in the study accounted for approximately 85 percent of the state's UI claims.

The replication of state characteristics in the enrollment sites was increased by doubling the sampling rate at one site, Rainier. Because of the elimination of Pierce County (Tacoma and Lakewood Job Services), a large concentration of the state's black population was eliminated. To compensate, enrollment in Rainier, located in King County adjacent to Pierce County and also containing a large concentration of the black population, was doubled. As a result, the enrolled claimant population had the racial mix of the state as a whole (i.e., about 85 percent non-Hispanic white, 4 percent black, and 11 percent other).

Site selection in Pennsylvania

An early decision was made to conduct the Pennsylvania experiment in 12 sites, both for operational reasons and because analysis showed that 12 sites was a sufficient number to reduce site-specific effects on the variance to an acceptable size. Desiring to enroll participants in only 12 of the state's 87 UC offices and able to eliminate only 24 for cause (mostly for being too small or not having collocation of Unemployment Compensation and Job Service offices), the researchers adopted a process of stratified random sampling to select the 12 out of the 63 eligible sites. The principle was to assure that each eligible claimant in the 63 sites had an equal chance of being selected into the experiment. With only 12 sites to be selected, the researchers wanted to guard against an accidentally skewed selection of sites with regard to administrative region of the state or duration of UI benefits. The latter stood as proxy for employment conditions in the local labor market. Seven regions and four duration categories provided the potential for stratification into 28 cells, which exceeded the number of sites to be selected. As described by Metcalf and Kerachsky (1988), the 28 cells were condensed into 12 clusters with approximately equal size UI caseloads. One site was randomly selected from each cell.

CHARACTERISTICS OF THE ENVIRONMENT

Characteristics of the States of Illinois, Pennsylvania, and Washington

Table 2.5 provides information on the three states in which bonus experiments were conducted, permitting comparison among states and over the two years for each state that were most relevant for the operational phases of the experiments. What do we learn from this table that is of importance to understanding the working of the bonus experiments?

Illinois and Pennsylvania were close in size and population density and experienced little population change over the relevant period. Washington was considerably smaller and less dense, but it experienced some modest population growth in the period. Illinois had the

**Table 2.5 Characteristics of the Illinois, Pennsylvania, and Washington
States in Selected Years**

	Illinois		Pennsylvania		Washington	
Characteristic	1984	1985	1989	1990	1988	1989
Population (000)	11,511	11,535	12,040	11,882	4,648	4,761
Pop/sq. mile	207	207	268	265	70	72
Racial groups (%)[a]						
Black	14.7		9.2		3.1	
Hispanic	5.6		2.0		4.4	
Asian	0.2		1.2		1.3	
Nat. American	0.1		0.1		1.7	
Labor force (000)	5,604	5,673	5,857	5,901	2,295	2,451
Employment (000)	5,093	5,160	5,592	5,583	2,153	2,300
Insured unemployment rate (%)	2.5	2.7	2.4	3.1	3.0	2.9
Total unemployment rate (%)	8.4	8.9	4.8	5.8	5.8	5.5
Labor force participation (%)						
Male	76.8	78.2	73.4	73.2	74.1	76.9
Female	54.3	54.4	52.8	53.5	59.5	61.4
UI claims (000)	835	836	1044	1184	465	457
Exhaust. rate (%)	39.4	38.7	23.3	25.1	27.9	25.7
Avg. weekly wage ($)	364	377	419	441	393	403
Avg. compensation duration (weeks)	18.6	17.2	14.5	14.8	14.8	15.3
Avg. WBA ($)	134	136	182	189	151	156
WBA/weekly wage	0.368	0.361	0.434	0.429	0.384	0.387

SOURCE: U.S. Dept. of Labor, Bureau of Labor Statistics (1984, 1985, 1988, 1989, 1990); U.S. Dept. of Commerce (1986, 1987, 1989, 1990, 1991, 1992); U.S. Dept. of Labor, Employment and Training Administration (1984, 1985, 1988, 1989, 1990).
[a] Available only for census years: Illinois 1980; Pennsylvania 1990; Washington 1990.

largest non-Caucasian population proportions and Washington the smallest. The proportion of blacks in Washington was considerably below the national average.

Labor force participation was similar, although male labor force participation was somewhat higher in Illinois than in the other two states and female labor force participation was somewhat higher in Washington than in the other two. Employment grew in both Illinois and Washington in the relevant periods but declined slightly in Pennsylvania. The total unemployment rate (TUR) was much higher in Illinois in the period, which reflects the conditions at the time. However, the insured unemployment rate (IUR) did not differ much across the states, despite the differences in TUR.

Relative to the sizes of the labor forces in the three states, it would appear that initial claims were lower in Illinois and were fairly stable across the two-year period. The much higher exhaustion rate in Illinois is consistent with the relatively low ratio of IUR to TUR in the state, as one explanation for the low ratio is a large number of exhaustees who remain unemployed. However, the low initial claims in Illinois may reflect a lower rate of layoffs in the early phases of a recovery that had not yet translated into significant job growth. The longer duration of compensation in Illinois was consistent with greater exhaustion of benefits and with the lingering effects of the recession. (The durations are for regular benefits and, therefore, do not include the effects of the extended benefit program.)

The lower weekly wage rate in Illinois is consistent with the difference in timing of the experiments, fully reflecting the 3 percent rate of inflation that characterized the period. Overall, the Pennsylvania UI program appears to be the more generous as displayed by the higher WBA/weekly wage ratio, known as the "replacement rate."

What does this information tell us about possible differences in impact of the bonus offer among states? The higher exhaustion rates and longer durations of insured unemployment in Illinois imply either 1) worse job prospects for covered workers in this state, at that time, than in the other two states or 2) a much greater tendency to use the UI system to voluntarily extend unemployment. The much higher TUR suggests the former. Employment growth was very modest, and the increasing labor force participation led to increases in unemployment rates—not suggestive of a situation in which increased job search would be productive. However, to the extent it is successful, there were potentially greater savings in Illinois, as the bonus responder would be, on average, making a greater reduction in the length of the unemployment spell than his peer in Pennsylvania or Washington. Thus, the economic data from the states are ambiguous as a basis for explaining the larger impact of the bonus offer in Illinois.

The higher wage replacement rate in Pennsylvania implies that a bonus offer representing the same ratio of bonus offer to WBA in the three states is more generous in terms of earning equivalence in Pennsylvania, which leads to an expectation of greater response in Pennsylvania.

Comparison of Control Groups across the Three Experiments

The control group represents the population from which the experimental sample is drawn. Differences and similarities among the control groups of the three experiments can help explain differences in the effects of the experimental treatments. Table 2.6 displays characteristics (including basic demographic and economic characteristics) of the control group members. There are some potentially important similarities and differences worth mentioning. The Illinois sample was slightly more female than the Washington or Pennsylvania samples, which both show a 60/40 male/female split—not unlike the working population. The age distributions are remarkably similar in Pennsylvania and Washington but differ by design in Illinois, which set 55 as the maximum age for enrollment. Nevertheless, the Illinois sample is even younger than indicated by the design, because it differs from the other two in the proportion of those under age 35.

In terms of racial differences, Illinois had a much lower proportion of white non-Hispanics and a much higher proportion of blacks than either Pennsylvania or Washington. The proportion of blacks is particularly low in Washington, consistent with its population mix. The basic manufacturing/nonmanufacturing industrial mixes are essentially the same in the three experiments.

The UI characteristics differ somewhat among the states. The lower WBA and base period earnings in Illinois probably reflects timing, since this experiment preceded the Pennsylvania and Washington experiments by about four years. An annual increase at a compound

**Table 2.6 Characteristics of Control Group Members
in the Three Experiments**

Characteristic	Illinois	Pennsylvania	Washington
Total members	3,952	3,354	3,082
Gender (%)			
Male	45.3	40.5	39.5
Female	54.7	59.5	60.5
Age (%)			
Less than 35	62.2	53.5	52.2
35 to 54	37.8	36.7	39.8
55 and above	0.0	9.7	8.0
Race (%)			
White, non-Hispanic	63.2	83.8	83.3
Black	27.1	12.1	4.3
Hispanic	7.6	3.5	7.0
Other	2.1	0.6	5.4
Industry (%)			
Manufacturing	26.4	25.8	23.1
Nonmanufacturing	73.6	74.2	76.9
Occupation (%)			
White-collar	42.1		34.2
Other occupations	57.9		65.8
Weekly benefit amount ($)	119.93	164.08	150.51
Entitled duration (weeks)	26.0	25.9	26.9
Base period earnings ($)	12,753	14,126	15,475
UI Benefits			
Weeks of insured unemployment	20.1	14.9	14.3
Benefits drawn ($)	2,487.00	2,387.00	2,066.00
Exhaustion rate (%)	47.2	27.7	23.9
Initial UI spell (weeks)	18.3	12.5	11.4

rate of 5.8 percent would bring the Illinois WBA up to the Washington level at the time the Washington experiment was launched. This rate of increase is not inconsistent with the wage growth rates in this period.

Pennsylvania had a somewhat more generous UI program than Washington, as indicated by the higher WBA, despite somewhat lower base period earnings. The average weeks of entitled duration are roughly 26 in all states. In Illinois and Pennsylvania, 26 weeks is the standard (although a few UI recipients get only 16 weeks, making the average for Pennsylvania 25.9 weeks), whereas in Washington it represents the average over a potential range of 10 to 30 weeks.

The poorer economic climate in Illinois at the time is indicated by the considerably longer average weeks of UI benefits, the longer initial spell of weeks on UI, and the much higher exhaustion rate than in either Pennsylvania or Washington. These differences do not carry over to much higher dollars of benefits drawn, however, because of the lower WBA.

EFFECTIVENESS OF THE RANDOMIZATION PROCESS

The objective of random assignment is to create groups that are homogeneous in terms of the characteristics that affect outcomes. If this is accomplished, a simple comparison of mean outcomes among treatment and control groups provides an unbiased estimate of the treatment effects. The characteristics of claimants in the different groups, within each experiment, are compared to test the effectiveness of the assignment process in creating homogeneous groups. Homogeneity is achieved if differences in the distribution of characteristics among the treatment and control groups are small and generally statistically insignificant. Chance alone will create some statistically significant differences. At a 90 percent confidence level, chance alone would be expected to produce a statistically significant difference in one out of ten characteristic comparisons. Tables 2.7, 2.8, and 2.9 show the distribution of characteristics generally found to affect the outcomes of interest—weeks of unemployment or UI benefit payments—in each of the experiments.

For Pennsylvania, the mean values of characteristics across the six treatment groups and the control group are shown in Table 2.7. Sixty-six treatment/control differences were calculated. Seven of the comparisons are statistically different at the 90 percent confidence level, which is what you would expect by chance alone. The three differences at the 95 percent confidence level are what you would expect. In all, the Pennsylvania results are not inconsistent with random assignment.[26]

For Washington, 14 characteristic means are compared across 6 treatment groups and the control group, providing a total of 84 treatment/control group comparisons (Table 2.8). Chance alone could account for as many as four statistically significant differences at the 95 percent confidence level and eight at the 90 percent confidence level. These are essentially the number of statistically significant differences shown in the table.

For Illinois, the means of 11 characteristics are compared in Table 2.9 for the single treatment and the control groups. These results are somewhat less supportive of the conclusion as to the effectiveness of random assignment, since 4 of the 11 means differed statistically at the 95 percent confidence level, considerably more than the 0 or 1 statistically significant differences that chance alone should account for.

However, validating the random process does not necessarily mean that the samples are sufficiently homogenous to warrant use of unadjusted mean comparisons. It is shown in Chapter 4 that treatment/control differences in UI compensation are affected by the inclusion of WBA (and base earnings) in the Pennsylvania and Washington estimating equations, requiring use of regression-adjusted treatment/control comparisons to provide unbiased estimates of treatment.

Table 2.7 Tests of Randomization in the Pennsylvania Experiment, Control and Six Treatment Group Means[a]

		Treatment group					
Variable	Control	Low/ short[b]	Low/ long	High/ short	High/ long	Declin./ long	High/ long
Female (%)	40.5	40.9	39.3	40.2	40.0	40.7	39.8
		(0.22)	(0.94)	(0.19)	(0.37)	(0.16)	(0.46)
Age less than 35 (%)	53.5	53.2	54.7	56.4**	56.4**	53.2	52.7
		(0.23)	(0.93)	(2.02)	(1.99)	(0.23)	(0.50)
Age 55 and above (%)	9.7	9.8	9.1	9.8	9.8	10.3	8.6
		(0.05)	(0.81)	(0.02)	(0.11)	(0.63)	(1.12)
Black (%)	12.1	10.3*	11.5	12.3	12.4	11.5	10.7
		(1.83)	(0.69)	(0.16)	(0.25)	(0.71)	(1.31)
Hispanic (%)	3.5	3.9	3.8	3.9	2.7	3.8	3.9
		(0.66)	(0.45)	(0.68)	(1.50)	(0.55)	(0.53)
Other non- Whites (%)	0.6	0.5	0.4	0.5	1.0**	0.4	0.7
		(0.42)	(0.58)	(0.18)	(2.10)	(0.67)	(0.36)
Manufacturing (%)	25.8	25.5	26.0	25.8	25.7	26.1	25.5
		(0.20)	(0.25)	(0.00)	(0.01)	(0.24)	(0.15)
Weekly benefit ($)	164.1	165.5	166.4	167.1	165.1	167.8*	166.9
		(0.65)	(1.27)	(1.52)	(0.50)	(1.82)	(1.23)
Base earnings ($)	14,126	14,375	14,650*	14,352	14,317	14,695*	14,301
		(0.72)	(1.83)	(0.73)	(0.60)	(1.83)	(0.49)
Maximum WBA (%)	18.6	19.3	20.7**	18.3	20.0	20.5	20.7
		(0.49)	(1.99)	(0.27)	(1.16)	(1.63)	(1.57)
Expected recall (%)	10.8	10.1	10.4	10.9	11.4	10.1	11.7
		(0.78)	(0.47)	(0.05)	(0.61)	(0.85)	(0.82)

SOURCE: Corson et al. (1991), Table III.7, p. 46; used with permission of Mathematica Policy Research, Inc.

[a] The t-statistic of the difference from the control group mean is in parentheses.

* = Significantly different from the control group mean at the 90 percent level of confidence; ** = significantly different from the control group mean at the 95 percent level of confidence.

[b] Treatment groups are described by the bonus amount (e.g., "Low") and the qualification period (e.g., "Short").

Table 2.8 Tests of Randomization in the Washington Experiment, Control and Six Treatment Group Means[a]

		Treatment group					
Variable	Control	Low/ short	Middle/ short	High/ short	Low/ long	Middle/ long	High/ long
Female (%)	39.5	38.9 (0.42)	39.3 (0.17)	38.7 (0.55)	38.5 (0.74)	39.8 (0.22)	38.0 (0.99)
Age less than 35 (%)	52.2	53.3 (0.84)	52.8 (0.43)	51.9 (0.20)	52.2 (0.02)	52.4 (0.14)	53.8 (1.01)
Age 55 and above (%)	8.0	7.7 (0.48)	7.8 (0.36)	8.0 (0.01)	8.2 (0.21)	8.4 (0.49)	6.8 (1.47)
Black (%)	4.3	5.2 (1.48)	4.7 (0.65)	4.0 (0.43)	4.7 (0.67)	4.1 (0.42)	4.2 (0.23)
Hispanic (%)	7.0	6.8 (0.40)	6.4 (0.96)	6.8 (0.28)	7.0 (0.00)	6.8 (0.42)	5.3** (2.18)
Other non-Whites (%)	5.4	4.9 (0.76)	4.6 (1.27)	4.7 (0.92)	4.9 (0.84)	5.1 (0.36)	4.4 (1.47)
Manufacturing (%)	23.1	22.0 (0.92)	22.8 (0.28)	21.9 (0.91)	22.8 (0.24)	22.3 (0.69)	22.5 (0.43)
Weekly benefit ($)	150.5	150.5 (0.02)	152.1 (1.12)	152.8 (1.40)	153.5** (2.11)	152.8 (1.58)	154.0** (2.12)
Entitlement (weeks)	26.9	26.7 (1.22)	27.0 (0.91)	26.8 (0.75)	26.9 (0.62)	26.8 (0.06)	27.0 (1.16)
Base earnings ($)	15,475	15,486 (0.03)	15,860 (1.22)	15,537 (0.17)	15,872 (1.27)	16,073* (1.90)	16,148* (1.88)
Maximum WBA (%)	33.0	32.7 (0.18)	33.5 (0.43)	33.5 (0.40)	34.8 (1.40)	34.0 (0.83)	36.0** (2.03)
Search exempt (%)	22.5	21.7 (0.66)	21.8 (0.64)	20.9 (1.23)	22.3 (0.18)	20.7 (1.58)	22.7 (0.14)
White collar (%)	34.2	33.3 (0.70)	35.6 (1.05)	34.8 (0.39)	35.3 (0.83)	36.7* (1.87)	35.6 (0.94)
Years of education	12.3	12.3 (0.34)	12.4* (1.80)	12.3 (0.43)	12.3 (0.34)	12.4 (1.00)	12.4 (1.61)

SOURCE: Spiegelman, O'Leary, and Kline (1992), Table 5-1, p. 85.

[a] The t-statistic of difference from the control group mean is in parentheses. * = Statistically significant at the 90 percent confidence level for a two-tailed test; ** = statistically significant at the 95 percent confidence level for a two-tailed test.

Table 2.9 Tests of Randomization in the Illinois Experiment, Control and Treatment Group Means[a]

Variable	Control mean	Treatment mean
Female (%)	45.3	43.7 (1.45)
Age less than 35 (%)	62.2	61.8 (0.32)
Black (%)	27.1	25.1** (2.10)
Hispanic (%)	7.6	7.4 (0.27)
Other non-Whites (%)	2.1	2.5 (1.01)
Manufacturing (%)	26.4	24.8 (1.62)
Weekly benefit ($)	119.9	118.8 (1.27)
Base earnings ($)	12,753	12,888 (0.65)
Maximum WBA(%)	35.3	33.1** (2.15)
White collar (%)	42.1	45.2** (2.79)
Years of education	11.5	11.8** (6.03)

SOURCE: Spiegelman and Woodbury (1987).

[a] The t-statistic of difference from the control group mean is in parentheses. ** = Significantly different from the control group mean at the 95 percent level of confidence for a two-tailed test.

OPERATIONS

In this section, the operational design and procedures of the three experiments are described and compared. All experiments start from the premise that participation in the experiment is limited to individuals who file claims for UI benefits. Thus, before embarking on a journey through the bonus experiment, we will digress to describe in some detail the process of filing a UI claim.

The UI Filing Process

To start the UI filing process, a prospective UI claimant enters a UI office and files a claim to establish a benefit year. A benefit year is the 12-month period in which the claimant can draw benefits before having to reestablish entitlement. Filing usually occurs the week immediately after the claimant becomes unemployed.[27]

In all three states, the claimant returns to the UI office to establish the waiting week and to claim the first week of compensation two weeks after filing to establish the benefit year. In all three states, as in most states, an eligible claimant must serve a waiting week before benefits can be paid for subsequent weeks of unemployment.

To receive UI benefits, the claimant must be unemployed at the start of the benefit year and must be both monetarily and nonmonetarily eligible for benefits. The two terms have technical definitions. *Monetarily eligible* means that there are sufficient wage credits in the base year (usually the first four of the five quarters prior to filing for benefits) to establish monetary entitlement. *Nonmonetarily eligible* means that separation from employment did not occur under conditions that made the claimant ineligible to receive benefits and that the claimant is "able and available" to work.

In all three states, a claimant is required to register with the ES some time in the two-week period between filing the initial claim and claiming the first week of benefits. Registration with the ES is tied to the requirement that a UI claimant must be actively seeking work in order to be eligible for UI benefits. The registration requirement is not enforced in Pennsylvania. In Washington, all UI and ES offices were joint, so that ES registration occurred at the same time as filing a claim for benefits. In Illinois, some offices were joint and other were not.

Claimants there were required to register with the ES before returning to the UI office to claim the first week of benefits (plus the waiting week credit).

Assignment and Enrollment

Assignment into the experiment took place in the UI office in the Pennsylvania and Washington experiments, but occurred in the Employment Service office in Illinois. In all three states, however, eligibility was limited to those claimants filing initial claims to establish a benefit year.

We will start with Washington, because the enrollment process there was simplest and most closely linked to the filing for UI benefits. For all UI applicants, an on-line computer file was accessed which provided the status of monetary eligibility and printed an initial statement of entitlement. Software was written exclusively for the experiment. It used the agency data file to randomly select some of the UI-eligible claimants according to last two digits of their social security number and assigned them to treatment or control status. A computer-generated form that was provided to every worker filing a claim would also contain information on the bonus offer if the claimant was assigned to an experimental treatment. A treatment-assigned claimant was tentatively enrolled into the experiment; the enrollment was confirmed by letter when both monetary and nonmonetary UI entitlement were determined. This process was also followed in Illinois.

The process in Pennsylvania differed somewhat, especially with regard to the timing of assignment and enrollment. Upon UI application, local office staff entered information from the UI application form into the state computer. A computer file was then created on the state system to extract information on all claimants in the demonstration offices who were determined to be monetarily eligible for UI benefits during the past week. The file was transferred to the special demonstration data system (the Participant Tracking System), and experiment eligibility screens were applied (described below). Once the screening was completed, a weekly maximum number of individuals was selected randomly from each office from among the pool of eligible claimants. The selected claimants were then assigned randomly to treatment and control groups (by the last two digits of their social security number).

Enrollment in Pennsylvania differed from that in Washington because it occurred at the time the claimant filed a claim to establish waiting week credit and collect benefits for the first week of compensated unemployment. Thus, enrollment into the experiment occurred two weeks after a claimant filed for benefits and excluded claimants who did not return to claim a waiting week (and a compensable week if also earned).

Illinois differed from the other two in that assignment and enrollment into the experiment occurred in the ES office at the time the claimant, who had previously filed for benefits, registered for job search assistance. Thus, only UI claimants who registered with the ES were eligible to participate, thereby de facto excluding most claimants exempt from job search. At the end of the registration process, the ES counselor would inform the selected claimant that he or she was eligible to participate in an experimental program. The claimant would then be asked to wait for a specially trained counselor who would hand the claimant a printed, one-page instruction sheet and explain the experiment. Unique to Illinois, the claimant would be asked to sign an agreement to participate, but the agreement did not really commit the claimant to any particular actions. This requirement was dropped in Pennsylvania and Washington.

The enrollment process in all three states was one of attempting to communicate the nature of the bonus offer and the necessary requirements to receive the bonus. Either in individual counseling sessions or in group enrollment sessions, the assigned claimant was given a single-page information sheet and a verbal description of the experiment, including an explanation of the participant's actions that would lead to a bonus. In Washington, the UI interviewer would end by asking a series of four questions designed to ensure that the claimant understood the program. The low rate at which apparently eligible participants collected bonuses in Illinois led to increased efforts in Pennsylvania and Washington to improve claimant's understanding of the program. (As described in Chapter 3, there was some improvement in the take-up rate in Washington over that in Illinois, but not in Pennsylvania.)

Differences in timing and location of enrollment among the experiments were not merely administrative details; they affected the characteristics of the sample in each experiment. In Washington, where enrollment took place in the UI office at the time the claimant filed for UI benefits, every claimant eligible for UI benefits was a potential participant. In Pennsylvania, where enrollment took place at the time the claimant submitted his or her first claim for waiting week credit or compensation, claimants who obtained jobs within the first two weeks after filing the initial claim were unlikely to file for the waiting week or the first compensable week and were thus ineligible for a bonus (Pennsylvania data indicated that 6 percent of initial filers didn't return to file a continued claim). The same situation would arise in Illinois for those claimants who did not register for job search assistance at the same time as filing an initial claim—this would differ among ES centers, depending upon whether or not the UI and ES offices were unified.

An external validity problem arises in the Pennsylvania design, because in a real program—unlike the experiment—knowledge of the bonus offer would be universal and claimants could postpone taking jobs until they had served the waiting week and established entitlement to the bonus. The Illinois design also has an external validity issue in that knowledge of the bonus offer could attract some of those exempt from job search to register with the ES. In general, all three experiments have an external validity problem of unknown dimension in that nonfilers who do not expect to be unemployed very long might file anyway in a real program to get the bonus.

Determination of Full Eligibility to Participate

To be fully eligible to participate, the monetarily eligible claimant must not have had a separation issue on the claim that would prevent payment of UI benefits. In Illinois and Washington, but not in Pennsylvania, central office personnel reviewed the claims files of claimants assigned to experimental treatment groups. If there were "issues" on the claim regarding separation from the previous employer, then eligibility for a bonus would be held up until the issue was resolved, and it was denied if the resolution was against the claimant or was not resolved prior to the end of the reemployment period. When the review showed the claimant to be eligible to receive UI benefits, the agent sent an enrollment letter to the assigned claimant, informing that person that he or she was eligible to participate in the experiment.[28] A Notice of Hire form accompanied the letter, with instructions regarding the procedures for submission. In Pennsylvania, the review for nonmonetary eligibility did not occur unless the bonus was claimed.

Submitting the Notice of Hire

The next step in the process occurred when the participating claimant obtained a full-time job within the qualification period. In all three experiments, the claimant informed the central UI office of a job acquisition that would establish eligibility for a bonus by submitting a Notice of Hire (NOH) form. In Illinois, the NOH was actually sent by the employer, thereby providing instant verification of employment. The employer verified that the claimant was hired in a job for 30 hours a week or more, starting on a particular date. The UI claim file was then accessed to verify that the hiring date was within the qualification period and that the claimant stopped receiving UI benefits. In Washington and Pennsylvania, the NOH was submitted directly by the claimant. The interposition of the employer was eliminated to reduce the possible stigmatizing effect of requiring the participating claimant to enlist the support of the employer in his or her quest for a bonus.

In Pennsylvania and Washington, the NOH provided information about the claimant's prior and new jobs, permitting a comparison to assure that the new job was not a recall to a previous job—a non-issue in Illinois. If the employer, occupation title, and wage rates of the prior and new jobs matched, there was a presumption of a recall and the employer would be contacted. Affirmative answers to the query as to whether the claimant was self-employed or placed on the job by his or her union would generate letters requesting clarification. A self-employed individual could receive a bonus but had to provide proof that he or she had a business license and some business income. The NOH process in Washington and Pennsylvania was more complicated than in Illinois because claimants could change jobs and still qualify for a bonus—with the condition that the claimant did not claim benefits and did not take more than a week between jobs. A claimant changing jobs in Washington and Pennsylvania would file an NOH for each job.

Submission of the Bonus Voucher

Sixteen or 17 weeks after reemployment, if the claimant had remained fully employed for the entire period (or changed jobs in Pennsylvania and Washington, with no more than a week interlude and no filing for benefits), the claimant submitted a voucher for the bonus payment. In Illinois, a valid voucher was certified by the employer before submission. In Washington and Pennsylvania, the voucher was submitted without such certification, but office personnel contacted employers to verify continual employment for the reemployment period and checked the UI claim file to ascertain that UI benefits had not been drawn during the reemployment period.

For payment of the bonus to be authorized, verification had to show the following: the claimant had not drawn benefits during the four-month qualification period; he or she had been employed on a full-time job (30 hours in Illinois and Pennsylvania, 34 hours per week in Washington); the first post-unemployment job was not a recall to the job held prior to filing for benefits or a placement through a union hiring hall; and that any self-employment was documented. If any of these issues were not favorable, the claimant would be contacted to resolve the discrepancies. When the agent was assured that the conditions for bonus payment had been met, a check would be issued for the amount of the bonus.

Participation in the Three Experiments

Table 2.10 shows the numbers of claimants offered enrollment into the bonus offer experiments and the proportions who participated at various levels (by submitting NOHs and vouchers for payment of bonuses). The proportion of eligibles submitting valid NOHs was highest in Illinois and lowest in Pennsylvania, as was the case with payment of bonuses. In all three experiments, only a small proportion of eligible enrollees fully participated by receiving a bonus.

The Illinois results pertain only to the claimant experiment. If the employer experiment had been included, the number of assignees would be double the number in the table. The drop-off in number of enrollees was much larger in Illinois than in the other experiments and was due to refusal to participate. Since the assignees included only

Table 2.10 Participation in the Three Experiments[a]

	Illinois		Pennsylvania		Washington	
Participation	Number	%	Number	%	Number	%
Assigned	4,186		11,410		14,080	
Enrolled	3,527		10,694		14,080	
Eligible	3,527	100	10,694	100	12,140	100
Submitted NOH	NA[b]		1,604	15.0	2,533	20.9
Valid NOH	765	21.7	1,315	12.3	2,255	18.6
Submitted bonus voucher	NA		1,155	10.8	1,946	16.0
Voucher paid	570	16.2	1,123	10.5	1,816	15.0

SOURCE: Spiegelman and Woodbury (1987), Table 5-1; Corson et al. (1991), Table III.3, p. 40 and Table VI.1, p. 77; Spiegelman, O'Leary, and Kline (1983), Table 3-1, p. 50 and Table 3-2, p. 52.

[a] In Illinois, the number assigned includes only those eligible to participate and the number enrolled includes those who agree to participate. In Pennsylvania, some of the eligible assignees did not return to claim a waiting week and therefore were not enrolled. All those enrolled were eligible. In Washington, assignment and enrollment occurred simultaneously at the time of filing for benefits for all those monetarily eligible. Some of those "tentatively" enrolled were found to be ineligible due to nonmonetary issues.

[b] NA = not available.

those eligible to participate, there is no difference in the number of enrollees and number of eligibles. In Pennsylvania, the decline from assigned to enrolled represents the nonmonetary ineligibility of some participants. In Washington, all who were monetarily eligible for UI were enrolled, but the ineligibles were then eliminated from the sample. Thus, much of the difference shown prior to "eligibility" represents differences in timing of dropping ineligibles from the sample and is not substantive.

Despite differences in procedure (discussed above) regarding NOH submissions that should have disadvantaged Illinois, the proportion of valid NOFs submitted was greatest in Illinois. The drop in the number of participants submitting valid NOHs to the number submitting bonus vouchers could be accounted for by failure to remain fully employed for the reemployment period (there might also be some take-up failure, as discussed in Chapter 3). In the end, the procedures adopted to increase participation in Pennsylvania and Washington were for naught, as Illinois had the highest proportion of eligible enrollees collecting bonuses.

Monitoring for Operational Performance

In all three experiments, the enrollment rates at the various offices were monitored to assure compliance with the experimental design. Monitoring occurred at two levels. In Pennsylvania and Washington, there was an on-line Oracle system developed to manage the paper flow (e.g., tracking claimants and sending out letters and forms) and to track enrollment rates in the offices. Staffs of the state agencies and of the evaluation contractors visited each of the offices, armed with information regarding performance. Real operational problems were uncovered in only one office in Washington—the claimstaker assigned to enroll bonus-eligible claimants into the experiment had been transferred and no one had yet taken her place. This lapse was immediately corrected.

A concern was the possible dwindling of interest and parallel reduction in information flow to the assigned claimant. Monitoring of sites did not uncover this tendency. Overall, it was concluded that the experiment operated according to design and that any lapses were very minor.

THE FEDERAL SUPPLEMENTAL COMPENSATION (FSC) PROGRAM IN ILLINOIS: AN UNPLANNED EXPERIMENT

As will be seen in Chapter 4, the impacts of the Illinois experiment were about double those experienced in similar size treatments in the other two experiments. A possible explanation for the large impacts of the bonus offer in Illinois was the presence in Illinois of a temporary extended benefit program that did not exist in the other states. FSC was a federally funded, national program that existed between 1982 and 1985. Its discontinuation in Illinois in the middle of the experimental enrollment period had not been anticipated by the research designers and resulted in a "natural experiment." The FSC program nationally extended benefits for most recipients by 10 to 16 weeks, depending upon the state's unemployment rate. For Illinois, the extension for those eligible was 12 weeks. Most of those claimants enrolled in the experiment in July and August 1984 had available the 12 weeks of extended UI benefits in addition to their 26 weeks of state regular benefits. After that date, all claimants had only the 26 weeks of regular benefits available.

Because the criteria for receiving extended benefits was somewhat more stringent than that for regular benefits, about 6 percent of the claimants eligible for regular benefits were not eligible for extended benefits. In Chapter 4, we compare the effects of the bonus offer on two groups: the first group is comprised of those claimants enrolled in the experiment (or controls) who were eligible for FSC ("FSC-eligibles"), and the second group is comprised of those experimentals and controls enrolled in the second period who, though not eligible for FSC, would have been eligible if it had been available ("FSC-ineligibles").

A natural experiment exists because each of these groups has its own control group and differs largely because of the FSC availability. Of course, there are also some other differences between the two groups due to differences in timing of enrollment, but the average difference in date of enrollment of two to three months is probably not substantive.

Table 3.1 in Chapter 3 shows that the FSC-eligible group participated to a greater degree than the FSC-ineligible group. The results in Chapter 4 show that indeed, the impacts were greater on the FSC-eligible group, explaining a large part of the differences in impact among the three experiments.

Notes

1. Obtaining unbiased estimates of program impact by a process that is essentially "model free" is the major motivation for an experimental design. We draw on the discussion by Hausman and Wise (1985) to present the argument. Starting with the premise that any evaluation goal is to estimate an equation of the following simple form

   (1) $Y = XB + e,$

where **B** is a vector of parameters to be estimated, with each element of **B** measuring the effect on Y of a unit change on the corresponding element of X, and e are the unmeasured determinants of Y, referred to as the error term. **B** will be an unbiased estimate of the effect of X on Y if X is uncorrelated with e. In the operations of a program, so-called "self-selection" is almost invariably going to create this correlation.   For example, a government training program (the X variables) offered to those unable to obtain employment attracts those most motivated to get jobs (part of the e term), thus X and e are correlated, and if motivation affects outcomes, then Y and e are correlated, and **B** is a biased estimate of the effect of X on Y. At best, according to Hausman and Wise (1985, p. 189), you can never be sure that the estimates are unbiased.

Randomization is a means for assuring that the estimates of **B** are unbiased. Suppose there is a treatment, T, and random assignment is used to select persons to receive the treatment. Then in the following equation

(2) $Y = TB + u,$

where T is the treatment and u is the error term, T will be uncorrelated with u, and therefore **B** will be an unbiased estimate of the effect of T on Y.

2. Extending the eligibility for an experiment to include potentially eligible as well as actually eligible persons would permit measurement of such an effect. For instance, in the income maintenance experiments, all adults were potentially eligible and families with incomes considerably above the benefit cut-off point were enrolled although they would receive no benefits. Such families, however, could reduce income in order to become eligible for income maintenance payments.

3. The exception in Washington occurred when claimants obtained employment that qualified them for a bonus without having established a waiting week for UI benefits. In this case, issues that might have resulted in the claimant being ineligible for benefits were not resolved, but the bonus was paid anyway; 7.6 percent (138/1,813) of those collecting the bonus did not serve a waiting week.

4. A reason advanced for excluding standbys in Pennsylvania was the desire to avoid antagonizing employers, who would not like standbys to be encouraged to take other jobs. Programmatically, the issue is difficult, because exclusion of standbys from bonus eligibility might simply encourage workers not to report standby status.

5. For a participant to receive a bonus payment while returning to a previous employer, the claimant must complete a form demonstrating that the position was different (e.g., different department, different job title, different salary level).

6. For the first two months of experimental enrollment in Washington (until May 9, 1988), the start of the qualification period for backdated claims was also backdated, reducing the length of the effective qualification period. After that date, the qualification period started with the filing date, the same as for other enrolled claimants. Although the proportion of backdated claims of experimental subjects increased substantially—from 10 percent to over 20 percent—between the two periods, the change could not be attributed to the treatment. This conclusion is

based on the absence of any statistically significant difference between experimental and control group members in the proportions backdating (see Appendix B in Spiegelman, O'Leary, and Kline 1992). At any rate, the proportion of claimants backdating claims more than two weeks was very small; only 1.4 percent of treatments and 1.2 percent of controls in Washington.

7. Of the 12,452 treatment-enrolled claimants in Washington, 1,445 were exempt from job search because of standby status or membership in full referral unions. The impact analysis showed essentially no difference in measured outcome including or excluding the exempt group. Compare Tables 5-4 and 5-5 in Spiegelman, O'Leary, and Kline (1992).

8. The workfare experiments are exceptions. These were a set of state-level experiments in which randomly selected AFDC recipients were placed into an experimental program and required to work or accept training in order to continue receiving welfare benefits. See Gueron and Pauly (1991) for a detailed description of these experiments.

9. The Pennsylvania and Illinois experiments had other components. The Pennsylvania experiment offered a voluntary job-search workshop of four half-days in combination with five of the bonus offer treatments. A sixth treatment was identical to one of the other treatments but did not include the workshop offer (labeled "PT4," a high-bonus, long-qualification-period treatment). While the workshop was implemented as designed, so few claimants chose to participate (less than 3 percent) that the workshop was discontinued. For analysis purposes, the samples from the two treatments with identical bonus offers were combined and presented herein as a single high-bonus, low-qualification-period treatment.

The Illinois experiment actually comprised two experiments—a claimant experiment in which a $500 bonus was offered to assigned UI claimants and an employer experiment in which the $500 bonus was paid to the employer of the participating UI claimant who obtained a job under the same conditions. The employer experiment is not discussed further in this book, but it is described fully in the final report of the Illinois experiment (Spiegelman and Woodbury 1987) and more briefly in Woodbury and Spiegelman (1987).

10. In Illinois, the fixed bonus offer of $500 was equivalent to an offer 4.2 times the mean WBA ($120) and ranged in value from 9.8 times the minimum WBA of $51 to 3.1 times the maximum WBA of $161.

11. Pennsylvania used a parsimonious two-level experiment because of the need to have treatments that offered job workshops (see note 6 above) and the desire to experiment with a declining bonus offer. In this treatment, the bonus offer was set initially at $6 \times$ WBA, and the offer declined over the qualification period. This treatment is not easily compared with the fixed bonus amount offers and furthermore had no effect on UI outcomes. Therefore, it is not discussed further in this monograph. For details, see Corson et al. (1991).

12. In Pennsylvania, a small proportion of claimants (less than 2 percent) are only eligible for 16 weeks of benefits; the rest are eligible for 26 weeks.

13. Although some claimants could be expected to accept temporary jobs just to qualify for the bonus, it was difficult, given the rules regarding voluntary quits, for a claimant to go on and off jobs at will and still collect UI benefits or the bonus. The evidence from Illinois showed no tendency to shift unemployment from the first spell to later spells in the benefit year.

14. The mathematical programming model used for SIME/DIME is described in Conlisk and Kurz (1972).

15. Administration and research were paid for out of state funds not subject to these budgetary constraints.

16. As discussed previously, the two treatments in Illinois were actually two experiments, the claimant experiment in which bonuses were offered to claimants and the employer experiment in which bonuses were offered to employers to hire claimants.

17. Although logic suggests that a bonus offer would only serve to reduce the length of the unemployment spell, that is not necessarily the case. For those who would normally find jobs within the qualification period, the bonus could create an income effect that would lengthen the unemployment spell. Only if there is a compelling case to consider only reductions in unemployment as of interest should a one-tailed test be adopted.

18. At that time, a one-tailed statistical significance test was considered appropriate because of the belief that the bonus could only serve to reduce the length of the unemployment spell. Subsequently, theoretical considerations led to an interest in possible adverse effects of the bonus offer for at least some groups, which suggests a preference for a two-tailed test.

19. The effect size is a pure number index (called d in Cohen) that is the difference between the treatment and control group means measured in standard deviation units. For a two-tailed test, the effect size index is $d = |M_A - M_B|/s$, where d = effect size index for t tests of means in standard deviation units, M_A and M_B = population means expressed in original units, and s = standard deviation of either population.

20. The power of the test in the table refers to the power of a two-cell test. If there is more than one treatment and it is desired to know the joint power of the tests on all treatments (i.e., what is the probability of rejecting a true effect of any of the treatments), then one must look at the joint probability. Thus, if there are three treatments and each has a power of 0.8, the joint probability of rejecting at least one true effect is 0.51, i.e., $(0.8)^3$.

21. These sample size considerations do not take into account the desire to learn about the effectiveness of the experimental treatment on subgroups of the relevant population, but the costs of having independent treatment groups representing each interesting subgroup is too large. The reasons for needing knowledge about subgroup impacts are either that a policy that strongly affects some population subgroups and not others may not be politically desirable or that it may suggest the need for some restructuring of the treatment to better serve some groups. For instance, a policy ineffective for some racial groups (or one gender) may not be

good policy, even if the overall effect is positive. It must be accepted, however, that estimating subgroup impacts on fully separated samples reduces the reliability of estimates considerably. For instance, dividing the sample into four subgroups (say, two ethnic and two gender groups) implies that, for each of the four groups, only an effect size twice that for the group as a whole will be detectable at the same significance level and power. As discussed in Chapter 4, more parsimonious means of estimating subgroup impacts can be used.

22. See note 10 above for discussion of why the workshop treatment is not being further discussed in this book.

23. A detailed discussion of the sample allocation model is provided in Metcalf and Kerachsky (1988).

24. Another advantage of a larger number of sites, which is not as yet well understood, is related to the displacement effect discussed in Chapter 6. The possibility that displacement would contaminate the control group, thereby compromising the internal validity of the experiment, is small if the sample size relative to the size of the relevant labor market is small. This speaks in favor of smaller samples in many sites rather than larger samples in fewer sites. However, this does not reduce the possibility of displacement in a full-blown program, thereby affecting the generalizability of experimental results.

25. Of the 22 ES offices in which the experiment was conducted, 8 were unified (none of which were in Chicago); 2 others were not unified but were housed in the same building (both in Chicago); and the other 12 were in separate buildings (7 of which were in Chicago).

26. This conclusion is reinforced because not all of the 48 tests are independent. The most important interdependency occurs because each of the six treatment group means are compared with the same control group mean. If one treatment/control test fails, there is an increased likelihood that other treatment/control tests for the same characteristic will fail. As a possible demonstration of this point, among the six statistically significant differences, there are two pairs.

27. It may occur before the claimant becomes unemployed based upon an expectation of imminent unemployment and a desire to establish a benefit year before the event, or it may occur after the week of becoming unemployed. In this case, the benefit year may start in a week prior to the filing week, referred to as a "backdated claim."

28. There was an exception to this rule in the Washington experiment. Unlike in Pennsylvania, claimants who filed and were monetarily eligible for benefits but who did not proceed to claim a waiting week were still eligible for a bonus. This created a small group who might have been ineligible for nonmonetary reasons, which would only have been determined if the claimant claimed a waiting week.

References

Cohen, Jacob. 1977. *Statistical Power Analysis for the Behavioral Sciences.* Revised ed. Orlando, Florida: Academic Press.

_____. 1988. *Statistical Power Analysis for the Behavioral Sciences.* Second ed. Hillsdale, New Jersey: Erlbaum Associates.

Conlisk, J., and M. Kurz. 1972. *The Assignment Model of the Seattle and Denver Income Maintenance Experiments.* SRI Research Memorandum no 15, Menlo Park, California, July.

Corson, Walter, Paul Decker, Shari Dunstan, and Stuart Kerachsky. 1991. *Pennsylvania Bonus Demonstration: Final Report.* Mathematica Policy Research, Inc., Princeton, New Jersey, September.

Fisher, R.A. 1960. *The Design of Experiments.* Seventh ed. New York: Oliver and Boyd.

Fisher R.A. 1968. *Encyclopedia of the Social Sciences*, Vol 5. New York: MacMillan and Co.

Gueron, Judith, and Edward Pauly. 1991. *From Welfare to Work.* New York: Russell Sage Foundation.

Hausman, Jerry, and David Wise, eds. 1985. *Social Experimentation.* Chicago: University of Chicago and NBER.

Hicks, Charles R. 1982. *Fundamental Concepts in the Design of Experiments.* New York: Holt, Rinehart and Winston, Inc., p. 1.

Kershaw, David, and Jerilyn Fair. 1977. *The New Jersey Income Maintenance Experiment*, vol. 8, p. xv, Academic Press, New York.

Metcalf, C., and S. Kerachsky. 1988. "Sample Allocation and Office Selection." Memorandum dated March 25, 1988, Mathematica Policy Research, Inc., Princeton, New Jersey.

Moffitt, Robert. 1992. "Evaluation Methods for Program Entry Effects." In *Evaluation Welfare and Training Programs*, C. Manski and I. Garfinkel, eds. Cambridge: Harvard University Press.

Ross, Heather. 1966. "A Proposal for a Demonstration of New Techniques in Income Maintenance," Memorandum, December, Data Center Archives, Institute for Research on Poverty, University of Wisconsin, Madison.

Rossi, Peter H., and Howard E. Freeman. 1989. *Evaluation: A Systematic Approach.* Newbury Park, California: Sage Publications.

Spiegelman, Robert G., Christopher J. O'Leary, and Kenneth J. Kline. 1992. *The Washington Reemployment Bonus Experiment: Final Report.* Unemployment Insurance Occasional Paper 92-6, Washington, D.C.: U.S. Department of Labor, Employment and Training Administration.

Spiegelman, Robert G., Philip K. Robins, and Richard West. 1983. *Final Report of the Seattle-Denver Income Maintenance Experiment,* SRI International, Menlo Park, California, May.

Spiegelman, Robert G., and Stephen A. Woodbury. 1987. *The Illinois Unemployment Insurance Incentive Experiments: Final Report.* Kalamazoo, Michigan: W.E. Upjohn Institute for Employment Research.

U.S. Department of Commerce, Bureau of the Census. Various years. *Statistical Abstract of the United States.*

U.S. Department of Labor, Bureau of Labor Statistics. Various years. *Geographic Profile of Employment and Unemployment.*

U.S. Department of Labor, Employment and Training Administration, *UI Data Summary.* Various years. Fourth quarter. Unemployment Insurance Service, Division of Actuarial Services.

U.S. Department of Labor. 1984 and 1985. *Quarterly Unemployment Insurance Compilation and Characteristics.* Fourth quarter.

Woodbury, Stephen, and Robert G. Spiegelman. 1987. "Bonuses to Workers and Employers to Reduce Unemployment: Randomized Trials in Illinois." *American Economic Review* 77(4): 513–530.

3

Participation in the Reemployment Bonus Experiments

Paul T. Decker
Christopher J. O'Leary
and
Stephen A. Woodbury

Participation in a social experiment—the proportion of program-eligible individuals who actually participate—is of interest for two main reasons. The first is external validity, or the relevance of an experiment's results to implementing a program based on the experiment. If participation in an experiment differs from participation in an actual program, then the experiment's results, however valid they may be on their own grounds, may yield poor estimates of the costs, the number of individuals served, and the outcomes for individuals that could be expected in an actual program. The issue of translating experimental results into estimates that are useful for policy is central to experimentation, and we explore it both here and more fully in Chapter 6.

Second, differences in the extent to which different groups respond to an experimental treatment are intrinsically interesting to both policymakers and experimenters. The policymaker's interest in participation stems mainly from a need to design policies that are "target efficient," i.e., that benefit groups believed to be most in need of assistance. Other things equal, a program that benefits workers with high earnings would generally be less desirable than a program that benefits workers with low earnings. Similarly, the experimenter's interest in participation stems from a need to understand how a treatment "works." In the case of a reemployment bonus, for example, if workers with long expected spells of unemployment participate in the program—that is, respond to the treatment and accept the bonus offer—then the bonus will be effective in reducing the duration of unemployment spells.

Understanding which groups of workers respond to a bonus treatment can shed light on the extent to which a bonus is effective.

Many of these issues overlap the issues of treatment impact discussed in Chapters 4 and 5. Although it could be argued that impact, not participation, is the central issue in evaluating and understanding an experimental treatment, we hope that it will be clear from both this chapter and Chapter 6 that participation is central to understanding what the costs of a reemployment bonus program would be and how the reemployment bonuses in Illinois, Pennsylvania, and Washington operated.

The next section of this chapter provides a descriptive look at participation in the three reemployment bonus experiments. In particular, we focus on three measures of participation: the rate at which claimants partially qualified for a bonus (as defined below), the bonus receipt rate, and the bonus take-up rate. We then offer an attempt to model and explain the differences in participation among the experiments using various regression models.

BONUS QUALIFICATION, RECEIPT, AND TAKE-UP RATES

What percentage of UI claimants enrolled in the three experiments qualified for a bonus? What percentage actually received a bonus? What was the bonus take-up rate—that is, what percentage of those who qualified chose to collect a bonus?

Table 3.1 displays basic data on participation in the three reemployment bonus experiments and allows one to trace the progress of claimants through the bonus experiments. As discussed in Chapter 2, both the Pennsylvania and Washington experiments had multiple treatments: each of these treatments is referred to by its bonus amount (low or high in Pennsylvania; low, medium, or high in Washington) and its qualification period (short or long). In Illinois, there was only one treatment, but about half the claimants assigned to the single $500 bonus treatment were eligible only for 26 weeks of regular state UI benefits, whereas the other half were eligible for an additional 12 weeks of Federal Supplemental Compensation (FSC), for a total of 38

Table 3.1 Reemployment Bonus Qualification, Receipt, and Take-Up Rates, by Treatment Group

			Claimants in group who	
				Received bonus
Group[a]	Sample size (1)	Partially qualified[b] (%) (2)	Total (%) (3)	Given partially qualified (%) (4)
Illinois experiment				
All treatment groups[c]	4,186	42.9	13.6	31.8
Treatment—FSC-elig.	2,337	46.0	15.7	34.3
Treatment—FSC-inelig.	1,589	39.1	11.5	29.4
Control—FSC-elig.	2,106	39.6	—	—
Control—FSC-inelig.	1,600	34.0	—	—
Pennsylvania experiment				
All treatment groups	8,834	56.6	10.6	18.6
Low bonus/short qual. period	1,395	46.1	6.9	14.9
High bonus/short qual. period	1,910	47.5	8.4	17.3
Low bonus/long qual. period	2,456	61.6	10.7	17.6
High bonus/long qual. period	3,073	63.1	13.5	21.4
Control/short qual. period	3,392	42.8	—	—
Control/long qual. period	3,392	58.1	—	—
Washington experiment				
All treatment groups	12,452	55.7	14.6	26.1
Low bonus/short qual. period	2,246	47.0	8.7	18.6
Medium bonus/short qual. period	2,348	48.2	12.4	25.8
High bonus/short qual. period	1,583	50.2	15.0	29.8
Low bonus/long qual. period	2,387	63.0	13.9	22.1
Medium bonus/long qual. period	2,353	61.3	17.8	29.0

High bonus/long qual. period	1,535	65.9	22.0	33.3
Control/short qual. period	3,082	48.0	—	—
Control/long qual. period	3,082	61.3	—	—

SOURCE: Tabulations from the Illinois, Pennsylvania, and Washington Reemployment Bonus Experiment Public-Use data files.

[a] See text for full description of each group and the bonus take-up rate.

[b] Stopped receiving UI by qualification date.

[c] The number of claimants assigned to "All treatment groups" in the Illinois experiment exceeds the sum of FSC-eligible and FSC-ineligible treatment-assigned claimants because claimants who were monetarily ineligible for FSC have been dropped from the FSC-eligible and FSC-ineligible subgroups. See Chapters 2 and 4 for further discussion.

weeks of benefits. Since the effects of the bonus offer differed significantly between these two groups (see Chapter 4), it is important to distinguish between FSC-eligible and FSC-ineligible claimants.

Table 3.1 also displays data on the control groups from each experiment. The Illinois control group is divided into those who were eligible and those who were ineligible for FSC. For Pennsylvania and Washington, the percentages of each control group who satisfied the criteria of the short and long bonus qualification periods are reported.

Column 2 of Table 3.1 shows that between 39 and 66 percent of the eligible UI claimants who were assigned to one of the bonus treatments stopped receiving UI benefits within their bonus qualification period. We refer to these claimants as having "partially qualified" for the bonus, because in order to fully qualify for a bonus they also needed to be reemployed (and submit a Notice of Hire) and stay employed for four months. We adopt this definition of qualification because the available administrative data do not allow us to construct a reliable measure of full qualification that is consistent across the three experiments·

We would expect variation in the percentage of claimants who partially qualified for a bonus to be influenced by three factors: the length of the qualification period, the bonus amount, and a variety of other factors such as individual characteristics and labor market conditions.

A longer qualification period clearly makes it easier to qualify for a bonus. Hence, it is not surprising that, in both the Pennsylvania and

Washington experiments, a higher percentage of claimants partially qualified for the bonus offers that had long qualification periods (11 or 12 weeks). In Pennsylvania, 62 to 63 percent of claimants partially qualified for the bonus offers that had a long (12-week) qualification period. In Washington, 61 to 66 percent of claimants partially qualified for the bonus offers that had a long (11-week) qualification period.

Surprisingly, though, only 43 percent of claimants in the Illinois experiment stopped receiving UI benefits within its 11-week qualification period, which was roughly the same as the long qualification periods in Pennsylvania and Washington. It seems likely that general labor market factors played a role in reducing the number of Illinois claimants who stopped receiving UI within the qualification period. Only 34 and 40 percent of the Illinois controls stopped receiving UI by the qualification date, whereas the comparable figures for long-qualification-period controls in Pennsylvania and Washington are 58 percent and 61 percent (Table 3.1).[1] That is, the labor market and other factors unrelated to the bonus experiment reduced the rate at which claimants escaped from UI during the Illinois experiment.

Higher bonus amounts appear to lead to a higher percentage of claimants ending insured unemployment within the qualification period, although the relationship is not strong. The high bonus treatment led to a slightly higher percentage of claimants ending UI within the short-qualification-period treatments in Pennsylvania (47 percent in the high bonus treatment versus 46 percent in the low bonus treatment). Comparisons across the long-qualification-period treatments in Pennsylvania suggest a similar result. The results are again similar in the Washington experiment: larger bonus amounts led to higher percentages of claimants who stopped receiving UI within the short-qualification-period treatments (47, 48, and 50 percent). The most generous bonus also led to the highest percentage of claimants who stopped receiving UI within the long-qualification-pepriod treatment (65.9 percent), although the relationship between low and medium bonus treatments is anomalous.

Differences between the control groups and the corresponding treatment groups in the percentage of claimants who stopped receiving UI by the qualification date foreshadow differences in treatment effects discussed in Chapters 4 and 5. For example, in Illinois, the difference in qualification rates between the FSC-eligible control and FSC-eligible treatment groups is about 6 percentage points (46.0 vs. 39.6), and the Illinois bonus had a large effect on unemployment and reemployment outcomes of the FSC-eligible treatment group. In contrast, there are only small differences between the qualification rates of the control group and the short-qualification-period treatment groups in Washington (–1.0, 0.2, and 2.2 percentage points). These Washington treatments had relatively small effects on unemployment and reemployment outcomes.

Column 3 of Table 3.1 reports the percentages of claimants who ultimately collected a bonus. Overall, 13.6 percent of the claimants assigned to the Illinois treatment, 10.6 percent of the Pennsylvania claimants, and 14.6 percent of the Washington claimants received a bonus. In both Pennsylvania and Washington, the highest rates of bonus receipt occurred for the high-bonus/long-qualification-period bonus offers. In Illinois, the bonus receipt rate was higher among FSC-eligible claimants than among those ineligible for FSC.

What is striking about the bonus receipt rates is that in Illinois, where the rate of ending UI by the qualification date was low as compared with both Pennsylvania and Washington, the overall bonus receipt rate was 13.6 percent—nearly as high as in Washington. In Pennsylvania, where the rate of ending UI by the qualification date was similar to that in Washington (and much higher than in Illinois), the overall bonus receipt rate was only 10.6 percent. Compared with either Pennsylvania or Washington, then, more of the Illinois claimants who ended UI by the qualification date ultimately collected a bonus.

Why did the Illinois treatment-assigned claimants overtake the Pennsylvania claimants and nearly catch up with the bonus-receipt rate of the Washington claimants? There are two possible reasons. First, they may have been more likely to fully satisfy the bonus qualification requirements (that is, by staying employed for four months) once they found a job within the qualification period. Second, they may have been more likely to claim a bonus when they fully qualified for one. Whether a worker stays employed for four months after reemployment (so as to fully qualify for a bonus) is at least partly a question of labor demand conditions during a bonus experiment. Collecting a bonus after qualifying for one, however, is a matter of voluntary participation. Unfortunately, the available data are inadequate to distinguish between the above two possibilities in a convincing way.[2]

We refer to the propensity of claimants who partially qualify for a bonus to collect a bonus as the *bonus take-up rate*. The rate is calculated as the number of bonus-offered claimants who received a bonus, divided by the number who stopped receiving UI benefits by the qualification date (that is, partially qualified), expressed as a percentage. The denominator of this bonus take-up rate overstates the number of claimants who qualified for a bonus, because some claimants who ended UI within the qualification period were not reemployed in a job that they held for at least four months. But again, the available data do not permit construction of a convincing indicator of full bonus qualification.

Column 4 of Table 3.1 displays estimates of the bonus take-up rate for each experiment. The figures again suggest that participation in the Illinois and Washington experiments was greater than in the Pennsylvania experiment. Take-up rates were 32 percent in Illinois (which had a qualification period of 11 weeks), 18 and 21 percent for the long-qualification-period treatments in Pennsylvania, and 22, 29, and 33 percent for the long-qualification-period treatments in Washington. We explore possible explanations of these differences in the next section.

These observations on bonus qualification, receipt, and take-up can be tied together by observing that there is a simple relationship among the three. Specifically, the probability that a worker receives a bonus is the product of the probability that she partially qualifies for a bonus and the probability that she collects a bonus given that she partially qualified:

Pr(bonus received) = Pr(partially qualified for bonus)
  × Pr(bonus received | partially qualified)

In Table 3.1, these probabilities translate into the proportions (expressed as percentages) shown in columns 3 (bonus receipt), 2 (partial bonus qualification), and 4 (bonus take-up).

The above relationship makes clear that bonus receipt depends partly on a probability that is to some degree beyond the control of a worker—the probability of partially qualifying for a bonus, which depends on the existence of job vacancies as well as on a worker's job search efforts. Bonus receipt also depends on a probability that is to a significant extent a matter of voluntary program participation—the probability of collecting a bonus conditional on ending UI by the qualification date. In the next section, we examine the correlates of each of these three probabilities.

EXPLAINING VARIATIONS IN BONUS QUALIFICATION, RECEIPT, AND TAKE-UP

To what extent can the differences in partial bonus qualification, bonus receipt, and bonus take-up rates among the three experiments be explained by the characteristics of claimants who enrolled in each of the three experiments and other observable variables? We approach this issue by using the data on individual claimants from each of the three experiments to estimate linear probability models of participation in the bonus experiments. Each of the models we estimate has a zero-one dependent variable indicating some form of participation in the reemployment bonus experiment—partial qualification for a bonus, bonus receipt, or bonus receipt conditional on partial qualification (that is, bonus take-up).

Partial Qualification for the Bonus

We first examine the correlates of partial qualification for the bonus. Columns 1, 2, and 3 of Table 3.2 report estimates of a model in which the dependent variable equals 1 if a claimant stopped receiving UI benefits by the qualification date, zero otherwise. In view of the data limitations described in note 1 to this chapter, this measure of partial qualification is the best available measure of qualification for a bonus. For each of the three experiments, we regress partial qualification on the following explanatory variables:

- Gender of the claimant.
- Ethnicity of the claimant.
- Age of the claimant.
- Whether the claimant was employed in manufacturing before the current UI claim spell.

- Whether the claimant expected to be recalled to the previous job (in Pennsylvania or Washington only) or received job referrals only through a union (in Washington only).

- Base period earnings of the claimant (in $10,000s)—that is, earnings in roughly the year preceding the initial claim for UI benefits.

- Basic features of the UI benefits received by the claimant—the weekly benefit amount (in $100s) and the potential duration of UI benefits. In Illinois, the latter is a dummy variable equal to 1 if the worker was eligible for FSC—that is, a total of 38 weeks of benefits rather than only 26 weeks of regular state benefits. In Pennsylvania, potential duration of benefits is modeled by a dummy variable equal to 1 if the worker was eligible for 26 weeks of benefits, rather than the 16 weeks of benefits for which about 1 percent of Pennsylvania claimants were eligible. In Washington, potential duration is modeled as the number of weeks of benefits for which the worker was eligible (times 10, which scales the variable to make its coefficient roughly comparable to those of the Illinois and Pennsylvania potential duration variables).

- In Pennsylvania and Washington, characteristics of the bonus offer made to the claimant, modeled in each case as a set of dummy variables. As in Table 3.1, treatments are referred to by their bonus amount (low or high in Pennsylvania; low, medium, or high in Washington) and the qualification period (short or long).

- A set of site dummy variables indicating the ES office where the claimant was assigned to treatment status and informed of the bonus offer. These site variables may capture a variety of effects, including differences from site-to-site in the way the bonus experiment was applied as well as regional differences in the labor market, which would affect the difficulty of obtaining reemployment. (Coefficients of the site dummies are not reported in the table.)

Table 3.2 Linear Probability Models of Partial Qualification, Bonus, Receipt, and Bonus Take-Up[a]

	Dependent variable								
	Partially qualified			Received bonus			Bonus take-up		
Explanatory variable	Illinois (1)	Pennsylvania (2)	Washington (3)	Illinois (4)	Pennsylvania (5)	Washington (6)	Illinois (7)	Pennsylvania (8)	Washington (9)
Gender									
Female	-0.024 (0.016)	-0.053 (0.011)	-0.046 (0.009)	0.007 (0.011)	-0.002 (0.007)	-0.003 (0.007)	0.038 (0.023)	0.019 (0.012)	0.034 (0.011)
Ethnicity									
Black	-0.103 (0.024)	0.054 (0.021)	-0.042 (0.022)	-0.074 (0.017)	-0.064 (0.013)	-0.072 (0.016)	-0.121 (0.037)	-0.114 (0.021)	-0.120 (0.028)
Hispanic	-0.016 (0.034)	0.021 (0.030)	0.005 (0.020)	-0.084 (0.023)	-0.058 (0.019)	-0.044 (0.015)	-0.176 (0.050)	-0.099 (0.030)	-0.076 (0.023)
Other	-0.063 (0.052)	0.870 (0.067)	0.011 (0.021)	-0.036 (0.036)	-0.039 (0.042)	-0.039 (0.015)	-0.032 (0.076)	-0.073 (0.065)	-0.074 (0.024)
Age									
<35	0.061 (0.016)	0.010 (0.012)	0.059 (0.009)	0.026 (0.011)	-0.001 (0.007)	0.025 (0.007)	0.006 (0.024)	-0.024 (0.012)	0.011 (0.011)
≥55	NA[b]	-0.096 (0.018)	0.001 (0.016)	NA	-0.058 (0.011)	-0.042 (0.012)	NA	-0.082 (0.021)	-0.073 (0.019)
Industry before unemployment									
Manufacturing	-0.015 (0.018)	0.054 (0.012)	0.073 (0.011)	-0.011 (0.013)	-0.019 (0.008)	-0.014 (0.008)	-0.018 (0.026)	-0.045 (0.013)	-0.050 (0.012)

Unknown	−0.091 (0.025)	0.030 (0.018)	0.149 (0.106)	−0.028 (0.017)	0.018 (0.012)	0.182 (0.077)	−0.020 (0.039)	0.023 (0.019)	0.199 (0.115)
Job attachment								
Expect recall or union referral	NA	−0.056 (0.017)	0.247 (0.011)	NA	−0.068 (0.011)	−0.088 (0.008)	NA	−0.116 (0.018)	−0.240 (0.012)
Base period earnings ($10,000s)	−0.004 (0.012)	0.016 (0.008)	−0.004 (0.005)	0.000 (0.000)	0.027 (0.005)	−0.004 (0.004)	0.010 (0.018)	0.050 (0.009)	−0.002 (0.006)
UI benefits								
Weekly benefit amount ($100s)	−0.022 (0.028)	−0.067 (0.013)	−0.090 (0.012)	0.037 (0.019)	0.007 (0.008)	0.041 (0.009)	0.099 (0.041)	0.028 (0.013)	0.128 (0.015)
Illinois: FSC-elig.	0.062 (0.016)	NA	NA	0.035 (0.011)	NA	NA	0.038 (0.023)	NA	NA
Pennsylvania: long duration	NA	0.045 (0.051)	NA	NA	0.005 (0.032)	NA	NA	−0.007 (0.053)	NA
Washington: potential duration (×10)	NA	NA	0.127 (0.012)	NA	NA	0.058 (0.009)	NA	NA	0.049 (0.015)

(continued)

Table 3.2 (continued)

Explanatory variable	Partially qualified			Received bonus			Bonus take-up		
	Illinois (1)	Pennsylvania (2)	Washington (3)	Illinois (4)	Pennsylvania (5)	Washington (6)	Illinois (7)	Pennsylvania (8)	Washington (9)
Bonus characteristics[c] (Penn. and Wash. only)									
Low bonus/ short qual. period	NA	NA	reference[d]	NA	NA	reference	NA	NA	reference
Medium bonus/short qual. period	NA	reference	0.011 (0.014)	NA	reference	0.034 (0.010)	NA	reference	0.070 (0.018)
High bonus/ short qual. period	NA	0.003 (0.017)	0.036 (0.016)	NA	0.015 (0.011)	0.061 (0.011)	NA	0.032 (0.020)	0.100 (0.019)
Low bonus/ long qual. period	NA	NA	0.160 (0.014)	NA	NA	0.050 (0.010)	NA	NA	0.024 (0.017)
Medium bonus/long qual. period	NA	0.142 (0.016)	0.148 (0.014)	NA	0.036 (0.010)	0.088 (0.010)	NA	0.030 (0.018)	0.089 (0.017)

Dependent variable

89

High bonus/long qual. period	NA	0.157 (0.016)	0.183 (0.016)	NA	0.068 (0.010)	0.129 (0.011)	MA	0.071 (0.018)	0.131 (0.018)
Low bonus	NA	NA	reference	NA	NA	reference	NA	NA	reference
Medium bonus	NA	reference	−0.003 (0.010)	NA	reference	0.036 (0.007)	NA	reference	0.067 (0.012) (continued)
High bonus	NA	0.004 (0.011)	0.026 (0.011)	NA	0.023 (0.007)	0.068 (0.008)	NA	0.036 (0.011)	0.103 (0.013)
Short qual. period	NA	reference	reference	NA	reference	reference	NA	reference	reference
Long qual. period	NA	0.149 (0.011)	0.147 (0.008)	NA	0.044 (0.007)	0.055 (0.006)	NA	0.033 (0.012)	0.021 (0.010)
Intercept	0.376 (0.045)	0.385 (0.062)	0.160 (0.055)	0.038 (0.031)	−0.004 (0.039)	−0.073 (0.040)	0.111 (0.067)	0.047 (0.065)	0.008 (0.069)
Sample size	4,186	8,748	12,452	4,186	8,748	12,452	1,795	4,947	6,939
R^2	0.040	0.054	0.092	0.036	0.045	0.048	0.047	0.078	0.124
MSE	0.235	0.232	0.224	0.113	0.090	0.118	0.206	0.140	0.169

[a] OLS coefficients, with standard errors in parentheses.

[b] "NA" indicates that the variable does not apply to the analysis.

[c] The Pennsylvania and Washington bonus characteristics are not strictly comparable, but the medium and high bonus amounts are similar, as are the short and long qualification periods. There was no low bonus amount in Pennsylvania. Also included in each regression is a set of site dummy variables indicating where the claimant was assigned to the bonus experiment.

[d] "Reference" refers to the reference category in a set of categorical variables.

We estimate a separate model of bonus receipt for each of the three experiments because pairwise tests for pooling the samples (Chow tests) strongly reject pooling.

Although many of the relationships between the explanatory variables and partial bonus qualification differ across the three experiments, some patterns do emerge (see columns 1, 2, and 3 of Table 3.2). These patterns reflect widely observed patterns of unemployment duration by ethnicity, age, and so on. For example, ethnic minorities tend to be less likely to partially qualify for a bonus (in Illinois and Washington), and younger workers are more likely than older workers to partially qualify for a bonus. Both outcomes reflect the shorter spells of unemployment that white workers and younger workers generally experience. Higher weekly benefit amounts (in Pennsylvania and Washington) tend to reduce the probability of partially qualifying for a bonus, and greater potential duration of benefits (in Illinois and Washington) tends to increase the probability of partially qualifying.

The estimates suggest that larger bonus offers and longer qualification periods lead to higher probabilities of partially qualifying for a bonus. The increases in partial qualification resulting from increased bonus amounts are rather small and are statistically significant only in the case of the high bonus amount in Washington (compare the coefficients of the low, medium, and high bonus amounts under the bonus characteristics in Table 3.2). It is much clearer that partial qualification rates rise with the length of the qualification period (compare the coefficients of the short and long qualification periods under the bonus characteristics in Table 3.2).

In regressions that are not reported, we included the bonus amount and the qualification period as continuous variables in models that are otherwise the same as those reported in Table 3.2. These regressions suggest that a $1,000 increase in the bonus amount increased the probability of partially qualifying by about 3 percentage points in Pennsylvania and by about 6 percentage points in Washington. They also suggest that extending the bonus qualification period by one week increased the probability of partially qualifying by about 1.5 percentage points in both Pennsylvania and Washington.

Bonus Receipt

Columns 4, 5, and 6 of Table 3.2 display estimates of models in which a dummy variable equal to 1 if a claimant received a bonus (zero otherwise) is regressed on the same explanatory variables used in the partial qualification equations reported in columns 1–3. The bonus receipt equations have less explanatory power than do the partial qualification equations (see the lower adjusted R^2 values at the bottom of Table 3.2). Again we estimate a separate model for each of the three experiments because pooling is rejected for the model of bonus receipt, as it was for partial qualification.

Most of the relationships between bonus receipt and the explanatory variables are similar to the those observed for partial qualification. Ethnic minorities are less likely to receive a bonus (in all three experiments), and younger workers are more likely to receive a bonus than are older workers (again in all three experiments). Workers who expect recall are less likely to receive a bonus (in Pennsylvania and Washington). Greater potential duration of benefits (in Illinois and Washington) tends to increase the probability of bonus receipt. Although higher weekly benefit amounts tend to reduce the probability of partially qualifying for a bonus, higher weekly benefit amounts tend to increase the probability of bonus receipt (in Illinois and Washington). (We return to this point in the discussion of bonus take-up rates below.) Also, although there is an ambiguous relationship between the industry from which a worker was laid off and partial qualification, workers laid off from manufacturing jobs seem less likely than others to receive a bonus (in Pennsylvania and Washington).

The probability of bonus receipt increases strongly both with larger bonus offers and with longer qualification periods—compare the coefficients of the low, medium, and high bonus amounts and those of the short and long qualification periods under the bonus characteristics in Table 3.2. In regressions not reported, we find that a $1,000 increase in the bonus offer increased the probability of bonus receipt by 4.5 percentage points in Pennsylvania and by 10 percentage points in Washington. Extending the bonus qualification period by one week increased the probability of bonus receipt by about 1 percentage point in both Pennsylvania and Washington.

Bonus Take-Up Rates

The third issue we seek to understand is what factors influenced whether a claimant who partially qualified for a bonus ultimately collected a bonus. This propensity of claimants who partially qualified for a bonus to collect a bonus is the bonus take-up rate. Columns 7, 8, and 9 of Table 3.2 display estimates of take-up rate models for Illinois, Pennsylvania, and Washington.[3] In each, we have regressed a dummy variable equal to 1 if a claimant received a bonus (zero otherwise) on the same explanatory variables that were used in the partial qualification and bonus receipt equations already discussed. The difference between the take-up rate models and the partial qualification and bonus receipt models is that the sample used in the take-up rate models includes only treatment-assigned claimants *who partially qualified for the bonus* (that is, ended UI benefit receipt by the qualification date).

These estimates show several patterns. Women tend to have higher take-up rates than men, other things equal, although the relationship is strong and statistically significant only in Washington. Ethnic minorities have much lower take-up rates than whites in all three experiments. Workers laid off from manufacturing jobs have lower take-up rates than other workers (in Pennsylvania and Washington). These effects arguably reflect differences in tastes—including possible differences in the extent to which workers trust the experimenters—that exist among different groups of workers.

Workers who expected to be recalled or (in Washington) to be placed by a union had much lower take-up rates than others, all else equal. In Pennsylvania, this effect was in addition to a lower tendency of workers who expected recall to qualify for a bonus. In Washington, this effect offsets the (rather surprising) positive effect of recall expectations on partial qualification and produces a net negative impact of recall expectations on the probability of bonus receipt.

Higher weekly benefit amounts (in all three experiments) are associated with higher take-up rates. This result seems counterintuitive, at least in Illinois, where a given bonus provides a smaller payoff (in relative terms) to a worker who receives high weekly benefits than to a worker who receives low weekly benefits. A possible interpretation, however, is that workers with higher weekly benefits tend to have relatively higher human capital and earnings. In other words, workers with high weekly benefit amounts are likely to be more productive, better able to make use of the UI system, and more likely to collect a bonus for which they qualify.[4]

A potentially interesting result is the relatively weak relationship between the potential duration of benefits and the bonus take-up rate. Recall that (except in Pennsylvania) longer potential duration of benefits lead to higher probabilities of qualifying for and receiving a bonus. The relationship between potential duration and bonus take-up is weaker in both Illinois and Washington, however, which suggests that the gross relationship between potential duration and bonus receipt results from search behavior, not bonus take-up behavior. That is, the evidence is consistent with the idea that bonus offers lead to a significant increase in the search intensity of workers for whom the potential duration of benefits is longer. Their propensity to collect a bonus is no greater than that of workers whose potential duration of benefits is shorter, but because they increase their search intensity more than do workers with shorter potential duration of benefits, a higher proportion of workers with a long potential duration of benefits qualifies for and ultimately collects a bonus.

The results in Table 3.2 suggest that larger bonus offers lead unambiguously to larger bonus take-up rates. In regressions not reported, we find that a $1,000 increase in the bonus offer would have increased the take-up rate by 8 percentage points in Pennsylvania and by 17 percentage points in Washington.

We have seen that larger bonus offers result in a higher probability of receiving a bonus, but they are only weakly related to the probability of qualifying for a bonus. The results in columns 7, 8, and 9 of Table 3.2 show that the observed positive effect of a larger bonus offer on bonus receipt occurs because larger bonus offers increase the take-up rate. That is, larger bonuses raise the probability of bonus receipt mainly because they raise the bonus take-up rate, not because they raise the probability of qualification. The point is potentially important in designing a reemployment bonus program. If higher bonus offers raise the bonus take-up rate without significantly raising the probability of partial qualification for a bonus (that is, of cutting short the spell of unemployment), then a higher bonus would lead to larger bonus payments without the benefit of shortening unemployment spells. This question is considered further in Chapter 4 when we consider the optimal size of a bonus offer.

Extending the bonus qualification period has a relatively weak effect on the probability of bonus take-up. Although statistically nonzero, the coefficients on the long qualification period variable are rather small in the take-up equations compared with those in the qualification equations. In unreported regressions, we find that extending the bonus qualification period by one week would have increased the take-up rate by less than 1 percentage point in Pennsylvania and Washington. A longer qualification period makes it easier to qualify for a bonus but does not increase a worker's incentive to collect a bonus (as does an increase in the bonus amount). Accordingly, it makes sense that the take-up rate should be weakly affected by the length of the qualification period.

EXPLAINING DIFFERENCES AMONG THE EXPERIMENTS

How would partial qualification for the bonus, bonus receipt, and bonus take-up have differed if the workers in one experiment (Illinois, say) had faced the "structure" of partial qualification, bonus receipt, and bonus take-up that existed in either of the other experiments (Pennsylvania or Washington)? Answering this question can suggest the extent to which differences among the experiments in partial qualification, bonus receipt, and bonus take-up can be explained by differences in observable factors associated with the experiments, such as the characteristics of claimants and characteristics of the labor market where the experiments were conducted.

For example, we could ask how many of the workers assigned to the Illinois treatment would have received a bonus if their probability of receiving a bonus had been determined by the structure of bonus receipt estimated in the Pennsylvania experiment. First, let x_{PA} denote the vector of mean observed characteristics of the workers who were assigned to a treatment in Pennsylvania and let b_{PA} denote the vector of estimated coefficients from the Pennsylvania bonus receipt equation. Then the proportion of Pennsylvania claimants who actually received a bonus (y_{PA}) can be expressed as:

$$y_{PA} = x_{PA} \cdot b_{PA}$$

Next, we can simulate the proportion of Illinois claimants who would have received a bonus if their bonus receipt were determined by the structure of bonus receipt observed in the Pennsylvania experiment. We denote this simulated proportion by $y_{IL|PA}$ and compute it by substituting the mean characteristics of the Illinois claimants (x_{IL}) into the Pennsylvania bonus receipt equation:

$$y_{IL|PA} = x_{IL} \cdot b_{PA}$$

The dot product $x_{IL} \cdot b_{PA}$ is a simulated proportion of Illinois bonus recipients because it applies the model of bonus receipt that was estimated for the Pennsylvania experiment to the characteristics of workers assigned to the Illinois experiment. A similar approach can be used to simulate the proportion of Washington claimants who would have received a bonus if they had been assigned to the Pennsylvania experiment, and so on.

Implementing the above procedure requires that the partial qualification, receipt, and take-up equations reported in Table 3.2 be modified in three ways. First, in the Illinois and Pennsylvania models, the dummy variables indicating the potential duration of UI benefits are replaced with continuous variables for the potential duration of UI benefits. Second, in the Pennsylvania and Washington models, the bonus amount and qualification period dummy variables are replaced with continuous variables indicating bonus amount and length of the qualification period (there was no variation in either the bonus amount or qualification period in Illinois). Third, in the models for all three experiments, we replace the site dummies with two sets of variables that attempt to capture the state of the labor market in which workers sought reemployment:

- The unemployment rate in the local area and quarter in which the worker filed his or her initial claim for UI benefits (entered as four dummy variables: less than 5 percent, from 5 to 7 percent, from 7 to 10 percent, and greater than 10 percent).

- The percentage change in employment in the local area where the worker filed the initial claim during the three months following the initial claim.[5]

The above modifications are needed so that the mean characteristics of the workers in each experiment can be substituted into the structure of partial qualification, bonus receipt, and bonus take-up estimated for the other experiments. The dummy variables that were used to characterize the potential duration of UI benefits, bonus characteristics, and sites in the models reported in Table 3.2 are not conformable across the three experiments.

Table 3.3 displays the results of simulating the partial qualification, bonus receipt, and take-up rates for each of the three experiments using the approach outlined above. The actual bonus receipt rate in Illinois was 13.6 percent, in Pennsylvania 10.6 percent, and in Washington 14.6 percent (column 2). The differences among the three experiments can be explained in either of two ways. First, recall that the probability of bonus receipt is the product of the probability of partially qualifying for a bonus and the probability of taking up a bonus for which one partially qualifies (see pp. 83). Column 1 of Table 3.3 shows that the partial qualification rates were higher in Pennsylvania and Washington than in Illinois. However, Illinois made up for its low partial qualification rate by having the highest take-up rate, and Pennsylvania was pulled down by the lowest take-up rate. This much we already knew from Table 3.1.

The simulations in Table 3.3 allow a second, potentially more revealing, kind of explanation of the differences among the three experiments. The simulations let us speculate about whether the differences among the three experiments in partial qualification and take-up rates can in turn be explained by differences among the three in the characteristics of the experimental claimants or the labor market conditions they faced. If claimant characteristics and labor market conditions don't explain much of the differences, then we would have to conclude that the differences in partial qualification and take-up stem from factors that are not captured in the variables that we can quantify and observe.

The partial qualification rates in column 1 suggest that more of the Illinois claimants would have partially qualified for a bonus if they had been in either the Pennsylvania or the Washington experiment (57.2 or 65 percent, instead of the actual 42.9 percent). Fewer Pennsylvania claimants would have partially qualified for a bonus in Illinois (46.1 percent, instead of the actual 56.6 percent), and a somewhat higher percentage of Pennsylvania claimants would have partially qualified for a bonus in Washington (58.3 percent, instead of the actual 56.6 percent). Finally, fewer of the Washington claimants would have partially qualified for a bonus in either Illinois (47.3 percent, instead of the actual 55.7 percent) or in Pennsylvania (49.1 percent, instead of the actual 55.7 percent).

However, differences among the experiments in the observable characteristics of the claimants and the labor market explain little if

Table 3.3 Actual and Simulated Partial Qualification, Bonus Receipt, and Bonus Take-Up Rates[a] (%)

	Partially qualified[b] (1)	Received bonus (2)	Bonus take-up[c] (3)
Illinois means applied to			
Illinois model (actual)	42.9	13.6	31.8
Pennsylvania model	57.2	10.1	19.8
Washington model	65.0	20.8	32.8
Pennsylvania means applied to			
Illinois model	46.1	19.7	42.5
Pennsylvania model (actual)	56.6	10.6	18.6
Washington model	58.3	19.1	25.3
Washington means applied to			
Illinois model	47.3	19.4	41.7
Pennsylvania model	49.1	10.3	17.3
Washington model (actual)	55.7	14.6	26.1

[a] The simulated take-up rates were obtained by substituting the mean characteristics of, for example, the Illinois treatment group into the take-up equations that were estimated for the Pennsylvania and Washington treatment groups. Actual values are shaded. See the text for further discussion.
[b] Partial qualification is defined as ending UI receipt by the bonus qualification date.
[c] The take-up rate is defined as the percentage of workers who actually collected a bonus given that they stopped receiving UI benefits by the qualification date.

any of the differences between Illinois and the other two experiments in partial qualification rates. For example, the actual difference between the Illinois and Pennsylvania partial qualification rates is 13.7 percentage points (56.6 minus 42.9). If the Illinois claimants had been assigned to the Pennsylvania experiment, the simulations suggest that their partial qualification rates would have increased to 57.2 percent—similar to what was actually observed in Pennsylvania. Hence, none of the difference between the Illinois and Pennsylvania partial qualification rates is explained by differences between the two experiments in observed variables. Rather, the differences depend wholly on how observed variables map into the probability of partially qualifying in each of the two experiments.

The conclusion is slightly less negative if we ask what would have happened to the Pennsylvania claimants if they had been assigned to the Illinois experiment. If the Pennsylvania claimants had been assigned in Illinois, their partial qualification rate would have fallen to 46.1 percent—3.2 percentage points higher than was observed in Illinois. Hence, observed variables explain less than one-quarter of the total observed difference between partial qualification rates in Illinois and Pennsylvania (3.2 points out of the total 13.7-point difference)—the rest is unexplained. (A decomposition of this simulation, which we do not report, shows that this 3.2 percentage point difference can be explained roughly half and half by more favorable labor market conditions in Pennsylvania and by Pennsylvania claimants having characteristics that are more favorable to partially qualifying for a bonus.)

Comparison of the Illinois and Washington partial qualification rates gives similar results. The actual difference between the Illinois and Washington partial qualification rates is 12.8 percentage points (55.7 minus 42.9). If the Illinois claimants had been assigned to the Washington experiment, their partial qualification rates would have been 65 percent, which suggests that observables explain none of the differences in partial qualification between Illinois and Washington. On the other hand, if the Washington claimants had been assigned to the Illinois experiment, their qualification rates would have been 47.3 percent, which suggests that observables can explain only about one-third of the total difference between the partial qualification rates in Illinois and Washington (4.4 points out of the total 12.8-point difference).

Given that the Illinois experiment occurred during the early stages of a recovery (late 1984 and early 1985), whereas the Pennsylvania and Washington experiments occurred after the recovery had matured (1988–1989), it is tempting to suggest that relatively slack labor demand played an important role in lowering the Illinois qualification rates. However, given that we have tried to control for labor market conditions in the partial qualification models, this is purely a speculative and post hoc rationalization of the apparent difference between Illinois and the other two experiments in how partial qualification came about. (There may be deficiencies in the labor market controls we have included, but they are standard measures of the health of the labor market.)

Consider next the take-up rates shown in column 3 of Table 3.3: the observed take-up rate was 31.8 percent in Illinois, 18.6 percent in Pennsylvania, and 26.1 percent in Washington. Was the take-up rate lowest in Pennsylvania and highest in Illinois as a result of differences in observable characteristics of claimants and the labor market conditions they faced, or do the differences stem from factors that are not captured in the observed variables?

The take-up rate was lower in Pennsylvania than in Illinois and Washington for reasons that are not accounted for by observed variables. Far fewer Illinois claimants would have taken up a bonus if they had been in the Pennsylvania experiment (just 19.8 percent, instead of the actual 31.8 percent). Similarly, fewer of the Washington claimants would have taken up a bonus if they had been in the Pennsylvania experiment (17.3 percent, instead of the actual 26.1 percent). That is, given individual and labor market characteristics mapped into much lower take-up rates in Pennsylvania than in either Illinois or Washington, and differences among the three experiments in measurable characteristics of claimants or labor market conditions do not explain the differences in take-up behavior. As with the partial qualification rates, differences in the take-up rates depend on the "structure" of bonus take-up—that is, on how observables map into the probability of bonus take-up in each of the experiments—rather than on individual characteristics or measurable features of the labor market.

Another way to see the point is to note that the Pennsylvania claimants would have had a much higher take-up rate either in Illinois (42.5 percent) or in Washington (25.3 percent) than they actually did (18.6 percent). The simulated take-up rate for Illinois (42.5 percent) is well above the actual take-up rate in Illinois (31.8 percent), and the simulated rate for Washington (25.3 percent) is very close to the actual take-up rate in Washington (26.3 percent), indicating again that the differences among the three experiments in take-up behavior cannot be explained by measurable characteristics of claimants or labor market conditions. It is clear that something about the Pennsylvania experiment—other than claimants' characteristics and the state of the labor market, at least to the extent that we have been able to control for these variables—resulted in lower take-up rates in Pennsylvania than in either Illinois or Washington.

Our inability to explain the large difference between the bonus take-up rates in Pennsylvania on the one hand, and Illinois and Washington on the other, suggests again the difficulty in predicting and understanding participation in a bonus program. It is difficult to quantify, or even to characterize descriptively, differences in a program's implementation from state to state and site to site. Yet differences in implementation of the three experiments would seem to be the most likely source of the large gap between the take-up rates of Pennsylvania and the other two experiments.

Anecdotal evidence on the Illinois experiment illustrates the potential importance to program participation of variables that are intangible and hard to quantify. In the Illinois experiment, each claimant who was assigned to a treatment was asked to sign a form indicating willingness to participate in the experiment. At one of the experimental sites, the treatment was administered by a woman who was reported to be enthusiastic about the reemployment bonus and readily trusted by the experimental claimants. (She was described to one of us as "grandmotherly.") At this site, the rates of willingness to participate and bonus take-up were higher than the average for the experiment as a whole, even after adjusting for measurable correlates of willingness to participate and bonus take-up. This sort of evidence is a reminder that a bonus treatment—like any treatment—includes more than a financial incentive. It also includes the way the incentive is presented and the attitude and trustworthiness of those who are assigned the job of administering the treatment.

DISCUSSION AND SUMMARY

This chapter has attempted to sort out differences among the Illinois, Pennsylvania, and Washington reemployment bonus experiments in what we have referred to generally as "participation." By participation in the bonus experiments, we mean three things: qualifying (in this case, partially) for a bonus, actually receiving a bonus, and collecting a bonus given partial qualification for a bonus (bonus take-up). These three concepts of participation are related by a simple identity: the probability of a worker receiving a bonus is the product of the probability that she partially qualifies and the probability that she collects a bonus given that she partially qualified. Table 3.1 shows each of these as empirical probabilities (expressed as percentages) of claimants qualifying for a bonus (column 2), receiving a bonus (column 3), and taking up a bonus (column 4).

Table 3.1 and the discussion on pp. 78–84 showed that the partial qualification rate in Illinois (43 percent) was much lower than in either Pennsylvania (57 percent) or Washington (56 percent). Ultimately, however, nearly as high a percentage of claimants received a bonus in Illinois (13.6 percent) as in Washington (14.6 percent), whereas only 10.6 percent of the Pennsylvania claimants received a bonus. The simple explanation is that the bonus take-up rate was higher in Illinois (31.8 percent) than in either Pennsylvania (where it was just 18.6 percent) or Washington (where it was 26.1 percent). At a rather superficial level, then, we were able to explain the bonus receipt rate.

But we are much less successful in quantifying the large differences across the experiments in the partial qualification and take-up rates that underlie the bonus receipt rate. The qualification models suggest, not surprisingly, that the correlates of partial qualification are similar to the correlates of short spells of unemployment (see Table 3.2). For example, younger workers and white workers are more likely than older workers and ethnic minorities to qualify for a bonus. Also, not surprisingly, higher bonus amounts and longer qualification periods tend to increase the probability of qualifying for a bonus. The bonus receipt models offer similar findings.

The bonus take-up estimates differ in some ways from the partial qualification and receipt estimates. The probability of collecting a bonus conditional on qualifying is influenced again by ethnicity (with racial minorities less likely to take up a bonus) and the bonus amount (with larger bonuses more likely to be collected), but several additional relationships also emerge. Women, nonmanufacturing workers, and workers who do not expect to be recalled are more likely to take up a bonus. Workers with higher weekly benefit amounts are more likely to take up a bonus. Those who face a longer qualification period are only slightly more likely than others to take up a bonus.

Nevertheless, it would be an understatement to say that puzzles remain in explaining differences in partial qualification, receipt, and take-up among the three experiments. In the last section, we use estimated models of partial qualification, receipt, and take-up to simulate the percentages of claimants who would have partially qualified for, received, and taken up a bonus if they had been assigned to one of the other experiments (see Table 3.3). Such simulations can suggest the extent to which differences among the experiments in observed participation are accounted for by observable differences in the characteristics of claimants (or in the labor market conditions they faced). We find that measurable differences in claimants' characteristics or labor market conditions explain very little of the differences across the three experiments in partial qualification and bonus take-up behavior. Instead, the differences depend on the "structure" of partial qualification and bonus take-up—that is, on how claimants' characteristics map into the probability of partial qualification or bonus take-up in each of the experiments

We are left with rather ad hoc explanations of the differences in participation across the three experiments. Perhaps partial qualification for the bonus was lower in Illinois than in Pennsylvania or Washington because the Illinois experiment took place during the early part of the 1980s recovery (whereas the Pennsylvania and Washington experiments occurred after the recovery had matured) or because of some other difficult-to-quantify feature of the labor market in Illinois. Perhaps the bonus offer was presented to claimants differently (and less attractively) in Pennsylvania than in Illinois or Washington. In fact, there is no convincing quantitative evidence for or against either of these views. The conclusion is that the estimated models of partial qualification and take-up offer little help in explaining the differences among the three experiments in the observed partial qualification and take-up rates.

Notes

1. The figures for the control group in Pennsylvania ("Control/short qual. period" and "Control/long qual. period") were obtained by observing the number of claimants in the Pennsylvania control group who stopped receiving UI benefits within 6 weeks and 12 weeks, respectively. A similar approach yielded the figures for the Washington control group.

2. Two types of administrative data were used in the analysis: UI claims records, which provide data on the timing and amounts of UI benefits paid to claimants; and wage records, which provide data on each worker's quarterly earnings in UI-covered employment in the state where the worker claimed UI benefits. Because the wage records are quarterly, they do not provide information on the exact timing of reemployment or whether employment was continuous during the required four months. Also, because wage records provide information only on UI-covered employment in the state where each worker claimed benefits, they miss reemployment in jobs that are in another state or are not covered by UI.

   Note that the partial qualification measure used in this chapter differs from the full qualification concept that is used elsewhere in this volume (especially Chapter 6). As a result, the bonus take-up rates that are calculated in this chapter cannot be compared with those derived in Chapter 6. In Chapter 6, the take-up rate is defined as the proportion of UI claimants who received a bonus given that they 1) were eligible for UI benefits, 2) became reemployed and stopped receiving UI benefits by the qualification date, and 3) remained employed for four months. In other words, the bonus take-up rate is the proportion of claimants who fully qualified for the bonus who then collected a bonus. Conceptually, this latter definition is the correct definition of the bonus take-up rate.

3. Pooling of the three experiments was rejected for the bonus take-up rate models as it was for the models of partial qualification and bonus receipt.

4. A possible problem with this interpretation is that the regressions already control for base period earnings. But base period earnings and the weekly benefit amount are systematically related and may be collinear. Indeed, the coefficients on base period earnings are essentially zero in Illinois and Washington (in Pennsylvania the coefficient is positive), so it is tempting to suggest that the weekly benefit amount variable is capturing most of the effect of higher earnings capacity on bonus take-up.

5. The employment level used is a three-month moving average of employment in the local area where the worker filed for UI benefits.

4

Bonus Impacts on Receipt
of Unemployment Insurance

Paul T. Decker
Christopher J. O'Leary
and
Stephen A. Woodbury

This chapter presents estimates of how a reemployment bonus affected three different outcomes of policy interest: weeks of unemployment insurance (UI) receipt during the benefit year, dollars of UI received during the benefit year, and the percentage of persons who exhaust their benefits. An assessment of how the reemployment bonus affected reemployment wages is made in Chapter 5.

To provide a deeper understanding of the reemployment bonus effects, this chapter also presents impact estimates based on slightly more involved computations. As shown in Chapter 2 in the discussion of the results of randomization (pp. 56–57), the characteristics of the treatment and control groups were quite similar in the Washington and Pennsylvania experiments; however, numerous statistically significant differences existed between the control and treatment groups in Illinois. Since the control and treatment groups were not completely homogenous, "regression adjustment" was done to account for differences between the treatments and controls in observable characteristics and improve the precision of treatment impact estimates.

Taken together, the Illinois, Pennsylvania, and Washington experiments examined a wide variety of bonus levels and qualification period lengths. In the third section of this chapter, we examine the marginal response to variations in these parameters. The analysis is done using a "continuous variables model" with the bonus amount and qualification period entered linearly.[1] Results are presented for the experiments separately and then for a pooled sample using evidence from all three.

To examine how the bonus offers changed behavior regarding the timing of unemployment, we present a hazard analysis of leaving insured unemployment. We then report treatment impacts in the three experiments for various subgroups: treatment impact estimates are presented by gender, age, race, previous industry, area unemployment rate, and weekly benefit entitlement. Some evidence from the Washington experiment about the effectiveness of the reemployment bonus for dislocated workers is also presented. The final section offers some conclusions.

Evidence from the three experiments suggests that a cash reemployment bonus offer can be expected to modestly shorten the average spell of insured unemployment, but the likely impacts seem to be too small for the bonus offer to be an optimum strategy for reducing UI costs. A full cost-benefit analysis investigating this question is provided in Chapter 7. No particular population subgroups had distinctly stronger reactions to the bonus than other groups; however, the bonus was more effective at times and places where the unemployment rate was lower.

TREATMENT IMPACTS ON INSURED UNEMPLOYMENT

The three experiments differed in the number and type of treatments examined and in the samples given a bonus offer. Figure 4.1 summarizes the characteristics of the treatment designs for the three experiments (which are more fully described in Chapter 2).

While there was only a single claimant treatment in the Illinois experiment—$500 for reemployment within 11 weeks on a job held 4 months—the availability of Federal Supplemental Compensation (FSC) was ended about halfway through the enrollment period. This resulted in a "natural experiment" in which 53 percent of the claimants offered a bonus in the Illinois experiment had a maximum entitled benefit duration of 38 weeks, while the others had a maximum duration of 26 weeks. According to Davidson and Woodbury (1991), the different entitled durations lead to significantly different response to the bonus offer. We present estimates separately for the different duration entitlement groups.

Figure 4.1 Design of the Reemployment Bonus Offers

A. Illinois Job Search Incentive Experiment

Bonus amount	Qualification period
$500	11 weeks

B. Pennsylvania Reemployment Bonus Experiment

	Qualification period	
Bonus amount	6 weeks	12 weeks
3 × WBA	Low bonus/short qual.	Low bonus/long qual.
6 × WBA	High bonus/short qual.	High bonus/long qual.

C. Washington Reemployment Bonus Experiment

	Qualification period	
Bonus amount	(0.2 × potential UI duration) + 1 week	(0.4 × potential UI duration) + 1 week
2 × WBA	Low bonus/short qual.	Low bonus/long qual.
4 × WBA	Med. bonus/short qual.	Med. bonus/long qual.
6 × WBA	High bonus/short qual.	High bonus/long qual.

As described in Chapter 2, the four treatments in Pennsylvania involved either a low or high bonus amount and either a short or a long qualification period. The low bonus (set at three times the weekly benefit amount [WBA]) had a mean of $502, while the high bonus (set at 6 × WBA) had a mean of $1,000. The short qualification period was set at 6 weeks and the long qualification period was set at 12 weeks. With WBAs ranging from $35 to $260, bonus offers in Pennsylvania ranged from $105 to $1,560. For all treatments in Pennsylvania, the reemployment period was set at 16 weeks.

In Washington, there were three formulas for the bonus amount (low, medium, and high) and two formulas for the qualification period (short and long). The bonus amounts were figured as 2, 4, or 6 times the WBA, and the qualification periods were computed as either 20 percent or 40 percent of the entitled duration of benefits plus one week.[2] The mean low bonus amount offered was $307, the mean medium amount was $615, and the mean high amount was $925. The

mean short qualification period was 7 weeks, and the mean long qualification period was 12 weeks. The bonus offers in Washington ranged
from $110 to $1,254. The reemployment period for all treatments was
set at four months.

For the Pennsylvania and Washington experiments we present estimates of the impact of each separate offer. For each of those experiments, we give an estimate of the mean effect of the short-
qualification-period offers, the long-qualification-period offers, and the
different bonus level offers, as well as an estimate for each experiment
of the overall mean impact of all treatments.

Unadjusted Treatment Impacts

For a classically designed experiment involving random assignment and large sample sizes, treatment impact estimates may be computed as the simple difference between treatment and control group
means of outcome measures. Simple experimental impact estimates
are not constrained by econometric models and may be very convincing and easy to understand if randomization was effective in creating
homogenous control and treatment group samples. This simplicity is
one of the fundamental appeals of experiments for program evaluation.

Table 4.1 presents unadjusted estimates of the response to the bonus
offer. The overall mean estimates indicate that the bonus offer reduced
weeks of UI benefit receipt by 1.15 weeks in Illinois, 0.62 weeks in
Pennsylvania, and 0.34 weeks in Washington (Woodbury and Spiegelman 1987; Corson et al. 1992; O'Leary, Spiegelman, and Kline 1995).
For Illinois and Pennsylvania, the null hypothesis of no impact can be
rejected at the 95 percent confidence level. The estimates also show
that the bonus offer reduced UI benefits received by $194 in Illinois,
$81 in Pennsylvania, and $22 in Washington. The bonus offer also
reduced the probability of UI benefit exhaustion by 3.3 percent in Illinois, 0.8 percent in Pennsylvania, and 1.0 percent in Washington.[3]

This pattern of results—bonus impacts in Illinois being markedly
larger than those in Pennsylvania, and impacts in Pennsylvania being
somewhat larger than those in Washington—holds up throughout the
comparison of various measures of treatment impact across the three
experiments. The relative impacts from the three experiments may be
examined in comparison to the parameters of the bonus offers. The

Table 4.1 Unadjusted Differences between Experimental and Control Group Means in the Illinois, Pennsylvania, and Washington Reemployment Bonus Experiments[a]

	Insured weeks	UI compensation ($)	Exhaustion rate	Sample size[b]
ILLINOIS				
Control	20.1 (0.19)	2,786 (33)	0.472 (0.008)	3,952
Treatment	−1.15** (0.27)	−194** (46)	−0.033** (0.011)	4,186
Control—FSC-elig.	21.6 (0.30)	3,094 (51)	0.490 (0.011)	2,106
Treatment—FSC-elig.	−1.78** (0.41)	−316** (70)	−0.054** (0.015)	2,337
Control—FSC-inelig.	18.3 (0.23)	2,520 (41)	0.447 (0.012)	1,600
Treatment—FSC-inelig.	−0.71** (0.34)	−90 (59)	−0.015 (0.018)	1,589
PENNSYLVANIA				
Control	14.9 (0.18)	2,388 (36)	0.277 (0.008)	3,392
Low bonus/short qual.	−0.42 (0.34)	−26 (68)	0.012 (0.014)	1,395
Low bonus/long qual.	−0.41 (0.28)	−44 (56)	−0.001 (0.012)	2,456
High bonus/short qual.	−0.51* (0.31)	−66 (61)	−0.001 (0.013)	1,910
High bonus/long qual.	−0.95** (0.27)	−146** (54)	−0.026** (0.011)	3,073
Mean bonus/short qual.	−0.47 (0.26)	−49 (52)	0.004 (0.011)	3,305
Mean bonus/long qual.	−0.71** (0.23)	−100** (46)	−0.015 (0.010)	5,529
Low bonus/mean qual.	−0.41 (0.25)	−38 (50)	0.003 (0.011)	3,851
High bonus/mean qual.	−0.78** (0.24)	−115** (47)	−0.016* (0.010)	4,983
Mean bonus/mean qual.	−0.62** (0.22)	−81* (43)	−0.008 (0.009)	8,834

(continued)

Table 4.1 (continued)

	Insured weeks	UI compensation ($)	Exhaustion rate	Sample size[b]
WASHINGTON				
Control	14.3	2,066	0.239	3,082
	(0.19)	(34)	(0.008)	
Low bonus/short qual.	−0.05	30	0.011	2,246
	(0.30)	(52)	(0.012)	
Med. bonus/short qual.	−0.19	5	−0.004	2,348
	(0.30)	(51)	(0.012)	
High bonus/short qual.	−0.62*	−69	−0.012	1,583
	(0.33)	(58)	(0.013)	
Low bonus /long qual.	−0.50*	−58	−0.030**	2,387
	(0.29)	(51)	(0.011)	
Med. bonus/long qual.	−0.14	12	−0.014	2,353
	(0.30)	(51)	(0.012)	
High bonus/long qual.	−0.73**	−86	−0.023*	1,535
	(0.34)	(58)	(0.013)	
Low bonus/mean qual.	−0.28	−16	−0.010	4,633
	(0.25)	(43)	(0.010)	
Med. bonus/mean qual.	−0.16	9	−0.009	4,701
	(0.25)	(43)	(0.010)	
High bonus/mean qual.	−0.67**	−77	−0.018	3,118
	(0.27)	(47)	(0.011)	
Mean bonus/short qual.	−0.25	−5	−0.000	6,177
	(0.24)	(41)	(0.009)	
Mean bonus/long qual.	−0.42*	−39	−0.022**	6,275
	(0.24)	(41)	(0.009)	
Mean bonus/mean qual.	−0.34	−22	−0.011	12,452
	(0.22)	(38)	(0.008)	

[a] Standard errors in parentheses. * = Statistically significant at the 90% confidence level; ** = statistically significant at the 95% confidence level.

[b] The Illinois sample sizes for FSC-eligible and FSC-ineligible do not sum to the total Illinois sample size. This discrepancy is due to the FSC eligibility conditions, which differed depending on the date of the benefit claim, and our desire to use the largest possible sample in the full sample analysis. Further details are given in Chapter 3.

average bonus offer as a multiple of the average WBA was 3.6 in Illinois, 4.7 in Pennsylvania, and 3.8 in Washington. The average qualification period was 11.0 weeks in Illinois, 9.0 weeks in Pennsylvania, and 8.4 weeks in Washington. Pennsylvania had both an average bonus which was a higher multiple of the average WBA and a longer average qualification period than did Washington. Pennsylvania also had an average bonus which was a higher multiple of the average WBA than Illinois, but the average qualification period in Pennsylvania was two weeks shorter than the uniform 11-week qualification period in Illinois.

A variety of bonus levels and lengths of qualification periods were tested in Pennsylvania and Washington. The results found in each of these separate experiments tends to corroborate the conclusion which might be drawn from the above comparison of overall mean responses across experiments. For Pennsylvania, combining treatments with similar WBA multiples yields two groups that differ in the level of the bonus offer but have the same mean qualification period; a similar exercise yields three bonus level groups for Washington. For both Pennsylvania and Washington, the only combinations estimated with statistical significance are the high bonus treatments combined across qualification periods. For Pennsylvania, the high bonus offers had a mean impact of –0.71 weeks across qualification periods, while in Washington the mean impact of the high bonus treatments was –0.67. In both experiments, these impact estimates are greater than the point estimates for the lower bonus multiples. When the responses to the short and long qualification periods in Pennsylvania and Washington are compared, the estimated response to the long qualification period is statistically significantly greater than for the short qualification period. The largest and most statistically significant impact estimates in both Pennsylvania and Washington were for the high-bonus-multiple/long-qualification-period treatments, with the effect on UI compensation being –0.95 weeks in Pennsylvania and –0.73 weeks in Washington.

An interesting sub-analysis involves the natural experiment with varying entitled duration of benefits in Illinois. The average bonus response of –1.15 weeks of benefits was made up of a response of –1.78 weeks for those eligible for FSC (38 weeks of benefit entitlement) and –0.71 weeks for those not eligible (26 weeks of benefit entitlement). The average response of –0.71 for the FSC-ineligible sample in Illinois is close to the response observed in Pennsylvania and Washington, where the entitled duration of benefits was also similar.

When the Illinois FSC-ineligible results are compared with the findings in Pennsylvania and Washington, the patterns of bonus offer impacts on the UI exhaustion rate within and across the three experiments are also similar. The mean FSC-ineligible impact was −1.5 percent in Illinois, −0.8 percent in Pennsylvania, and in −1.0 in Washington. The overall impact on exhaustions in Illinois was −3.3 percent, with the impact for the FSC-eligible group in Illinois an astounding −5.4 percent. For the high bonus/long qualification treatments, the impact on exhaustion of benefits was −2.6 percent in Pennsylvania and −2.3 percent in Washington. In Illinois and for the high bonus/long qualification treatments in Pennsylvania and Washington, the reductions in exhaustion rate were statistically significant, indicating that some participants dramatically changed behavior by moving from benefit exhaustion to relatively short-term unemployment. The same general pattern of bonus offer impacts is observed on dollars of UI in the benefit year; however, the results in Pennsylvania and Washington were relatively weak compared with estimated impacts on the other outcomes.[4]

Adjusted Treatment Impacts

If treatment-control differences in outcome variables are due to factors other than the treatment, a simple comparison of means may not be adequate to identify treatment effects. As discussed in Chapter 2, for the Washington experiment there were no more differences between treatment and control groups in observable characteristics than would be expected to result from a random assignment process. Unfortunately, the variables on which there were the most pronounced differences—WBA and base period earnings (BPE)—may have affected the measurement of outcomes of interest.

An alternative procedure for computing the simple difference between treatment and control means on an outcome variable of interest that yields the same result involves estimating

(4.1) $Y = a + \mathbf{TB} + u,$

by ordinary least squares regression. In this equation the intercept, a, is the mean value of the outcome variable, Y, for the control group. $\mathbf{T}$ is a matrix of dummy variables representing the treatments, and u is a normally distributed mean zero error term. The parameter vector $\mathbf{B}$ contains estimates of the simple differences between treatment and control means on the outcome variable.

The model used to estimate treatment impacts while holding other factors constant is a straightforward generalization of Equation 4.1. The specification for computing adjusted treatment impacts involves adding terms for concomitant variables and is referred to as a covariance model. In the present case it takes the form

$$(4.2) \quad Y = a + \mathbf{T}B + ZC + u,$$

where the introduction of concomitant variables, Z, into the model reduces the experimental error caused by differences in the observable characteristics between the control and treatment groups.[5] When estimating this model, each concomitant variable is included as a deviation from its own mean, thereby allowing interpretation of the intercept as the mean value of the outcome variable Y for the control group given the mean observable characteristics of the whole sample.[6] By this approach, the vector $\mathbf{B}$ yields estimates of treatment impacts adjusted for differences across observations in the characteristics Z.

Investigation into the causes of the lack of homogeneity in the observable characteristics of the experimental and control groups in the Washington sample indicated that treatment impacts estimated without adjusting for the heterogeneity of the groups are likely to be biased. Variations in the WBA accounted for most of the important heterogeneity across the Washington groups. In particular, it was found that omission of WBA when estimating treatment effects on dollars of UI compensation in Washington is likely to yield biased impact estimates. Nonetheless, to avoid any possibility of omitted variable bias in estimating adjusted treatment impacts, a full set of concomitant or adjustment variables is included as covariates in estimation of treatment effects for Illinois, Pennsylvania, and Washington.[7]

The introduction of adjustment variables as covariates reduced the standard errors on parameter estimates, with a greater effect on dollars of UI compensation than the other outcomes (Table 4.2). The mean

Table 4.2 Adjusted Differences between Experimental and Control Group Means in the Illinois, Pennsylvania, and Washington Reemployment Bonus Experiments[a]

	Benefit weeks	UI compensation ($)	Exhaustion rate	Sample size[b]
ILLINOIS				
Control	20.0 (0.19)	2,763 (28)	0.468 (0.008)	3,952
Treatment	−1.04** (0.26)	−150** (40)	−0.026** (0.011)	4,186
Control—FSC-elig.	21.45 (0.30)	2,996 (45)	0.485 (0.011)	2,106
Treatment—FSC-elig.	−1.46** (0.41)	−228** (62)	−0.042** (0.015)	2,337
Control—FSC-inelig.	18.18 (0.24)	2,458 (37)	0.446 (0.012)	1,600
Treatment—FSC-inelig.	−0.65* (0.33)	−57 (51)	−0.009 (0.017)	1,589
PENNSYLVANIA				
Control	14.9 (0.18)	2,400 (31)	0.274 (0.008)	3,358
Low bonus/short qual.	−0.62* (0.34)	−99* (58)	0.001 (0.014)	1,388
Low bonus/long qual.	−0.35 (0.28)	−67 (48)	0.000 (0.012)	2,432
High bonus/short qual.	−0.44 (0.30)	−99* (52)	0.001 (0.013)	1,890
High bonus/long qual.	−0.82** (0.26)	−133** (45)	−0.014 (0.011)	3,038
Mean bonus/short qual.	−0.53** (0.26)	−99** (45)	0.000 (0.011)	3,278
Mean bonus/long qual.	−0.62** (0.23)	−104** (39)	−0.008 (0.010)	5,470
Low bonus/mean qual.	−0.43* (0.25)	−75** (43)	0.002 (0.010)	3,820
High bonus/mean qual.	−0.69** (0.24)	−123** (40)	−0.009 (0.010)	4,928
Mean bonus/mean qual.	−0.58** (0.21)	−102** (37)	−0.004 (0.009)	8,748

(continued)

	Benefit weeks	UI compensation ($)	Exhaustion rate	Sample size[b]
WASHINGTON				
Control	14.35	2,099	0.241	3,082
	(0.19)	(30)	(0.007)	
Low bonus/short qual.	−0.05	22	0.008	2,246
	(0.29)	(46)	(0.011)	
Med. bonus/short qual.	−0.23	−28	−0.005	2,348
	(0.29)	(45)	(0.011)	
High bonus/short qual.	−0.72**	−117**	−0.017	1,583
	(0.32)	(51)	(0.013)	
Low bonus/long qual.	−0.58**	−112**	−0.032**	2,387
	(0.29)	(45)	(0.011)	
Med. bonus/long qual.	−0.28	−44	−0.019*	2,353
	(0.29)	(45)	(0.011)	
High bonus/long qual.	−0.75**	−135**	−0.020	1,535
	(0.33)	(52)	(0.013)	
Low bonu/mean qual.	−0.33	−47	−0.013	4,633
	(0.24)	(39)	(0.010)	
Med. bonus/mean qual.	−0.25	−36	−0.012	4,701
	(0.24)	(38)	(0.009)	
High bonus/mean qual.	−0.74**	−126**	−0.018*	3,118
	(0.27)	(42)	(0.010)	
Mean bonus/short qual.	−0.29	−33	−0.003	6,177
	(0.23)	(37)	(0.009)	
Mean bonus/long qual.	−0.51**	−92**	−0.024**	6,275
	(0.23)	(36)	(0.009)	
Mean bonus/mean qual.	−0.40*	−63*	−0.014*	12,452
	(0.21)	(33)	(0.008)	

[a] Standard errors in parentheses.   * = Statistically significant at the 90% confidence level; ** = statistically significant at the 95% confidence level.

[b] The Illinois sample sizes for FSC-eligible and FSC-ineligible do not sum to the total Illinois sample size. This discrepancy is due to the FSC eligibility conditions, which differed depending on the date of the benefit claim, and our desire to use the largest possible sample size in the full sample analysis. Further details are given in Chapter 3.

regression-adjusted response across all treatments to a bonus offer was a reduction of $150 in Illinois, $102 in Pennsylvania, and $63 in Washington. The Illinois and Pennsylvania estimates are significant at the 95 percent confidence level, while the Washington estimate is significant at the 90 percent confidence level. The adjusted impact estimates are somewhat larger for Pennsylvania and Washington and somewhat smaller in Illinois than the unadjusted estimates, but in no case is the adjusted estimate significantly different from the unadjusted estimate.

Regression adjustment of impact estimates has the greatest effect on the high bonus/long qualification treatments in Pennsylvania (–$133) and Washington (–$135). Both estimates are statistically significant and larger than the unadjusted estimates, but they are not significantly different from the unadjusted estimates.[8]

Regression-adjusted estimates of the bonus impact on weeks of UI and benefit exhaustion were only modestly changed from the unadjusted estimates. The overall regression-adjusted mean estimates indicate that the bonus offer reduced UI benefit receipt by 1.04 weeks in Illinois, 0.58 weeks in Pennsylvania, and 0.40 weeks in Washington. The mean regression-adjusted estimate of the reduction in the probability of UI benefit exhaustion was 2.6 percent in Illinois, 0.4 percent in Pennsylvania, and 1.4 percent in Washington.

For Washington, where lack of homogeneity was most severe, regression adjustment allowed detection of statistically significant impacts on compensation and weeks for three of the individual treatments at the 95 percent level of confidence, whereas not a single treatment impact on dollars of compensation was estimated with significance before regression adjustment.

A CONTINUOUS VARIABLES MODEL OF
TREATMENT RESPONSE

In both Pennsylvania and Washington the bonus amount was defined in terms of the WBA. Since the WBA varies widely across claimants, the bonus amount may be used as a continuous variable when estimating bonus impacts. In Pennsylvania the qualification period was set at either 6 or 12 weeks, while in Washington it was defined as either 20 or 40 percent of the entitled duration of benefits plus 1 week. Therefore, the qualification period may also be used as a continuous variable. The variation in the bonus amount and qualification period in Pennsylvania and Washington is sufficient to allow estimation of the impact of incremental changes in the values of these parameters of a bonus offer. This section presents estimates from continuous variables models of bonus impacts for the separate Pennsylvania and Washington experiments and for these experiments combined with data from the Illinois experiment.

The continuous variables models represent a bonus offer as a given dollar amount paid for reemployment within a certain number of weeks. (These models are called continuous variables models because the treatments are represented by continuous variables rather than discrete indicator variables.) These models allow estimation of the effect of incremental changes in the bonus amount and the qualification period. The estimating equations have the following general linear specification:

$$(4.3) \quad Y = a + b_1 B + b_2 Q + ZC + u,$$

where, B is the bonus amount in dollars, Q is the qualification period length in weeks, and Z is a set of concomitant or adjustment variables centered around their mean.[9] The parameters to be estimated are a, b_1, b_2, and C. The random error term, u, is assumed to be normally distributed with mean zero. In Equation 4.3, B and Q take on the value of zero for members of the control group. Including the WBA as a control variable improves the within-treatment homogeneity of B and results in the parameter b_1 being estimated using variation in B across the treatments. The same effect is achieved in estimating the parameter on Q by including the entitled duration of benefits. Parameter estimates for Equation 4.3 are presented in Table 4.3 for five samples. The dependent variable for each regression model is weeks compensated in the benefit year.

In the models estimated separately on the Pennsylvania and the Washington samples, none of the parameter estimates on B nor Q are statistically significant. For the sample formed by pooling data from the two experiments, however, the standard errors on the estimated parameters on B and Q are smaller and the parameter on the bonus amount, B, is estimated with statistical significance. The pattern and magnitude of results is consistent across the Pennsylvania and Wash-

Table 4.3 Continuous Variables Models of Bonus Impacts (UI Weeks)[a]

Sample[b]	$100 Increase in bonus amt.	One-week increase in qual. period	Sample size
Pennsylvania	−0.035 (0.030)	−0.028 (0.026)	2,106
Washington	−0.044 (0.031)	−0.023 (0.024)	15,534
Pennsylvania and Washington (pooled)	−0.039* (0.021)	−0.026 (0.018)	27,640
Pennsylvania, Washington, and Illinois (pooled)	−0.031 (0.021)	−0.047** (0.016)	35,778
Pennsylvania, Washington, and Illinois FSC-inelig. (pooled)	−0.027 (0.021)	−0.034** (0.017)	30,829

[a] Standard errors are in parentheses. * = Statistically significant at the 90% confidence level in a two-tailed test; ** = statistically significant at the 95% confidence level in a two-tailed test.

[b] The Pennsylvania estimates were computed in a regression model which also included cohort indicators, office indicators, and demographic and economic variables. The Washington estimates were computed in a regression model which also included the WBA and the entitled duration of benefits. The pooled sample estimates were estimated in regressions which included cohort indicators, office indicators, indicators for Washington, Pennsylvania, and Illinois FSC where possible, and demographic and economic variables.

ington samples; a higher bonus amount and a longer qualification period both reduce the weeks of UI drawn in the benefit year by similar magnitudes.

Evidence from the pooled Pennsylvania and Washington sample suggests that a $100 increase in a bonus offer will reduce weeks of UI compensation in the benefit year by an average of 0.039 weeks, and a 1-week increase in the qualification period will reduce weeks of UI compensation in the benefit year by 0.026. These parameters, estimated on the combined data, have sampling errors about 50 percent smaller than parameters estimated on the separate samples. Using results of the pooled estimation, response to the bonus offer in Pennsylvania and Washington may be summarized by saying that with a 12-week qualification period, it would take a bonus of nearly $1,800 to induce an average 1-week decline in insured unemployment among those offered a bonus. To appreciate the meaning of this, recall that about 12.9 percent of those offered a bonus in Pennsylvania and Washington actually were paid a bonus (Table 3.1 in Chapter 3).[10] This means that, on average, it cost about $232 in bonus payments to save a week of UI benefit payments, which averaged about $159.[11]

For Illinois, because there is no variation in either the bonus amount or the qualification period, the separate influence of these parameters may not be estimated using a sample with data only from Illinois. Nonetheless, these effects may be inferred by combining the Illinois data with that from the other experiments. Adding the Illinois data to the combined Pennsylvania and Washington sample yields a total sample of nearly 36,000 UI beneficiaries. As seen in Table 4.3, combining the Illinois data with that from Pennsylvania and Washington results in an estimated increased effect of the qualification period and a reduced effect of the dollar bonus amount. In a formal statistical sense, however, the parameter estimates on the dollar bonus amount and the qualification period are not affected by adding the Illinois data to the Washington and Pennsylvania data.[12]

It was previously noted that the Illinois beneficiaries who were FSC-ineligible, and therefore had an initial benefit entitlement of 26 weeks, responded to the bonus offer in much the same way as beneficiaries in Pennsylvania and Washington. When the FSC-eligible group is excluded from the three-state sample, the results of estimating the continuous variables model indicate that the qualification period has a diminished impact on benefit duration. This impact is more in line with the combined Pennsylvania and Washington impact; however, even with the FSC-eligible group excluded, the impact of the dollar bonus amount for the three-state sample remains somewhat smaller than for the Pennsylvania and Washington sample. Even though there appears to be some underlying differences between Illinois and the other two experiments, the results of estimating the continuous variables model on the combined sample excluding the Illinois FSC-eligible group probably provides the best summary of bonus response across the three experiments.

In Table 4.4 we present estimates of the reduction in weeks of UI receipt for four hypothetical bonus offers based on parameter estimates for the sample formed by pooling data from Pennsylvania and Washington together with the FSC-ineligible sample from Illinois. The fol-

Table 4.4 The Predicted Impacts[a] of Four Hypothetical Bonus Offers on UI Receipt, Based on a Continuous Variables Model Estimated on the Pooled Pennsylvania, Washington, and Illinois Data[b]

Hypothetical bonus offer	Amount of the bonus offer ($)	Bonus qual. period (weeks)	Impact on weeks of UI benefits
1	500	6	-0.34*** (0.09)
2	1,000	6	-0.47*** (0.16)
3	500	12	-0.54*** (0.15)
4	1,000	12	-0.68*** (0.17)

[a] Predicted impacts are based on the regression-adjusted impact estimates presented in Table 4.3 for the pooled Pennsylvania, Washington, and Illinois FSC-ineligible sample, which included 30,829 observations.

[b] Standard errors of predicted impacts in parentheses. *** = Statistically significant at the 99% confidence level in a two-tailed test.

lowing four hypothetical bonus offers are examined: 1) $500 for reemployment within 6 weeks, 2) $1000 for reemployment within 6 weeks, 3) $500 for reemployment within 12 weeks, and 4) $1000 for reemployment within 12 weeks. For wage and benefit levels prevailing during the 1980s, these four hypothetical bonus offers span the range of policy-relevant bonus options reasonably approximated by use of a linear model.

As shown in Table 4.4, weeks of UI benefit receipt are predicted to decline for each of the separate hypothetical bonus offers. Furthermore, the impact on UI receipt of a hypothetical bonus offer increases as the bonus amount or the duration of the bonus increases. All of the impact estimates computed using this simulation methodology are significant at the 99 percent confidence level. The least generous hypothetical bonus offer—$500 with a six-week qualification period—would reduce UI receipt by one-third of a week. Since the continuous variables model involves a linear relationship between the bonus parameters and UI receipt, doubling the bonus amount and duration simply doubles the impact of the bonus offer on UI receipt. As shown

in Table 4.4, the offer with a $1,000 bonus amount and 12-week quali-
fication period has twice the impact of the offer with a $500 bonus
amount and 6-week qualification period. Hypothetical bonus offers 2
and 3, which combine a high dollar amount with a short qualification
period or a low dollar amount with a long qualification period, would
be likely to reduce UI receipt by a greater amount than the least generous offer but less than the most generous offer.

The offers reviewed in Table 4.4 are summarized graphically along
with all other possible dollar bonus amounts for the 6- and 12-week
qualification periods in Figure 4.2. The figure makes plain the linear
nature of the impact response surface estimated. It is also clear from
the diagram that, for any given dollar bonus amount, there will be a
greater response the longer the qualification period and, for any given
qualification period, there will be a greater response the higher the dollar bonus amount. The illustration does, however, mask the seemingly
different way that Illinois beneficiaries respond to the parameters of the
bonus in comparison with benefit recipients in Pennsylvania and Washington.[13]

THE TIMING OF TREATMENT IMPACTS

We now consider the impact of bonus offers on the time pattern of
ending receipt of UI benefits. To understand this pattern, we examine
the cumulative UI exit rate.[14] Since UI continued claim forms must be
filed every two weeks by claimants wishing to continue benefit receipt,
we analyze patterns over time measured in two-week intervals.

Estimates of cumulative UI exit rates through the end of any time
period, t, are computed by dividing the difference between the initial
risk pool of UI claimants and the remaining number of UI claimants at
the start of time period $t + 1$ by the initial risk pool of UI claimants.
The algebraic formula for the computation is simply:

$$(4.4) \quad c(t) = (R_0 - R_{t+1})/R_0$$

In this formula R_0 is the initial number of UI benefit recipients in
the separate treatment and control groups, and R_{t+1} is the number of UI

**Figure 4.2 Linearized Effect of the Bonus Offer on Benefit Year
            UI Weeks**

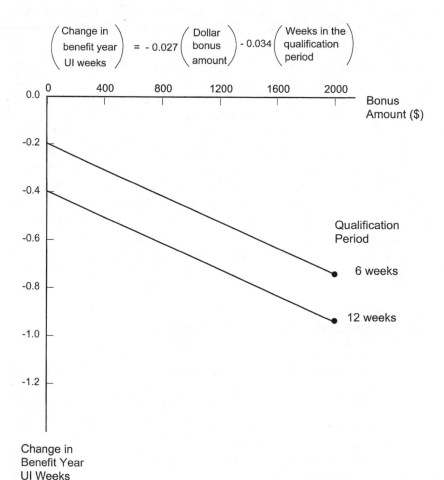

recipients in these groups at the start of time period $t + 1$. Throughout our discussion of the timing of treatment response, we focus on the first spell of UI benefit receipt that followed the initial claim for UI benefits. In none of the three experiments did as many as 5 percent of initial claimants have multiple spells of UI benefit receipt during their benefit year.

Cumulative exit rates for treatment and control groups for each of the three experiments are reported in Table 4.5 observed at two-week intervals for unemployment spells between 1 and 39 weeks in duration. This number of periods is considered because the longest entitled duration of benefits among the experiments was 38 weeks for FSC-eligible claimants in Illinois.

To clearly understand the ideas involved consider an example from Table 4.5. The cumulative UI exit rate through the fifth week in the benefit year for control subjects in Pennsylvania was 0.403. This means that out of 8,834 initial UI recipients, 40.3 percent of the control group had stopped drawing UI benefits by the start of the sixth week of their claim. The comparable percentage among those offered a bonus in Pennsylvania was 42.4. The difference in these cumulative UI exit rates was found to be statistically significant.

There is a common pattern in the cumulative UI exit rates across the three experiments. Cumulative exit rates are higher among the treatment groups, at least through the first several weeks of UI receipt. However, the general level of UI exit rates is considerably lower in Illinois than in either Pennsylvania or Washington and tends to be slightly lower in Pennsylvania than in Washington.[15] Four factors might account for these differences: 1) differences in the labor market structures of the three states (that is, differences in the mix of industries and occupations), 2) differences in demand for labor among the three states, 3) differences among the three states in the administration of UI, and 4) differences among the three states in the characteristics of workers who are eligible for UI.

An effective bonus offer would lead claimants in treatment groups to have higher UI exit rates than controls during the period over which the bonus could be earned. Comparison of exit rates for the control and treatment groups in Illinois clearly shows that exit rates were higher during the bonus qualification period for UI claimants who were offered the bonus.

Table 4.5 Cumulative Hazard Rates for Leaving Unemployment Insurance

Illinois	Control	Treatment	FSC-eligible control	FSC-eligible treatment
Initial risk set	3,952	4,186	2,106	2,337
Spell length (weeks)				
0–1	0.127	0.150**	0.138	0.154
2–3	0.197	0.230**	0.215	0.249**
4–5	0.252	0.287**	0.271	0.307**
6–7	0.298	0.343**	0.322	0.370**
8–9	0.339	0.389**	0.364	0.417**
10–11	0.372	0.427**	0.396	0.458**
12–13	0.406	0.460**	0.422	0.484**
14–15	0.432	0.488**	0.443	0.509**
16–17	0.457	0.513**	0.466	0.531**
18–19	0.483	0.537**	0.487	0.548**
20–21	0.515	0.559**	0.508	0.569**
22–23	0.541	0.584**	0.528	0.590**
24–25	0.578	0.616**	0.556	0.615**
26–27	0.816	0.833**	0.661	0.709**
28–29	0.825	0.843**	0.674	0.724**
30–31	0.835	0.853**	0.690	0.740**
32–33	0.841	0.859**	0.702	0.749**
34–35	0.851	0.869**	0.720	0.767**
36–37	0.863	0.877*	0.744	0.780**
38–39	0.998	0.997	0.996	0.995

Pennsylvania	Control	Mean treatment	High bonus/ long qual.
Initial risk set	3,392	8,834	3,073
Spell length (weeks)			
0–1	0.258	0.271	0.273
2–3	0.343	0.355	0.357
4–5	0.403	0.424**	0.428**
6–7	0.456	0.486**	0.487**
8–9	0.515	0.538**	0.542**
10–11	0.564	0.587**	0.591**
12–13	0.608	0.635**	0.649**
14–15	0.647	0.671**	0.681**
16–17	0.681	0.701**	0.713**
18–19	0.708	0.726*	0.740**
20–21	0.734	0.750*	0.763**
22–23	0.759	0.773*	0.786**
24–25	0.787	0.797	0.810**
26–27	0.986	0.989*	0.991*
28–29	0.993	0.993	0.993
30–31	0.994	0.994	0.994
32–33	0.995	0.995	0.995
34–35	0.995	0.996	0.996
36–37	0.996	0.996	0.997
38–39	0.997	0.996	0.997

(continued)

Table 4.5 (continued)

Washington	Control	Mean treatment	High bonus/ long qual.
Initial risk set	2,702	11,052	1,358
Spell length (weeks)			
0–1	0.206	0.196	0.221
2–3	0.333	0.337	0.364*
4–5	0.431	0.437	0.464**
6–7	0.506	0.508	0.526
8–9	0.564	0.563	0.588
10–11	0.611	0.613	0.653**
12–13	0.644	0.650	0.684**
14–15	0.679	0.681	0.720**
16–17	0.715	0.720	0.758**
18–19	0.748	0.756	0.781**
20–21	0.784	0.792	0.816**
22–23	0.813	0.821	0.838*
24–25	0.838	0.850	0.862**
26–27	0.862	0.873	0.888**
28–29	0.885	0.899**	0.909**
30–31	0.982	0.982	0.980
32–33	0.989	0.989	0.987
34–35	0.993	0.991	0.992
36–37	0.994	0.993	0.993
38–39	0.995	0.994	0.994

[a] * = Cumulative hazard rate significantly different from control group in a two-tailed test at the 90% confidence level; ** = cumulative hazard rate significantly different from control group in a two-tailed test at the 95% confidence level.

For the Pennsylvania experiment, the cumulative UI exit rate for the treatment groups taken as a whole was higher than for the control group through most of the bonus qualification period. Compared with Illinois, cumulative impacts appeared to be smaller, but were nevertheless big enough to produce a 0.62-week reduction in insured unemployment (as reported in Table 4.1). The cumulative impacts for the high bonus/long qualification treatment in Pennsylvania were modestly larger over the first 14 weeks following the start of UI benefits (Table 4.5, Pennsylvania, high bonus/long qualification).

In the Washington experiment, there is scant statistical evidence that bonus-offered workers gave up their UI benefits at a faster pace than did the control group. When all treatments are taken together, UI exit rates were higher for bonus-offered workers than for controls only by the week 28–29 period. This is consistent with the small (and statistically insignificant) 0.3-week reduction in insured unemployment that can be seen in Table 4.1 for the mean bonus offer. Isolating the most effective treatment in Washington, the high-bonus/long-qualification treatment (Table 4.5) there is some evidence that UI exit rates of the bonus-offered workers were higher than the exit rates of the control group. These results are consistent with the somewhat larger reduction in insured unemployment for this group (0.73 week) that can be seen in Table 4.1.

The basic conclusion to be drawn from the analysis of cumulative exit rates is that the Illinois and Pennsylvania bonus offers taken as a whole both acted to increase UI exit rates during their respective bonus qualification periods. There is also some evidence that the high bonus offers in the Washington experiment increased UI exit rates. These time patterns of cumulative exit rates for treatment and control subjects are presented graphically in Figure 4.3. Treatment impacts on cumulative exit rates are presented graphically in Figure 4.4, where the estimated impact is equal to the difference between the cumulative exit rate for the treatment group and the cumulative exit rate for the control group.

Cumulative UI exit rates are also useful for examining the extent to which the workers who took advantage of bonus offers were individuals who otherwise would have exhausted their benefits. For potential benefit exhausters, each bonus offer accepted would generate a large reduction in observed unemployment. In Illinois, for example, the reduction would be from 27 weeks of insured unemployment to at most 11 weeks. On the other hand, for workers who would have otherwise had relatively short durations of UI benefit receipt, each bonus offer accepted might generate only a relatively small reduction in observed unemployment.

After 11 weeks, 37.2 percent of the claimants in the Illinois control group had stopped receiving UI benefits, whereas 42.7 percent of the Illinois treatment group had stopped receiving benefits (Table 4.5). In other words, at the end of the bonus qualification period, an additional 5.5 percentage points (42.7 − 37.2) of the bonus-offered workers had ended their UI receipt as compared with the controls. Moreover, this 5.5 percentage point difference diminishes only slightly after the end of the bonus qualification period. Even immediately before exhaustion of regular UI benefits (weeks 24–25), the difference is nearly 4 percentage points. In other words, the control group fails to catch up with the treatment group in terms of exit from UI. This failure of the control and treatment cumulative exit rates to converge suggests that a large proportion of the workers who responded to the Illinois bonus offer would have had long spells of insured unemployment in the absence of the bonus offer. These results are consistent with estimates in Table 4.1, which show that the Illinois bonus reduced the UI benefit exhaustion rate by over 3 percentage points overall (and by over 5 percentage points among FSC-eligibles). Figures 4.3 and 4.4 illustrate that cumulative UI exit rates for treatment subjects remain above controls at 26 weeks and at 38 weeks for the FSC-eligible group. We conclude that the Illinois bonus reduced the duration of UI spells among workers who tended to have relatively long expected durations of UI receipt.

The evidence from Pennsylvania exhibits a different pattern. The difference between the control and combined treatment cumulative exit rates peaks at between 2 and 3 percentage points during weeks 6–7 and 12–13 (Table 4.5 and Figures 4.3 and 4.4). These peaks in cumulative UI exit coincided with the end of the short (6-week) and the long (12-week) bonus qualification periods. For the high bonus/long qualification treatment alone, the difference is larger, peaking at about 4 percentage points in weeks 12–13. Unlike for Illinois, however, the control and treatment cumulative exit rates do converge near the end of the qualification period. In terms of leaving UI, the control group caught up with the combined treatment groups by weeks 24–25 (the

Figure 4.3 Cumulative UI Exit Rates by Treatment and Control Groups

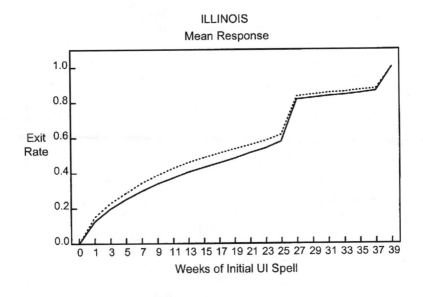

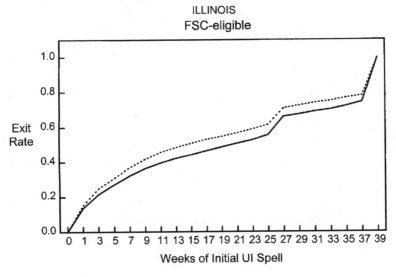

Figure 4.3 (cont.)

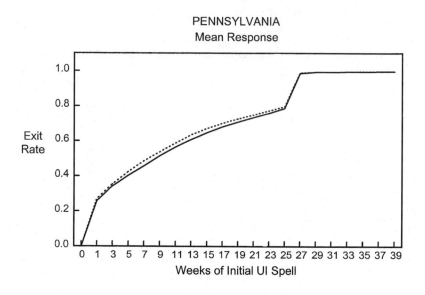

PENNSYLVANIA
Mean Response

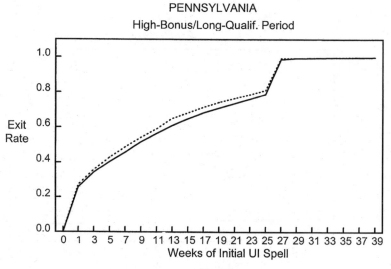

PENNSYLVANIA
High-Bonus/Long-Qualif. Period

Figure 4.3 (cont.)

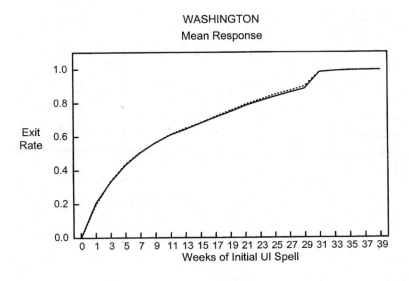

WASHINGTON
Mean Response

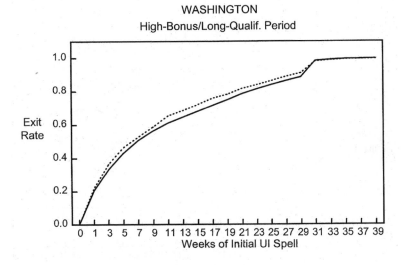

WASHINGTON
High-Bonus/Long-Qualif. Period

Figure 4.4 Simple Treatment Impacts on Cumulative UI Exit Rates

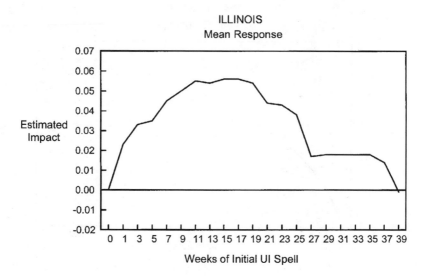

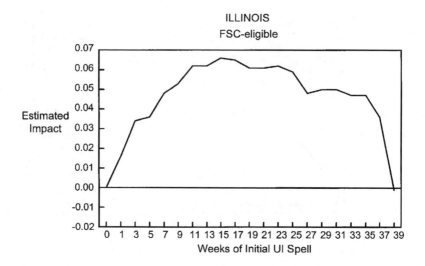

Figure 4.4 (cont.)

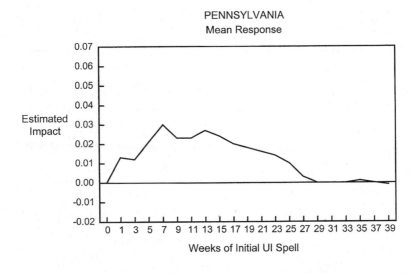

PENNSYLVANIA
Mean Response

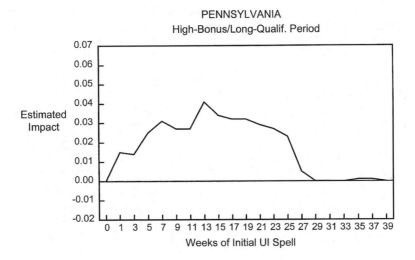

PENNSYLVANIA
High-Bonus/Long-Qualif. Period

Figure 4.4 (cont.)

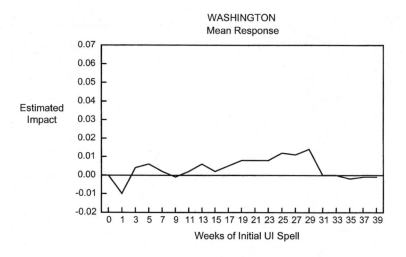

WASHINGTON
Mean Response

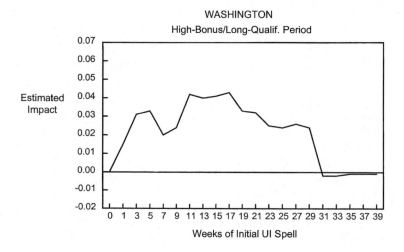

WASHINGTON
High-Bonus/Long-Qualif. Period

time period before exhaustion), but not until weeks 28–29 (just after benefit exhaustion) for the high-bonus/long-qualification treatment in Pennsylvania.

The decaying impact of the Pennsylvania treatments on the cumulative UI exit rate shows that much of the bonus-induced reduction in UI receipt occurred because the bonus effect was concentrated among claimants who would have had relatively short spells of UI receipt. The exception is the high bonus/long qualification treatment in Pennsylvania, which reduced the probability of a worker exhausting UI benefits by 2.6 percent as reported in Table 4.1. The point can also be seen in Table 4.5, which shows that in weeks 24–25 there is still a 2.3 percentage point difference between the cumulative exit rates of the control group and the high bonus/long qualification treatment group. Overall, though, the Pennsylvania treatments appear to have affected the behavior mainly of workers with relatively low expected durations of UI receipt.

The cumulative UI exit rate results for Washington show a weaker, but similar, pattern to that seen in Pennsylvania. For all treatments combined, the bonus initially creates an insignificant difference between the cumulative UI exit rates of the control and the experimental groups which diminishes before weeks 28–29 (the period before exhaustion). The exception is the high bonus/long qualification treatment, for which the cumulative UI exit rate remains 2.4 percentage points greater than controls in weeks 28–29 (Table 4.5). This is consistent with the significant 2.3 percentage point reduction in UI exhaustion reported in Table 4.1 for those with the high bonus/long qualification offer. The evidence indicates that the average Washington bonus offer reduced the UI receipt of workers who would have experienced relatively short spells of UI receipt in any event. The exception presented for Washington is the high bonus/long qualification offer, which reduced benefit exhaustion.

IMPACTS OF THE BONUS OFFER ON
POPULATION SUBGROUPS

There are two main reasons for examining treatment impacts by population subgroup. One is to provide information to policymakers who may consider targeting a reemployment bonus program to certain groups, such as dislocated workers or older UI claimants. Another is to identify possible biases in the effects—a program that benefits only one gender or certain ethnic groups may not be considered good policy even if it is cost-effective.

This section reports on treatment impacts for 12 subgroups defined by binary variables for six characteristics: gender, age, race, industry, area unemployment, and the WBA level. The dummy variables specified for the analysis were a variable indicating whether a claimant was female; an age variable indicating whether the claimant was 35 years old or over; a race variable indicating whether a claimant was black; an industry variable indicating whether the claimant's previous job was in manufacturing; an unemployment variable indicating whether the local unemployment rate was below 5 percent; and a variable indicating whether the claimant qualified for the maximum WBA.

It is standard practice to examine program impacts by gender, age, and race. We investigated differential treatment impacts by industry, area unemployment, and WBA for various reasons. Because manufacturing is a shrinking sector, workers leaving manufacturing are more likely than others to be displaced workers. Accordingly, examining impacts for manufacturing workers separately from others may shed light on the value of the reemployment bonus as a way of aiding displaced workers. Because the reemployment bonus could be implemented either as an ongoing or as a countercyclical program, it was important to examine whether the bonus had an impact only when reemployment prospects were good. Finally, existing evidence suggests that the disincentive effects of UI are greatest for workers whose prior earnings were relatively low; these claimants who typically have WBAs below the state maximum receive benefits which tend to replace a larger share of lost earnings. Accordingly, it seemed important to examine whether workers below the maximum WBA had greater treatment impacts than other workers. If so, then the reemployment bonus might be an effective way of mitigating the disincentive effects of the UI system for workers who are most adversely affected.

We estimate all subgroup treatment impacts in a single regression model. This means that the treatment response for each subgroup is estimated controlling for the influence of all other subgroup characteristics. For example, the model estimates the treatment impacts associated with being black controlling for the fact that blacks are less likely to be at the maximum WBA, less likely to claim benefits in areas with unemployment rates below five percent, and so on. If we did not proceed in this way, any differential impact associated with being black might be a result not of being black but rather of other characteristics that blacks possess.

The equation estimated for each outcome of interest is a straightforward generalization of Equation 4.2:

$$(4.5) \quad Y = a + \mathbf{TB} + \mathbf{ZC} + \mathbf{GD} + \mathbf{GTE'} + \mathbf{GZF'} + \mathbf{ZTH'} + u$$

where Y is the outcome measure (either weeks of insured unemployment, dollars of UI compensation, or the UI benefit exhaustion rate); $\mathbf{T}$ is the matrix of treatment dummies; $\mathbf{Z}$ is a matrix of concomitant variables in deviation form; $\mathbf{G}$ is the matrix of dummy variables which code for membership in a subgroup; a is the intercept; $\mathbf{B}, \mathbf{C}, \mathbf{D}, \mathbf{E}, \mathbf{F}$, and $\mathbf{H}$ are conformable parameter vectors, and u is a normally distributed random error term with mean of zero. Note that Equation 4.5 is written to include concomitant variables, $\mathbf{Z}$, that may have been correlated with assignment to treatment and control groups. In the models estimated for all three experiments, the concomitant variables, $\mathbf{Z}$, were entered linearly and interacted with all subgroup dummies.[16]

Equation 4.5 specifies a complete one-way interaction model—that is, all first-order products of subgroup dummy variables, treatment indicators, and concomitant variables with each other are included. This model allows simultaneous estimation of all subgroup treatment impacts, but imposes linear restrictions on those estimates.[17]

Table 4.6 displays the estimated bonus impacts on weeks of insured unemployment, dollars of UI benefits received, and the UI exhaustion rate for each of the 12 subgroups. Inspection of these results reveals one main finding: there is virtually no difference between any pair of subgroups shown that is both statistically signifi-

Table 4.6 Impacts of the Treatments on UI Receipt by Subgroup[a]

Subgroup	Illinois				Pennsylvania				Washington			
	Benefit weeks	$ of UI compensation	Exhaust. rate	Sample size	Benefit weeks	$ of UI compensation	Exhaust. rate	Sample size	Benefit weeks	$ of UI compensation	Exhaust. rate	Sample size
Males	-0.94** (0.36)	-135** (55)	-0.029* (0.015)	4,519	-0.40 (0.29)	-90* (49)	0.001 (0.012)	7,237	-0.69** (0.28)	-98** (47)	-0.012 (0.011)	9,471
Females	-1.37** (0.40)	-207** (61)	-0.029* (0.017)	3,619	-0.91** (0.36)	-123** (61)	-0.015 (0.015)	4,845	0.06 (0.35)	4 (51)	-0.018 (0.014)	6,063
Aged <35 yr.	-1.18** (0.34)	-177** (51)	-0.031** (0.014)	5,045	-0.87** (0.30)	-136** (51)	-0.010 (0.012)	6,682	-0.29 (0.30)	-30 (47)	-0.012 (0.012)	8,169
Age 35 yr. and over	-1.04** (0.44)	-151** (66)	-0.026 (0.018)	3,093	-0.29 (0.32)	-63 (55)	0.000 (0.014)	5,544	-0.52* (0.31)	-82* (49)	-0.017 (0.012)	7,365
Black	-0.89* (0.53)	-197** (80)	-0.017 (0.022)	2,122	-1.37** (0.63)	-202* (108)	-0.015 (0.026)	1,412	-0.48 (1.01)	45 (160)	-0.011 (0.040)	695
Non-black	-1.21** (0.31)	-156** (47)	-0.033** (0.013)	6,016	-0.50** (0.23)	-90** (39)	-0.004 (0.009)	10,670	-0.39* (0.21)	-59* (34)	-0.015* (0.008)	14,839
Manufacturing	-0.74 (0.53)	-134* (81)	-0.015 (0.022)	2,084	-1.81**## (0.43)	-257**# (74)	-0.027 (0.018)	3,111	-0.71 (0.45)	-104 (71)	0.000 (0.016)	3,505
Nonmanu-facturing	-1.26** (0.31)	-178** (47)	-0.034** (0.013)	6,054	-0.19 (0.25)	-50 (43)	0.002 (0.010)	8,971	-0.31 (0.24)	-40 (38)	-0.019** (0.009)	12,029
Low unemploy-ment	-1.33** (0.63)	-209** (96)	-0.040 (0.026)	1,459	-1.05**# (0.33)	-167** (56)	-0.015 (0.014)	5,332	-1.04** (0.37)	-203**## (58)	-0.048**## (0.015)	5,328
Not low unemploy-ment	-1.08** (0.29)	-158** (44)	-0.027** (0.012)	6,679	-0.25 (0.29)	-52 (50)	0.002 (0.012)	6,750	-0.06 (0.26)	23 (41)	0.003 (0.010)	10,206

Maximum WBA	-1.34** (0.65)	-236** (99)	-0.032 (0.027)	2,780	-1.03 (0.70)	-195 (120)	-0.010 (0.029)	2,377	0.99* (0.53)	155* (83)	0.001 (0.021)	5,252
Not maximum WBA	-1.02** (0.40)	-132** (62)	-0.027* (0.017)	5,358	-0.50* (0.27)	-81* (46)	-0.004 (0.011)	9,849	1.11** (0.33)	-161***## (51)	-0.022* (0.013)	10,282

[a] Standard errors in parentheses. * = Statistically significant at the 90% confidence level for a two-tailed test; ** = statistically significant at the 95% confidence level for a two-tailed test; # = statistically different from the complementary subgroup at the 90% confidence level for a two-tailed test; ## = statistically different from the complementary subgroup at the 95 percent confidence level for a two-tailed test.

cant at conventional confidence levels and consistent across the three experiments. The implication of this finding is quite striking. The reemployment bonus has a remarkably even impact on various subgroups of workers, whether delineated by gender, age, race, sector of employment, local unemployment rate, or maximum WBA eligibility.

The evidence suggests some differences that may be worth noting, however. For example, the evidence from Illinois and Pennsylvania (but not from Washington) suggests that women may be slightly more responsive than men to the reemployment bonus. This is consistent with research on female labor supply, which has found higher labor supply elasticities for women than for men, meaning that women's attachment to the labor force is more flexible than men's.

Results from Illinois and Pennsylvania (but again not from Washington) also suggest that younger workers may be somewhat more responsive than older workers to the reemployment bonus. An explanation for younger workers' relatively larger response is similar to that given for women—younger workers' labor force attachment is more flexible than older workers'.

There is no evidence to suggest that the reemployment bonus had a different impact on African Americans compared to other racial or ethnic subgroups. Impact estimation for each experiment was also done using a further disaggregation by race and ethnicity. The results suggested that the response of blacks differed from the overall mean response to a bonus offer by more than any other racial or ethnic subgroup. Yet, there were no significant differences between any of the more finely defined groups. In short, the impact of the reemployment bonuses did not vary by race or ethnicity.

In Pennsylvania and Washington, claimants whose previous jobs were in manufacturing had a stronger response to the bonus offer than workers whose previous job was not in manufacturing, with the difference in impact across groups being statistically significant in Pennsylvania. It may be the case that claimants who had lost a job in manufacturing tended to wait longer for recall, so that the bonus has more possibility to alter search behavior. However, this result is not obtained in Illinois, where the impact was even slightly greater for workers whose previous jobs were outside of manufacturing. Overall, there is no clear evidence for differential impacts across these subgroups.

The results from both the Pennsylvania and Washington experiments (although not from Illinois) suggest that UI claimants in low unemployment areas tended to respond more strongly to the bonus than did claimants in high unemployment areas. We have defined *low unemployment* as a 5 percent rate of total unemployment or lower, since this is at or below the rate previously considered to be associated with nonaccelerating inflation.[18]

That the bonus response appears to be greater in areas of low unemployment suggests that the bonus offer is more effective when increased search effort is more likely to generate additional job offers. This is an issue of labor demand and appeals to the notion that, in a labor market in which job prospects are neither good nor improving, the bonus impact can be expected to be low. That the bonus was effective in Illinois, where the unemployment rate was relatively high on average, may be a result of the improving labor market in northern Illinois during the experiment. We return to this issue in Chapter 6, which addresses the problems of interpreting the implications of experimental results for policy implementation.

It was expected that because the earnings replacement rate is relatively higher for those below the WBA maximum, the initial intensity of job search would be correspondingly low, and the reemployment bonus would have a greater impact. There is no evidence from the three experiments that claimants below the maximum WBA responded more strongly to the bonus than did claimants at the maximum WBA. In fact, in the Pennsylvania experiment (where the greatest difference in impact between the two groups occurred), those at the maximum WBA reduced weeks of insured UI by twice as much as those below the maximum.

SUMMARY

Field experiments were conducted in Illinois, Pennsylvania, and Washington in the 1980s to test the theory that the average duration of insured unemployment could be shortened if cash reemployment bonuses were offered to unemployment insurance beneficiaries. Claimants who were randomly assigned to treatment were told they would be given a lump sum cash payment if they started a new job by a certain date and stayed working full time for at least four months. In each of the three experiments, a randomly selected control group was compared with the various treatment groups.

While the first experiment, conducted in Illinois, yielded very encouraging results, the subsequent field tests provided less support for the bonus idea. The relatively weak response to the bonus offer in Pennsylvania and Washington led to a reexamination of the powerful Illinois results. It was discovered that within the designed experiment, a second experiment had unintentionally taken place. In 1984 as Illinois was recovering from a major recession, the availability of Federal Supplemental Compensation was terminated. This resulted in about half of the claimants studied having 38 weeks of UI benefit eligibility, with the remainder being eligible for only 26 weeks of regular UI benefits. It turns out that the mean bonus response of −1.15 weeks in Illinois was made up of a response of −1.78 weeks for those FSC-eligible and −0.54 weeks for those FSC-ineligible. The average response of −0.54 for the FSC-ineligible sample in Illinois is close to the response observed in Pennsylvania and Washington where the entitled duration of benefits was also similar.

Among the individual treatments, the impact on weeks of UI benefits ranged from −0.05 for the low bonus/short qualification offer in Washington to −1.78 for the bonus offer to FSC-eligible claimants in Illinois. Impacts for Pennsylvania tended to fall between those for Illinois and Washington. Overall a cash bonus can be expected to modestly shorten spells of insured unemployment—the mean effect of the offers made in the three states yielded about a one-half week reduction in weeks of UI benefits.

Evidence from a sample created by pooling data from Illinois, Pennsylvania, and Washington indicated that either lengthening the duration of the search period or increasing the bonus amount would lead to a greater reduction in weeks of UI benefits collected. Simulations based on data pooled from the three experiments suggest that offering a reemployment bonus with a $1,000 dollar amount, a 12-week qualification period, and a four-month reemployment period would result in an average reduction of 0.66 weeks of UI benefits.

The degree of response to the bonus offer was also examined for important subgroups within the sample. Results from Pennsylvania and Washington suggest that UI claimants in low unemployment areas and claimants whose prior employment was in manufacturing tended to respond more strongly to the bonus. However, close inspection of subgroup results reveals one main finding: there is no difference between any pair of subgroups shown that is both statistically significant at conventional confidence levels and consistent across the three experiments. The implication of this finding is quite striking—the reemployment bonus has a remarkably even impact on various subgroups of workers, whether delineated by gender, age, race, industrial sector of employment, level of local unemployment, or level of the weekly benefit amount.

Notes

1. Decker and O'Leary (1992) used the continuous variables model to analyze pooled Pennsylvania and Washington data. A summary article on the pooled analysis is Decker and O'Leary (1995).
2. One week was added in the computation of the qualification period in Washington to adjust for the presence of a waiting week. The *waiting week* is the first week after filing for benefits that a claimant would otherwise be eligible for compensation. It does not reduce total entitlement but does postpone payment, thereby discouraging casual entry into the system. The Washington experiment added a week to the qualification period because the treatments were intended to have qualification periods which were 20 and 40 percent of the compensable period.
3. The New Jersey UI reemployment experiment tested a declining bonus. A similar treatment was tried as part of the Pennsylvania experiment, but it is not reported in Tables 4.1 and 4.2 because it is not comparable to other treatments in Illinois, Pennsylvania, and Washington. The impact of the Pennsylvania declining bonus offer, which started at $6 \times$ WBA and declined by 10 percent of the original amount per week, had insignificant point estimate of a 0.2 weeks reduction in UI benefits.
4. See Chapter 6, p. 199, for an explanation of why the FSC-eligible and FSC-ineligible responses differ.
5. Netter and Wasserman (1974, Chapter 22) give a concise discussion of covariance analysis.
6. The effect of centering around the mean is that the intercept takes the value of the outcome measure for a hypothetical person in the sample who was not exposed to the experimental treatment and whose exogenous characteristics are at the mean value for each of the characteristics across the total sample (control and experimental groups combined). Therefore, the control group means reported in Table 4.2 are slightly different from the unadjusted values given in Table 4.1. Control group means may also differ because sample sizes differ due to missing data on

concomitant variables for some observations. The treatment effect is the impact of the treatment on the outcome measure for that hypothetical individual.

7. The appendix table (Table A4.1) presents complete regression results for each experiment from a model of weeks of UI benefits with a single treatment indicator and all concomitant variables. The full final project reports are Corson et al. (1992) for Pennsylvania, Spiegelman, O'Leary, and Kline (1992) for Washington, and Spiegelman and Woodbury (1987) for Illinois.

8. Because of the upper limit on dollars and weeks of UI compensation, a type of censoring is at work. Tobit models which explicitly accounted for censoring were therefore estimated. Tobit models yielded virtually the same results as the ordinary least squares models and are therefore not reported. Since the outcome in the exhaustion equation is a zero/one binary variable, a probit model for exhaustion was estimated. Again the results were extremely close to those computed by ordinary least squares.

9. The concomitant variables included when computing the estimates reported in Table 4.3 were gender, age, race, previous industry, the WBA, entitled maximum duration of benefits, base period earnings, work-search exempt status, enrollment site, and (for Pennsylvania) the quarter of enrollment into the experiment.

10. In Pennsylvania, 10.6 percent of 8,864 bonus offers were paid; in Washington, 14.6 percent of 12,452 offers were paid.

11. The mean WBA for the treatment-assigned beneficiaries was $166 in Pennsylvania and $154 in Washington.

12. While the design of the Illinois experiment prevents formal testing of differences in the parameters across all three samples, the "two-sigma rule" suggests the response is unchanged by adding the Illinois data since the parameter estimates are within twice the standard error of those estimated on the combined Pennsylvania and Washington data alone. Formal analysis of variance tests were performed by separately removing Pennsylvania and Washington from the full sample of data combined from the three experiments, and the parameter estimates were not found to be statistically different in either case. These tests also provide some justification for the exercise of estimating a bonus response surface on pooled data.

13. Estimation of a quadratic response surface for the pooled sample suggested that, for low dollar bonus amounts or very long qualification periods, the bonus could lead to increased UI benefit durations. The quadratic model included the dollar bonus amount, weeks in the qualification period, the bonus amount squared, the qualification period squared, and the bonus amount multiplied by the qualification period along with the concomitant variables included in the linear continuous variables model. Results from the quadratic model suggest that Figure 4.2 is an appropriate representation of response when the bonus amount is in the range $700 to $1,700 and the qualification period is between 5 and 12 weeks. The quadratic model suggests the minimum response occurs for a bonus amount of $700 with a 9.7-week qualification period.

14. More formally, the cumulative exit rate is computed by what Kiefer (1988) referred to as an integrated hazard function. In the present application, the hazard

function yields conditional UI exit rates which are not examined here since they are subject to selection bias resulting from response to the bonus offer by treatment group members. The cumulative hazard is not subject to such bias since the base for computation, the initial risk pool, does not change between periods.

15. The UI exit rates for the Illinois controls are roughly 50 to 70 percent of the UI exit rates in Pennsylvania and roughly 40 to 60 percent of the UI exit rates in Washington.

16. The concomitant variables, Z, included when performing subgroup impact estimation were WBA, entitled duration of benefits, base period earnings, work-search exemption status, an industry missing indicator, and five indicator variables for the quarter of enrollment in Pennsylvania.

17. Treatment impacts for a particular subgroup were computed as the sum of the parameter estimated on the product of the subgroup dummy variable and the treatment indicator added to the sum of estimates of parameters on subgroup dummies interacted with treatment indicators multiplied by their respective population shares (i.e., the proportion of the population having that characteristic). In each computation, parameter estimates for the complement to the subgroup of interest were omitted. For example, expressing population shares as the expected value of the subgroup dummy variables, $\mathcal{E}(G)$, the subgroup impacts would be computed as $\text{ß} + \mathcal{E}(G)\hat{E}$, where ß and $\hat{E}$ are the least squares estimates of $\boldsymbol{B}$ and $\boldsymbol{E}$ from Equation 4.5.

18. Rosen and Quandt (1988, p. 54) estimated the nonaccelerating inflation rate of unemployment (NAIRU) as 5.6 percent over the period 1932 to 1983, using a disequilibrium model of the aggregate labor market and setting the inflation rate at 5 percent.

References

Corson, Walter, Paul Decker, Shari Dunstan, and Stuart Kerachsky. 1992. *Pennsylvania Reemployment Bonus Demonstration: Final Report.* Unemployment Insurance Occasional Paper 92-1, Washington, D.C.: U.S. Department of Labor, Employment and Training Administration.

Davidson, Carl, and Stephen A. Woodbury. 1991. "Effects of a Reemployment Bonus under Differing Benefit Entitlements, or, Why the Illinois Experiment Worked." Unpublished manuscript. Kalamazoo, Michigan: W.E. Upjohn Institute for Employment Research.

Decker, Paul T., and Christopher J. O'Leary. 1992. *An Analysis of Pooled Evidence from the Pennsylvania and Washington Reemployment Bonus Demonstrations.* Unemployment Insurance Occasional Paper 92-7, Washington, D.C.: U.S. Department of Labor, Employment and Training Administration.

_____. 1995. "Evaluating Pooled Evidence from the Reemployment Bonus Experiments." *Journal of Human Resources* 30(3): 534–550.

Kiefer, Nicholas M. 1988. "Economic Duration Data and Hazard Functions." *Journal of Economic Literature* 26(2): 646–679.

Netter, John, and William Wasserman. 1974. *Applied Linear Statistical Models.* Homewood, Illinois: Richard D. Irwin.

O'Leary, Christopher J., Robert G. Spiegelman, and Kenneth J. Kline. 1995. "Do Bonus Offers Shorten Unemployment Insurance Spells? Results from the Washington Experiment." *Journal of Policy Analysis and Management* 14(2): 245–269.

Rosen, Harvey S., and Richard E. Quandt. 1988. *The Conflict between Equilibrium and Disequilibrium Theories: The Case of the U.S. Labor Market.* Kalamazoo, Michigan: W.E. Upjohn Institute for Employment Research.

Spiegelman, Robert G., Christopher J. O'Leary, and Kenneth J. Kline. 1992. *The Washington Reemployment Bonus Experiment: Final Report.* Unemployment Insurance Occasional Paper 92-6, Washington, D.C.: U.S. Department of Labor, Employment and Training Administration.

Woodbury, Stephen A., and Robert G. Spiegelman. 1987. "Bonuses to Workers and Employers to Reduce Unemployment: Randomized Trials in Illinois." *The American Economic Review* 77(September): 513–530.

Appendix

Definitions of variables in Appendix Table A4.1. Site indicators differ acrossthe experiments (see site definitions below).

Intercept	constant term
Treatment	dummy variable 1 if treatment assigned, else zero
WBA	weekly benefit amount
Female	dummy variable 1 if female, else zero
AGELT35	dummy variable 1 if less than 35 years, else zero
AGEGT54	dummy variable 1 if greater than 54 years, else zero
Black	dummy variable 1 if Black, else zero
Hispanic	dummy variable 1 if Hispanic, else zero
Other non-White	dummy variable 1 if not White, Black or Hispanic, else zero
Entitled duration	Illinois, dummy 1 if 26 weeks; Pennsylvania, dummy one if 15 weeks; Washington number of weeks of UI entitlement
BPE	base period earnings
Manufacturing	dummy variable 1 if prior job in manufacturing, else zero
SIC missing	dummy variable 1 if SIC code missing, else zero
Search exempt	dummy variable 1 if search exempt, else zero

Site 1 - Illinois, Springfield South; Pennsylvania, Coatesville; Washington, Auburn
Site 2 - Illinois, Springfield North; Pennsylvania, Philadelphia (North); Washington, Renton
Site 3 - Illinois, Danville; Pennsylvania, Philadelphia (Uptown); Washington, Lynnwood
Site 4 - Illinois, Kankakee; Pennsylvania, Reading; Washington, North Seattle
Site 5 - Illinois, Rockford East; Pennsylvania, Lewistown; Washington, Rainier
Site 6 - Illinois, Rockford West; Pennsylvania, Butler; Washington, Everett
Site 7 - Illinois, Peoria; Pennsylvania, Connellsville; Washington, Bellevue
Site 8 - Illinois, Moline; Pennsylvania, McKeesport; Washington, Bellingham
Site 9 - Illinois, Galesburg; Pennsylvania, Erie; Washington, Bremerton
Site 10 - Illinois, West Town; Pennsylvania, Pittston; Washington, Mt. Vernon
Site 11 - Illinois, Mt. Prospect; Pennsylvania, Scranton; Washington, Olympia
Site12 - Illinois, Waukegan; Pennsylvania, Lancaster; Washington, Lewis County
Site 13 - Illinois, Villa Park; Washington, Aberdeen
Site 14 - Illinois, Aurora; Washington, Cowlitz County
Site 15 - Illinois, Woodlawn; Washington, Spokane

Site 16 - Illinois, South Chicago; Washington, Moses Lake
Site 17 - Illinois, Chicago Heights; Washington, Wenatchee
Site 18 - Illinois, Bedford Park; Washington, Yakima
Site 19 - Illinois, Chicago Hotel and Restaurant workers; Washington, Sunnyside
Site 20 - Illinois, Chicago Professional and Sales workers; Washington,
             Tri-cities
Site 21 - Illinois, Ravenswood; Washington, Walla Walla
Site 22 - Illinois, Evergreen Park
Site missing - Illinois

NQ1 - enrolled in Pennsylvania in third quarter 1988
NQ2 - enrolled in Pennsylvania in fourth quarter 1988
NQ3 - enrolled in Pennsylvania in first quarter 1989
NQ4 - enrolled in Pennsylvania in second quarter 1989
NQ5 - enrolled in Pennsylvania in third quarter 1989

Table A4.1 Regression-Adjusted Treatment Impact Equations

Variable	Illinois Parameter estimate	Std. error	Pennsylvania Parameter estimate	Std. error	Washington Parameter estimate	Std. error
Intercept	20.00**	0.19	14.91**	0.18	14.35**	0.19
Treatment	−1.04**	0.26	−0.58**	0.21	−0.40*	0.21
WBA	0.02**	0.00	0.02**	0.00	0.03**	0.00
Female	0.38	0.27	1.04**	0.21	1.41**	0.19
AGELT35	−2.00**	0.28	−1.52**	0.21	−1.91**	0.18
AGEGT54	—	—	3.19**	0.34	1.27**	0.31
Black	3.96**	0.40	−1.90**	0.39	1.77**	0.45
Hispanic	1.86**	0.57	−1.57**	0.55	−0.09	0.40
Other non-White	0.82	0.93	−1.81	1.25	−0.34	0.40
Entitled duration	−2.83**	0.27	−1.82**	0.91	0.15**	0.02
BPE	0.08**	0.02	−0.07**	0.01	−0.03**	0.01
Manufacturing	0.68**	0.32	−0.48**	0.23	−1.61**	0.21
SIC missing	1.19**	0.42	0.16	0.34	0.87	1.98
Search exempt	—	—	−0.60*	0.31	−3.77**	0.22
Site 1	−2.46**	0.86	−1.15**	0.52	−1.99**	0.95
Site 2	−2.15**	0.88	1.36**	0.49	−2.44**	0.97
Site 3	2.35**	0.87	—	—	−3.80**	0.99
Site 4	0.04	0.95	−1.75**	0.51	−1.36	0.95
Site 5	−0.25	1.01	0.38	0.59	−0.90	0.92
Site 6	−0.74	0.94	1.00*	0.54	−2.06**	0.96
Site 7	0.55	0.78	1.85**	0.55	−2.79**	0.96
Site 8	0.14	0.82	1.12**	0.52	−1.45	1.01
Site 9	1.15	1.45	0.60	0.52	−0.30	1.04
Site 10	0.44	0.80	1.83**	0.58	−2.03**	1.00
Site 11	−5.78**	0.68	−0.10	0.52	−0.60	1.01
Site 12	−1.08	0.95	−2.38**	0.52	−3.01**	1.08
Site 13	−2.85**	0.79	—	—	−1.10	1.05
Site 14	−2.74**	0.84	—	—	−3.45**	1.06
Site 15	−0.69	0.70	—	—	−0.69	0.94
Site 16	−0.16	0.67	—	—	−2.92**	1.05
Site 17	0.37	0.78	—	—	−1.95**	0.99

Table A4.1 (continued)

| | Illinois | | Pennsylvania | | Washington | |
Variable	Parameter estimate	Std. error	Parameter estimate	Std. error	Parameter estimate	Std. error
Site 18	0.40	0.71	—	—	−1.01	0.94
Site 19	2.30	3.41	—	—	−0.15	1.02
Site 20	0.02	0.70	—	—	−0.62	0.99
Site 21	−0.51	0.77	—	—	—	—
Site missing	0.87	1.48	—	—	—	—
NQ1	—	—	−2.13**	0.97	—	—
NQ2	—	—	−1.44**	0.41	—	—
NQ3	—	—	−1.98**	0.40	—	—
NQ4	—	—	−1.80**	0.41	—	—
NQ5	—	—	−1.49**	0.40	—	—
Sample size	8,138		12,106		15,534	
R^2	0.08		0.05		0.06	

5
Impacts on Employment and Earnings

Paul T. Decker
Christopher J. O'Leary
and
Stephen A. Woodbury

The findings presented in the previous chapter demonstrate that the reemployment bonus offers in the Illinois, Pennsylvania, and Washington bonus experiments generally reduced unemployment insurance (UI) receipt. Presumably, the reductions in UI receipt occurred because the bonus offers induced claimants to return to work more quickly than they would have in the absence of the bonus offer. To receive a bonus, claimants not only needed to stop receiving UI, they also needed to prove that they held a job and that they held that job for a minimum period of time. We therefore expected, given the impacts on UI receipt, to also observe an increase in employment and earnings among claimants who received a bonus offer. In this chapter, we examine employment and earnings during the year following claimants' benefit applications to determine whether this impact occurred.

Although we expected the bonus offers to have positive impacts on average earnings among all claimants, the reemployment incentives generated by the bonus offers may have had potentially negative impacts on the characteristics of new jobs held by claimants who found a job. Because the UI system provides financial assistance to claimants who are looking for work, they can presumably be more selective in taking a new job than they would be in the absence of UI. Hence, UI may lead claimants to spend more time unemployed because they are searching for the best possible match between their skills and available jobs. The reemployment bonus creates an incentive to shorten search time, however, which may cause claimants to be less selective in their search, potentially resulting in a relatively less desirable match between the claimant and the job.

One way in which a less desirable job match might manifest itself is through a lower rate of earnings on the subsequent job. We therefore extend our analysis of employment and earnings to examine the rate of earnings among reemployed claimants and to test whether the bonus offers, by promoting rapid reemployment, induced claimants to accept lower-paying jobs.

Impacts of the bonus on the job match may also manifest themselves through changed rates of attachment to employers or to industries. To speed reemployment, UI claimants who received a bonus offer may have been more inclined to search for and accept jobs with new employers or in different industries. Greater employer or industry switching might imply that job-specific or industry-specific human capital possessed by claimants at their previous jobs was being abandoned to take advantage of the bonus offer. If the specific human capital was still potentially productive, the abandonment of it would represent a loss due to the reemployment bonus offer. On the other hand, if the specific human capital was no longer potentially productive, or if its potential productivity was not large enough to justify longer unemployment spells, employer and industry switching may be a benefit of the reemployment bonus offer. This would be especially true if claimants who switch employers or industries have more stable employment in the long run than if they had not switched. In this chapter we test for the effects of the bonus offers on employer and industry attachment by comparing the rates at which the treatment and control groups returned to their previous employers or industries.

DATA AND METHODOLOGY

Our analysis of the impacts of the bonus offers on employment and earnings is based on two quarterly measures drawn from UI wage records: 1) whether claimants reported earnings and 2) the amount of earnings received. The state UI wage records also contain direct data on employment for the Pennsylvania and Washington experiments. The Pennsylvania wage records report weeks of work in a quarter, and the Washington wage records report hours of work in a quarter. Using these data, we constructed an employment indicator that specifies whether a claimant had either positive weeks of work in the quarter (Pennsylvania) or positive hours of work (Washington). Because the Illinois records contain no direct employment data, we chose to use the earnings indicator as a proxy for an employment indicator for most of our analysis, so that we could investigate employment probabilities for all three experiments.

For all three experiments, we have a full set of wage records data on claimant earnings for the three calendar quarters following the claimants' entry into the UI system.[1] We also examined data for the quarter in which claimants filed their initial UI claims. Although earnings data for this quarter partly reflect claimants' experience with pre-UI employers, random assignment implies that pre-UI earnings during this quarter should not vary significantly across treatment groups within each demonstration. Hence, any significant cross-group differences in earnings in the quarter of benefit application should be attributable to the impact of the treatment on postapplication earnings. We can also control for any remaining cross-group differences in pre-UI earnings by controlling for base period earnings in our regression estimates.

UI wage records were used because these data were available for all three experiments.[2] Although we believe that UI wage records are a useful source of earnings data, they do have some shortcomings for our analysis. One important deficiency is that they are organized by calendar quarter and thus cannot be used to isolate the impacts that occurred immediately after the benefit application date. This inflexibility may be an important constraint, because previous studies of a reemployment bonus in the New Jersey UI Reemployment Demonstration Project showed that the impact of the bonus offer occurred soon after the benefit application date (see Corson et al. 1989; Corson and Decker 1990). In the present analysis, we attempt to address this shortcoming by reporting estimates for the quarter in which claimants applied for benefits, which encompasses the period immediately after the benefit application date.

Another shortcoming is that a variety of factors may have affected the accuracy of the wage records data. For example, the wage records exclude the earnings of claimants who were employed outside the state or outside the UI-covered sectors (such as those who were self-employed). Because our analysis of earnings would include such individuals as if their earnings were zero, the impact estimates would be biased toward zero. Furthermore, the UI wage records report earnings when they are received, not when they are earned. Claimants may have received severance pay or pension payouts from their pre-UI employer after they applied for UI benefits. These payments could be misinterpreted as earnings from a post-UI job, overstating the earnings received by claimants following their benefit application date.[3]

We attempted to minimize the effect of potential shortcomings of the wage records data by excluding extreme outliers—claimants whose earnings were greater than $100,000 in any quarter of observation. This restriction was intended to exclude high values that are caused by severance payments or pension payouts. The outliers may also be caused by coding errors in the wage records. The restriction on earnings values affected the Washington data much more than the Illinois or Pennsylvania data. In Washington, 66 observations were excluded from the data set because of this earnings restriction, compared with only one observation each in Illinois and Pennsylvania.[4]

EMPLOYMENT AND EARNINGS AMONG CONTROL GROUP MEMBERS

In the absence of the reemployment bonus, the control group claimants in Washington had the highest employment rates after their initial UI claims, followed by the Pennsylvania claimants and then the Illinois claimants. Because we had no direct employment information on the Illinois claimants, we used the presence of individual earnings during a period as a proxy for employment during the period. The use of earnings as a proxy for employment allows us to calculate employment rates for each experiment (Table 5.1). The Washington control group members were employed more than the Pennsylvania control group members, who in turn were employed more than the Illinois control group members throughout the observation period. We also present the direct employment indicators for Washington and Pennsylvania in Table 5.1. They are consistent with the proxy measure in demonstrating that the Washington control group tended to have higher employment rates than the Pennsylvania control group.

Table 5.1 Mean Employment and Earnings among Control Groups[a]

| | Period of observation | | | | | |
| | of initial UI claim | Quarter[b] | | | Total (all four quarters) | Sample size |
		1	2	3		
Claimants with reported employment (%)						
Illinois	ND[c]	ND	ND	ND		ND
Pennsylvania	84.1	59.0	67.3	70.6		3,353
Washington	81.7	65.9	70.5	72.0		3,082
Claimants with reported earnings (%)						
Illinois	86.0	53.7	56.0	61.9		3,866
Pennsylvania	88.1	63.4	71.1	74.4		3,392
Washington	88.6	71.5	76.2	77.3		3,064
Earnings ($)[d]						
Illinois	2,446	1,231	1,676	2,070	7,422	3,866
Pennsylvania	2,648	1,711	2,357	2,606	9,322	3,392
Washington	3,057	2,613	3,120	3,269	12,059	3,064

SOURCE: State UI wage records.
[a] The sample means presented in this table are not regression adjusted.
[b] Quarters 1, 2, and 3 are the first, second, and third full calendar quarters after the UI claim.
[c] ND = no data available.
[d] Excludes observations with earnings greater than $100,000 in any quarter.

The Washington control group members also had higher earnings than the Illinois and Pennsylvania control group members. Over the four-quarter observation period, Washington control group members earned an average of about $12,000, compared with $9,300 earned by the Pennsylvania control group members and $7,400 earned by the Illinois control group members.

Two factors help to explain the differential earnings of the control groups in the three demonstrations. First, on average, the Washington claimants were more highly paid than the Pennsylvania claimants prior to their respective layoffs, and the Pennsylvania claimants were more highly paid than the Illinois claimants (Table 2.5 in Chapter 2).[5] We would expect that this difference in earnings would continue to exist as claimants become reemployed, since the difference in base period earnings at least partly reflects inherent differences in characteristics (such as differences in skill levels) between the claimants in the different states. Second, Washington claimants appear to have become reemployed more quickly than the Pennsylvania or Illinois claimants. As shown in Table 5.1, the rate of employment for the three quarters following the initial claim was highest for Washington claimants and lowest for Illinois claimants.[6] Since unemployed claimants received zero earnings, the relatively low employment rates for the Pennsylvania and Illinois claimants contributed to the relatively low earnings levels experienced by these claimants.

ESTIMATED IMPACTS ON EMPLOYMENT AND EARNINGS

Estimates based on data from the UI wage records provide only weak evidence that the bonus offers enhanced the employment of claimants following their initial claim. The clearest evidence of positive employment impacts can be seen for Illinois (Table 5.2). The estimated impact of the Illinois bonus offer on the probability of employment is positive in each of the four quarters of observation. The impact is largest and statistically significant in quarter 2 (the second full calendar quarter after the initial claim)—the bonus offer increased the probability of employment by 3.9 percentage points, or by 7.0 percent of the control group employment rate (56 percent) shown in Table 5.1. The finding that the Illinois experiment had the clearest and largest employment impacts is consistent with the findings on UI receipt presented in the previous chapter, which showed that the Illinois experiment had the largest impact on UI receipt.

The estimated impacts of the Pennsylvania and Washington bonus offers on employment provide no strong evidence that the bonus offers increased the probability of employment in those two states. In Pennsylvania, only about half of the estimated impacts on the probability of employment have a positive sign, and none of the impacts is significantly greater than zero. The combined impacts of the Pennsylvania

Table 5.2 Estimated Impacts of the Bonus Offers on Probability of Employment[a,b] (percentage points)

Treatment	Bonus amt./ duration	of initial UI claim	Quarter[c]		
			1	2	3
Illinois					
IT	$500/11 weeks	0.8	1.6	3.9***	2.1
		(0.7)	(1.1)	(1.1)	(1.1)
Impact (as % of control group mean)[d]		0.9	3.0	7.0	3.4
Pennsylvania					
PT1	3 × WBA[e]/ 6 weeks	−1.2	−2.2	−1.4	−3.8***
		(1.0)	(1.5)	(1.4)	(1.4)
PT2	6 × WBA/ 6 weeks	−0.4	1.0	0.7	0.7
		(0.9)	(1.4)	(1.3)	(1.2)
PT3	3 × WBA/ 12 weeks	0.5	1.0	−0.7	−2.4**
		(0.9)	(1.3)	(1.2)	(1.1)
PT4	6 × WBA/ 12 weeks	−0.9	0.6	0.6	−0.7
		(0.8)	(1.2)	(1.1)	(1.1)
Combined treatments		−0.4	0.4	0.0	−1.4
		(0.7)	(1.0)	(0.9)	(0.9)
Impact of combined treatments (as % of control group mean)[d]		−0.5	0.6	0.0	−1.9
Washington					
WT1	2 × WBA/ (0.2 × UI duration) + 1 week	−0.9	−0.9	−2.9**	−0.7
		(0.9)	(1.2)	(1.2)	(1.1)
WT2	4 × WBA/ (0.2 × UI duration) + 1 week	−1.3	−1.5	−2.0*	−0.9
		(0.9)	(1.2)	(1.2)	(1.1)
WT3	6 × WBA/ (0.2 × UI duration) + 1 week	−0.5	0.2	−1.1	2.0
		(1.0)	(1.4)	(1.3)	(1.3)
WT4	2 × WBA/ (0.4 × UI duration) + 1 week	−0.6	0.3	−0.9	−0.4
		(0.9)	(1.2)	(1.2)	(1.1)

(continued)

Table 5.2 (continued)

Treatment	Bonus amt./ duration	Quarter[c] of initial UI claim	1	2	3
WT5	4 × WBA/ (0.4 × UI duration) + 1 week	−0.3 (0.9)	0.2 (1.2)	−0.2 (1.2)	0.1 (1.1)
WT6	6 × WBA/ (0.4 × UI duration) + 1 week	−0.7 (1.0)	1.9 (1.4)	0.6 (1.3)	1.1 (1.3)
Combined treatments		−0.7 (0.6)	−0.1 (0.9)	−0.9 (0.8)	0.0 (0.8)
Impact of combined treatments (as % of control group mean)[d]		−0.8	−0.1	−1.2	0.0

SOURCE: State UI wage records.

[a] Individuals are treated as being employed in a quarter if the wage records contain earnings data in that quarter. The estimates are based on regressions that include treatment indicators and other explanatory variables to control for claimant characteristics, UI benefit parameters, and local factors.

[b] Standard errors in parentheses. * = Statistically significant at the 90 percent confidence level in a two-tailed test; ** = statistically significant at the 95 percent confidence level in a two-tailed test; *** = statistically significant at the 99 percent confidence level in a two-tailed test.

[c] Quarters 1, 2, and 3 are the first, second, and third full calendar quarters after the initial UI claim.

[d] See Table 5.1.

[e] WBA = weekly UI benefit amount.

treatments demonstrate that the treatment group members had about the same probability of employment as did the control group members in each of the quarters. In Washington, the majority of the estimated impacts are negative, and none is significantly greater than zero. The combined impacts of the Washington treatments show that treatment group members and control group members had similar average earnings in each of the quarters.

The evidence on whether the bonus offers increased earnings is also mixed (Table 5.3). In Illinois, the bonus offer clearly caused a short-term increase in earnings. Over the full four-quarter observation

Table 5.3 Estimated Impacts of the Bonus Offers on Earnings[a,b] ($)

Treatment	Bonus amt./ duration	of initial UI claim	Quarter[c] 1	2	3	Total, all four quarters
Illinois						
IT	$500/ 11 weeks	−6 (57)	132*** (48)	120** (49)	5 (55)	250* (148)
Impact (as % of control group mean)[d]		−0.2	10.7	7.2	0.2	3.4
Pennsylvania						
PT1	3 × WBA/ 6 weeks	−11 (100)	8 (84)	−77 (78)	−188** (82)	−269 (235)
PT2	6 × WBA/ 6 weeks	−14 (89)	113 (75)	−18 (70)	52 (73)	133 (211)
PT3	3 × WBA/ 12 weeks	105 (83)	81 (70)	−15 (65)	−5 (68)	166 (195)
PT4	6 × WBA/ 12 weeks	−28 (78)	73 (66)	77 (62)	53 (64)	175 (185)
Combined treatments		15 (63)	74 (53)	6 (50)	−2 (52)	93 (149)
Impact of combined treatments (as % of control group mean)[d]		0.6	4.3	0.2	−0.1	1.0
Washington						
WT1	2 × WBA/ (0.2 × UI duration) + 1 week	19 (91)	−213** (95)	−58 (93)	13 (93)	−239 (257)
WT2	4 × WBA/ (0.2 × UI duration) + 1 week	−25 (90)	−93 (94)	−133 (92)	110 (92)	−141 (254)

(continued)

Table 5.3 (continued)

Treatment	Bonus amt./ duration	Quarter[c] of initial UI claim	1	2	3	Total, all four quarters
WT3	6 × WBA/ (0.2 × UI duration) + 1 week	−35 (101)	23 (106)	−18 (104)	184* (104)	155 (287)
WT4	2 × WBA/ (0.4 × UI duration) + 1 week	−73 (89)	4 (93)	−132 (92)	4 (92)	−197 (253)
WT5	4 × WBA/ (0.4 × UI duration) + 1 week	−80 (90)	−82 (94)	−66 (92)	36 (92)	−193 (254)
WT6	6 × WBA/ (0.4 × UI duration) + 1 week	−124 (102)	57 (107)	165 (105)	199* (105)	296 (290)
Combined treatments		−50 (66)	−61 (69)	−55 (68)	79 (68)	−88 (187)
Impact of combined treatments (as % of control group mean)[d]		1.6	−2.3	−1.7	2.4	−0.7

SOURCE: State UI wage records.

[a] The estimates are based on regressions that include treatment indicators and other explanatory variables to control for claimant characteristics, UI benefit parameters, and local factors. We excluded observations with earnings greater than $100,000 in any quarter.

[b] Standard errors in parentheses. * = Statistically significant at the 90 percent confidence level in a two-tailed test; ** = statistically significant at the 95 percent confidence level in a two-tailed test; *** = statistically significant at the 99 percent confidence level in a two-tailed test.

[c] Quarters, 1, 2, and 3 are the first, second, and third full calendar quarters after the initial UI claim.

[d] See Table 5.1.

[e] WBA = Weekly UI benefit amount.

period, the treatment group members earned $250, or 3.4 percent, more than control group members. This difference is statistically significant at the 90 percent confidence level. The increase in earnings occurred primarily in quarters 1 and 2. The quarterly impact estimates represent an 11 percent increase in earnings in quarter 1 and a 7 percent increase in quarter 2. Both of these quarterly estimates are significant at the 95 percent confidence level.

The magnitude and timing of the estimated earnings impacts in Illinois are consistent with the findings on UI receipt from the Illinois experiment. With respect to the magnitude of the impacts, we demonstrated in Chapter 4 (Table 4.2) that the Illinois bonus offer reduced average UI receipt by 1.04 weeks. If we use this impact to derive an expected impact on earnings based on the assumption that the 1.04-week reduction in UI receipt translates directly into a 1.04-week increase in employment, we find an expected impact on earnings of $258.[7] Our estimated impact for the full four-quarter observation period, $250, is similar to this expected impact. With respect to the timing of the impacts, the large and significant earnings impact in the second quarter after the initial UI claim implies that the bonus reduced unemployment among sample members who would have otherwise stayed unemployed into the second quarter. Hence, the Illinois bonus had at least some effect on claimants who faced substantial (up to 6 months) unemployment spells. This finding is consistent with the significant reduction in the rate of benefit exhaustion caused by the Illinois bonus offer, as demonstrated in Chapter 4.[8]

The estimates for the Pennsylvania experiment are more modest than the Illinois estimates and are not statistically significant in most cases. All but one of the Pennsylvania bonus offers (the low bonus/ short qualification treatment) have a positive estimated impact on earnings over the four-quarter observation period, but none of the estimates is statistically significant. The estimated impact of all of the treatments combined was to increase earnings by an average of $93, or 1.0 percent, per claimant, but this combined effect is also not statistically significant.

Despite the lack of consistently significant findings for earnings impacts, the estimated Pennsylvania impacts are consistent with the estimated impacts of the Pennsylvania treatments on UI receipt that were discussed in Chapter 4. Specifically, the magnitude of the estimated earnings impacts are similar to what one would expect based on the magnitude of the estimated UI impacts. For example, assuming that the 0.58-week reduction in UI receipt for the combined Pennsylvania treatments translates directly into a 0.58-week increase in employment, the expected impact of the combined treatments on earnings is $158 (0.58 times average pre-UI weekly earnings for the control group of $272). This expected impact is within the 95 percent confidence interval (approximately –$199 to $385) of the estimated combined treatment impact for Pennsylvania discussed above.

The comparison of the estimated UI impacts and the estimated earnings impacts demonstrates the difficulty in estimating earnings impacts for the bonus experiments. Although the Pennsylvania sample was large and the estimates relatively precise, the estimates are not precise enough to detect the modest earnings impact that would be consistent with the UI impacts. Given the standard errors in Table 5.3, the impact of the combined Pennsylvania treatments would need to be equal to about $250 per claimant to be statistically significant at the 90 percent confidence level, considerably higher than the $158 impact that is predicted based on the estimated UI impact as described above.

The Washington findings provide no evidence that the Washington bonus offers increased the earnings of claimants. Over the entire observation period, the treatment group members in Washington earned $88 less than did the control group members, as shown in Table 5.3. The estimated impacts of individual treatments on earnings were generally modest, both in each quarter and over the entire observation period, and many of these estimated impacts were negative rather than positive. The impacts of the most generous bonus offers on earnings are more positive than the impacts of the less generous bonus offers, which is consistent with the estimated impacts on UI receipt. However, none of the estimated impacts of the individual treatments on earnings is statistically significant.

The lack of consistently positive impacts on earnings of the Washington treatments is probably not surprising given that the estimated impacts of the Washington treatments on UI receipt are small, as discussed in Chapter 4. As in the case of the Pennsylvania estimates, even though the Washington sample is large and our earnings estimates are relatively precise, the estimates shown in Table 5.3 are not precise enough to detect the small earnings impacts that would be consistent with the small estimated UI impacts. If we generated expected earnings impacts based on the estimated UI impacts, these expected impacts would fall within the 95 percent confidence intervals around the actual impact estimates. For example, using the same method as we used for Pennsylvania, we generate an expected earnings impact for the combined Washington treatments of $119.[9] This expected impact is well within the 95 percent confidence interval (approximately –$455 to $279) of the estimated combined treatment impact on earnings in Washington (the –$88 impact described in the previous paragraph). The presence of errors in the Washington data, as demonstrated by the large number of extreme outliers, also makes it difficult to use the wage records data to detect impacts on earnings.

IMPACTS ON WAGES

Claimants may respond to a reemployment bonus offer by intensifying their job search so that they find a new job quickly enough to receive the bonus. Alternatively, a claimant may attempt to speed reemployment not by intensifying the job search but by relaxing standards for acceptable job offers. That is, claimants may, in an effort to receive a bonus, accept jobs that do not quite match their skills or do not offer the wages or benefits that they would command in the absence of the bonus offer. If such an effect were to occur, it should be considered a potential cost of the bonus offer since claimants would be matched to jobs in which they are potentially less productive.

Consider the possibility that claimants sacrifice wages in order to hasten reemployment and qualify for the bonus. Such an effect would have negative long-run consequences if it led to a decrease in lifetime earnings compared to what would occur in the absence of the bonus. In this section, we attempt to determine whether the bonus offers decreased wages at reemployment. We examine the sample of all claimants who reported earnings in two consecutive calendar quarters after their initial UI claim. This approach is intended to focus our analysis on a sample of claimants who found reemployment. We used this sample of reemployed claimants to estimate the impacts of the treatments on quarterly wages in the second quarter, or first full quarter, of employment after the initial UI claim.

In all three experiments, the reemployed treatment group members had quarterly wages that were similar to the earnings of reemployed control group members, suggesting that claimants who received a bonus offer did not sacrifice wages to become reemployed quickly. The estimated impacts of the combined treatments on wages based on the differences of means (model 1 in Table 5.4) are modestly positive but not statistically significant in the Pennsylvania and Washington experiments. The estimate for the Illinois experiment is negative, but it is also small and statistically insignificant.

Because the reemployed claimants are not a random sample of all claimants, the differences in wages between the reemployed treatment group members and the reemployed control group members do not necessarily provide an unbiased estimate of the effect of the bonus offers on wages. The impact estimates in model 1 of Table 5.4 may therefore be subject to selection bias because the wage equations can be estimated only with reemployed claimants. Selection bias occurs in the treatment/control comparisons if the reemployed claimants in the treatment group were either a more or less "select" group than the reemployed claimants in the control group, who became reemployed in the absence of the bonus offer. If the bonus offers induced relatively high-wage workers to become reemployed more quickly, the difference in wages between the treatment and control groups would represent an upwardly biased estimate of the impact of the treatments on wages. On the other hand, if the bonus offers induced relatively low-wage workers to become reemployed more quickly, the difference in wages between the groups would represent a downward biased estimate of the impact of the treatments on wages.

To control for the inherent differences between the reemployed treatment group members and the reemployed control group members, we estimated two additional wage models. The first of these models (model 2 in Table 5.4) includes additional explanatory variables to control for race, gender, age, weekly benefit amount (WBA), and base period earnings. The second of these models (model 3 in Table 5.4) is similar to model 2, but the dependent variable is defined as the difference between post- and pre-layoff quarterly earnings.

Table 5.4 Estimated Impacts of the Bonus Offers on Earnings among Reemployed Claimants[a] ($)

Treatment	Bonus amt./ duration	Model[b] 1	2	3
Illinois				
IT	$500/11 weeks	−18.0 (73.0)	8.0 (65.0)	37.0 (65.0)
Control group mean of depend. variable		3,326	3,326	69
Sample size		4,441	4,441	4,441
Pennsylvania				
PT1	3 × WBA[c]/6 weeks	7.0 (104.0)	−39.0 (81.0)	−43.0 (86.0)
PT2	6 × WBA/6 weeks	28.0 (92.0)	−40.0 (72.0)	−7.0 (76.0)
PT3	3 × WBA/12 weeks	130.0 (86.0)	28.0 (67.0)	−9.0 (71.0)
PT4	6 × WBA/12 weeks	162.0**[b] (80.0)	52.0 (63.0)	40.0 (66.0)
Combined treatments		100.0 (66.0)	11.0 (51.0)	3.0 (54.0)
Control group mean		3,560	3,560	114
Sample size		8,442	8,442	8,442
Washington				
WT1	2 × WBA/ (0.2 × UI duration) + 1 week	109.0 (119.0)	71.0 (100.0)	48.0 (104.0)
WT2	4 × WBA/ (0.2 × UI duration) + 1 week	66.0 (117.0)	8.0 (99.0)	−6.0 (102.0)
WT3	6 × WBA/ (0.2 × UI duration) + 1 week	−33.0 (131.0)	−6.0 (110.0)	23.0 (114.0)
WT4	2 × WBA/ (0.4 × UI duration) + 1 week	−8.0 (116.0)	−114.0 (98.0)	−107.0 (101.0)
WT5	4 × WBA/ (0.4 × UI duration) + 1 week	−39.0 (116.0)	−95.0 (98.0)	−116.0 (106.0)
WT6	6 × WBA/ (0.4 × UI duration) + 1 week	221.0* (132.0)	90.0 (111.0)	73.0 (115.0)

(continued)

Table 5.4 (continued)

Treatment	Bonus amt./ duration	Model[b]		
		1	2	3
Combined treatments		46.0	−15.0	−23.0
		(86.0)	(72.0)	(75.0)
Control group mean		4,281	4,281	454
Sample size		11,454	11,454	11,454

SOURCE: State UI wage records.

[a] Standard errors in parentheses. * = Statistically significant at the 90 percent confidence level in a two-tailed test; ** = statistically significant at the 95 percent confidence level in a two-tailed test.

[b] Model 1 uses earnings in the second quarter of earnings after the initial UI claim as the dependent variable and treatment indicators as explanatory variables. Model 2 is identical to model 1, but adds additional explanatory variables to control for race, gender, age, base period earnings, and WBA. Model 3 uses the change in quarterly earnings between the base period before the layoff and the second quarter of earnings receipt after the layoff as the dependent variable.

[c] WBA = Weekly UI benefit amount.

Based on these alternative models, it appears that claimants who received a bonus offer did not accept lower wages, on average, to become reemployed more quickly. The estimated impacts of the combined treatments are negative in Pennsylvania and Washington, but the estimates are small and statistically insignificant. The estimated impact of the combined Pennsylvania treatments is either positive or negative, depending on the model, but the estimates are consistently small and statistically insignificant.

IMPACTS ON EMPLOYER AND INDUSTRY ATTACHMENT

The bonus offers may have affected the probability that claimants returned to their previous employer. Claimants who had the opportunity to receive a reemployment bonus may have foregone the chance of returning to their previous employer in an effort to become reemployed within the qualification period. In addition, the Washington and Pennsylvania experiments paid bonuses only to reemployed claimants who were not recalled to their old jobs.[10]   This restriction provided an additional incentive to break any existing employer attachment.

Evidence from the experiments suggests that the bonus offers generally reduced the probability of returning to the previous employer.[11] Table 5.5 contains the estimated impacts on probability of recall based on two alternative models: model 1 is based on simple comparisons of reemployed treatment and control group members, while model 2 controls for other factors, including race, gender, age, previous industry, base period earnings, WBA, potential benefit duration, recall expectations, and local office. Approximately 40 percent of reemployed claimants in the control group in any of the states had returned to their previous employer. Surprisingly, the findings presented in Table 5.5 suggest that the Illinois bonus offer had a larger impact on the probability of returning to the previous employer than the combined Washington or Pennsylvania bonus offers. This finding is surprising because the Illinois experiment was the only one of the three experiments that did not have an explicit restriction on bonus payments to claimants who returned to their previous job.[12] Despite this factor, the estimated impact of the Illinois bonus was to decrease the probability of recall by an estimated 3 or 4 percentage points, significant at the 95 percent confidence level (model 2 in Table 5.5).

The estimated impact in Pennsylvania was smaller—the combined treatments reduced the probability of returning to the previous employer by 1.6 percentage points—and not statistically significant. Among the individual Pennsylvania treatments, the high bonus (6 × WBA) treatments had the largest estimated impacts on employer attachment (all significant at the 90 or 95 percent confidence level). Hence, in Pennsylvania the more generous bonus offers appear to have induced some claimants to take new jobs rather than wait to be recalled to their previous employer. The estimated impact of the combined treatments in Washington was similar to the Pennsylvania impact and was statistically insignificant in both models.[13,14]

The bonus offers may induce claimants to not only find jobs with new employers but also find jobs in new industries. Such an impact would occur if the financial incentive inherent in the bonus offer led claimants to search for jobs in other industries more intensively or accept jobs in other industries more readily than they would in the absence of the bonus offer. Industry codes were available to investigate

**Table 5.5 Estimated Impacts on the Probability
of Return to Previous Employer[a] (percentage points)**

Treatment	Bonus amt./ duration	Model 1	Model 2
Illinois			
IT	$500/11 weeks	−4.0***	−3.9**
		(1.3)	(1.3)
Control group mean		39.9	39.9
Pennsylvania			
PT1	3 × WBA[c]/6 weeks	0.0	0.4
		(1.8)	(1.7)
PT2	6 × WBA/6 weeks	−2.7*	−2.6*
		(1.6)	(1.5)
PT3	3 × WBA/12 weeks	−0.4	0.1
		(1.5)	(1.4)
PT4	6 × WBA/12 weeks	−2.5*	−2.7*
		(1.4)	(1.3)
Combined treatments		−1.6	−1.4
		(1.1)	(1.0)
Control group mean		41.4	41.4
Washington			
WT1	2 × WBA/ (0.2 × UI duration) + 1 week	−1.6	−1.0
		(1.5)	(1.4)
WT2	4 × WBA/ (0.2 × UI duration) + 1 week	−3.6**	−2.6*
		(1.5)	(1.4)
WT3	6 × WBA/ (0.2 × UI duration) + 1 week	1.8	2.9*
		(1.7)	(1.5)
WT4	2 × WBA/ (0.4 × UI duration) + 1 week	0.9	1.5
		(1.5)	(1.4)
WT5	4 × WBA/ (0.4 × UI duration) + 1 week	−2.3	−1.4
		(1.5)	(1.4)
WT6	6 × WBA/ (0.4 × UI duration) + 1 week	−1.9	−1.6
		(1.7)	(1.6)
Combined treatments		−1.2	−0.5
		(1.1)	(1.0)
Control group mean		40.2	40.2

Table 5.5 (continued)

SOURCE: State UI wage records.
[a] Standard errors in parentheses. * = Statistically significant at the 90 percent confidence level in a two-tailed test; ** = statistically significant at the 95 percent confidence level in a two-tailed test; *** = statistically significant at the 99 percent confidence level in a two-tailed test.
[b] All estimates are based on linear probability models. Model 1 includes only treatment indicators as explanatory variables. Model 2 includes treatment indicators and other variables to control for race, gender, age, base period earnings, and WBA.
[c] WBA = Weekly UI benefit amount.

this issue in the Illinois and Washington experiments. These codes were derived from the employer identification numbers from the wage records and UI administrative records.[15] We based our investigation on the two-digit level of industrial classification.

Findings from the Illinois and Washington experiments provide generally weak evidence that the bonus offers may have reduced the probability that claimants returned to their previous industry. About half of the control group members in either experiment returned to their previous industry, with the rate being somewhat higher in Washington. The impacts of the Illinois treatment and the combined Washington treatments on the probability of returning to the previous industry were small and negative (Table 5.6). In model 2, which adjusts for individual characteristics, the Illinois treatment reduced the probability of return to industry by an estimated 1.7 percentage points, and the combined Washington treatments reduced the probability of return by 1.0 percentage point. Neither of these estimates, however, is significant at conventional confidence levels. Two of the individual Washington treatments, WT2 and WT5 (Table 5.6), had significant impacts on the probability of return, but neither of these treatments is the most generous treatments in Washington, and neither has a significant impact on duration of UI receipt (Chapter 4). Hence, these data provide only weak evidence that claimants reduced their UI duration and received a bonus by increasing their industrial mobility slightly.

Whether the decreased employer and industry attachment that may be attributable to the bonus experiments would be considered undesirable is unclear. The effect is undesirable only if claimants, in their effort to receive the bonus, were so shortsighted in their reemployment decisions that they lost lifetime earnings by taking jobs that did not

**Table 5.6 Estimated Impacts on the Probability of Return to Previous
Two-Digit Industry[a] (percentage points)**

Treatment	Bonus amount/ duration	Model 1	Model 2
Illinois			
IT	$500/11 weeks	−2.2*	−1.7
		(1.4)	(1.3)
Control group mean		51.9	51.9
Washington			
WT1	2 × WBA/6 weeks	−0.7	−0.2
		(1.5)	(1.5)
WT2	4 × WBA/6 weeks	−3.2**	−2.6*
		(1.5)	(1.4)
WT3	6 × WBA/6 weeks	−0.2	0.5
		(1.7)	(1.6)
WT4	2 × WBA/12 weeks	−0.2	−0.1
		(1.5)	(1.4)
WT5	4 × WBA/12 weeks	−3.1**	−2.4*
		(1.5)	(1.4)
WT6	6 × WBA/12 weeks	−1.1	−0.8
		(1.7)	(1.6)
Combined treatments		−1.5	−1.0
		(1.1)	(1.0)
Control group mean		56.4	56.4

SOURCE: State UI wage records.

[a] Standard errors in parentheses. * = Statistically significant at the 90% confidence level in a two-tailed test; ** = statistically significant at the 95% confidence level in a two-tailed test.

[b] All estimates are based on linear probability models. Model 1 includes only treatment indicators as explanatory variables. Model 2 includes treatment indicators and other variables to control for race, gender, age, base period earnings, and WBA.

[c] WBA = Weekly UI benefit amount.

reward the employer- or industry-specific capital accumulated on their previous jobs. Presumably, rational claimants would only switch employers or industries to receive the bonus if the amount of the bonus compensated for any loss in lifetime earnings inherent in the switch.

CONCLUSION

Although the evidence is somewhat mixed, the three reemployment bonus experiments generally appear to have increased employment and earnings modestly. The clearest impacts on employment and earnings occurred in Illinois, where the $500 bonus offer increased earnings by an average of $250, or 3.4 percent, per claimant over the year following the initial UI claim. This finding is not surprising given that the Illinois experiment also had substantial impacts on UI receipt. The employment and earnings impacts in Pennsylvania were smaller than in Illinois and not statistically significant. Finally, the estimated earnings impacts in Washington were not consistently positive, although the estimated impacts of the most generous bonus offers were more positive than the impacts of the less generous offers.

Overall, the findings with respect to employment and earnings are consistent with the impacts on UI receipt presented in Chapter 4. The estimated employment and earnings impacts were modest, as would be expected given the modest impacts on UI receipt. In addition, the experiment with the largest impact on UI receipt (Illinois) also had the largest impacts on employment and earnings, while the experiment with the smallest impact on UI receipt (Washington) had the smallest impacts on employment and earnings.

We found no evidence that claimants responded to the bonus offers by sacrificing wages to speed their reemployment. In all three experiments, the reemployed treatment group members and the reemployed control group members had similar wages on their new jobs, other things being equal.

Finally, some claimants appear to have broken attachments with previous employers or industries to speed their reemployment. The clearest effects on employer and industrial mobility occurred in Illinois, where the bonus offer decreased the probability of returning to the previous employer by 3 to 4 percentage points and decreased the probability of returning to the previous industry by about 2 percentage points. Similar findings with respect to employer attachment were found in Pennsylvania, where the most generous bonus offers significantly reduced the probability of returning to the previous employer. The Washington bonuses had negative estimated impacts on both the probability of returning to the previous employer and the probability of returning to the previous industry, but the estimates were smaller than in Illinois and tended to be insignificant.

Notes

1. Earnings data for later quarters are available but not for the full samples.
2. Interview data on earnings were also available for the Pennsylvania experiment but not for the Washington and Illinois experiments. Corson et al. (1992) used both wage records and interview data to investigate earnings in the Pennsylvania experiment and found that wage records provide adequate information for evaluating the impacts of the bonus offers on earnings. See Appendix D of Corson et al. (1992) for a direct comparison of interview and wage records data on earnings.
3. Decker (1989) discussed these and related shortcomings of UI wage records data based on data from the New Jersey UI Reemployment Demonstration. He estimated that 9 percent of the claimants in the New Jersey demonstration sample lived outside New Jersey (and therefore may have been likely to find work outside New Jersey) at the time of the demonstration, 3 percent became self-employed in the year after their initial UI claim, and 28 percent received severance pay or a pension payout from their previous employer.
4. Investigation of the outliers in the Washington data suggested that they reflect errors in the data rather than actual receipt of earnings or other forms of compensation. The outliers for given individuals in given quarters were extremely inconsistent with the earnings reported in other quarters for those individuals.
5. Earnings are not adjusted for differences in price levels, so some of the earnings differences may not represent differences in real earnings.
6. The higher reemployment rates for Washington were due partly to the inclusion of stand-by recall claimants in the Washington experiment. Since these claimants expected to be recalled by their pre-UI employer after a brief period of unemployment, the inclusion of these claimants in the Washington experiment increased the overall employment rates for Washington claimants compared with the Illinois and Pennsylvania experiments, which excluded stand-by recall claimants. See Chapter 2 for a full discussion of eligibility requirements in the three experiments.
7. We calculate the expected impact on earnings by multiplying 1.04 weeks by average weekly earnings in the base period for the control groups, $248.

8. Decker (1994) examined in detail the impacts of reemployment bonuses on the short-term and long-term unemployed in the Illinois experiment and the New Jersey UI Reemployment Demonstration.

9. We calculated the expected impact by multiplying the combined treatment impact on UI weeks (0.40) by average weekly earnings in the base period ($298) in Washington.

10. In the Washington experiment, bonuses were paid to claimants hired by their previous employers only if they were hired for different jobs. In Pennsylvania, claimants recalled by their previous employers did not receive bonuses, regardless of the job.

11. Claimants were treated as returning to their previous employer if the identification number of the employer in the first quarter of earnings matches the identification number of the separating employer. If a claimant had multiple employers in the first quarter of earnings, we used the employer that paid the most earnings in the quarter.

12. Among those Illinois claimants who eventually received a bonus payment, 21 percent had returned to their previous employer.

13. Spiegelman, O'Leary, and Kline (1992) also used data from a follow-up interview to investigate the probability of returning to the previous employer. Estimates based on these interview data suggest that the bonus offers significantly reduced the probability of recall by 6 percent. As pointed out by Spiegelman, O'Leary, and Kline, the interview data differ from the wage records by explicitly identifying the previous and new employers, instead of relying on the matching of codes from the wage records. Interview data may be less accurate due to errors in self-reporting, however, and the sample of survey respondents is a smaller and probably nonrandom subset of the claimant population.

14. Anderson (1992) considered the impact of a reemployment bonus on recall in her study of the New Jersey Unemployment Insurance Reemployment Demonstration. She found that the bonus offer in New Jersey did not reduce recall rates significantly.

15. In Illinois and Washington, the industry code is part of the employer identification number. In Pennsylvania, the employer identification number does not contain an industry code.

References

Anderson, Patricia M. 1992. "Time-varying Effects of Recall Expectation, a Reemployment Bonus, and Job Counseling on Unemployment Duration." *Journal of Labor Economics* 10(1): 99–115.

Corson, Walter S., and Paul T. Decker. 1990. "The Impact of Reemployment Services on Unemployment Insurance Benefits: Findings from the New

Jersey Unemployment Insurance Reemployment Demonstration." Unpublished paper.

Corson, Walter, Paul T. Decker, Shari Miller Dunstan, and Anne R. Gordon. 1989. *The New Jersey Unemployment Insurance Reemployment Demonstration Project: Final Evaluation Report*. Unemployment Insurance Occasional Paper 89-3, Washington, D.C.: U.S. Department of Labor, Employment and Training Administration.

Corson, Walter, Paul Decker, Shari Dunstan, and Stuart Kerachsky. 1992. *Pennsylvania Reemployment Bonus Demonstration: Final Report*. Unemployment Insurance Occasional Paper 92-1, Washington, D.C.: U.S. Department of Labor, Employment and Training Administration.

Decker, Paul T. 1989. "Systematic Bias in Earnings Data Derived from Unemployment Insurance Wage Records and Implications for Evaluating the Impact of Unemployment Insurance Policy on Earnings." Unpublished paper.

Decker, Paul T. 1994. "The Impact of Reemployment Bonuses on Insured Unemployment in the New Jersey and Illinois Reemployment Bonus Experiments." *Journal of Human Resources* 29(3): 718–741.

Spiegelman, Robert G., Christopher O'Leary, and Kenneth J. Kline. 1992. *The Washington Reemployment Bonus Experiment: Final Report*. Unemployment Insurance Occasional Paper 92-6, Washington, D.C.: U.S. Department of Labor, Employment and Training Administration.

6

From Social Experiment to Program

The Reemployment Bonus

Carl Davidson and Stephen A. Woodbury

This chapter examines the problem of transferring the results obtained in the Illinois, Pennsylvania, and Washington reemployment bonus experiments to an actual reemployment bonus program. The results presented in the preceding three chapters suggest that a reemployment bonus program could reduce the duration of insured unemployment without adverse consequences for workers offered the bonus. On the whole, the results appear to be "internally valid"—that is, comparisons between the treatment and control groups generally provide unbiased estimates of the bonus impacts.

Experimental results alone, however, do not indicate whether implementing a reemployment bonus program would be desirable. Important questions still exist about the extent to which bonus experiments are "transferable" and give an accurate picture of what would happen if a bonus program were actually adopted. In any social experiment, whether experimental results are transferable to an actual program ("externally valid") is distinct from whether the results are valid on their own grounds (internally valid). The first section of this chapter develops a model-based classification of the problems that impede the transfer of experimental results to a policy setting.

In the second section, we characterize an equilibrium-matching model of the labor market that provides an organizing framework for analyzing the problems of transferring the reemployment bonus experiments' results to the setting of an actual program. (The full model is presented in the chapter appendix.) This section also presents the main results on spillover effects, classification changes, and behavioral changes that could follow adoption of a bonus program. The third section explores how the outcomes of a program that offered a bonus only to dislocated workers could differ from those observed in the bonus experiments. We also discuss how exogenous changes in economic and labor market conditions may alter the effectiveness of a reemployment bonus program. The final section summarizes the chapter's methods and main results.

THE TRANSFERABILITY PROBLEM IN THE REEMPLOYMENT BONUS EXPERIMENTS

A well-designed social experiment can offer a high degree of control over the variables that influence outcomes such as unemployment duration and earnings after reemployment, and as a result can yield unbiased, readily understandable, and convincing estimates of the impact of an economic incentive on behavior. A variety of problems may hamper the transfer of experimental results to what could be expected of an actual program, however. Existing treatments of the transferability of experimental results include Aigner (1985), Spiegelman and Woodbury (1990), Garfinkel, Manski, and Michalopoulos (1992), Moffitt (1992a), Davidson and Woodbury (1993), and Meyer (1995). However, there is no generally accepted categorization of problems underlying the transferability of experimental results. Accordingly, we offer the following catalog of transferability problems, based on the labor market model that we use to investigate those problems.

Briefly, the results of implementing an actual program may differ from the effects of a treatment as estimated in a social experiment for five reasons.

1) Spillover effects—the possibility that workers who respond to the bonus program would make it more difficult for other workers to find employment (that is, would crowd out or displace other workers from employment).

2) Classification changes without efficiency implications—in particular, the possibilities that if a program were adopted, more bonus-qualified workers would actually collect a bonus and more work-

ers eligible for unemployment insurance (UI) would claim benefits in order to collect a bonus.

3) Behavioral changes with efficiency implications—the possibility that under an actual bonus program, an increasing share of bonus-offered workers would participate and respond to the bonus offer by increasing their job-search intensity.

4) Scale effects—the possibility that program outcomes would differ from experimental outcomes if a bonus program were offered to a different population or adopted on a different scale than the experiments.

5) Exogenous economic changes—the possibility that different economic or labor market circumstances, which may not have been adequately controlled for in the experiments, would yield program outcomes that differed from the experimental outcomes.

Table 6.1 lists these five transferability problems and notes the features of the model that allow us to account for them. Each problem is discussed in turn.

Spillover Effects

Experimental impacts are usually estimated only for the subgroup of the population that would be eligible for the program, but a program may have indirect or spillover effects on other groups of workers. For example, an experimental training program to upgrade the skills of workers could improve the employment and earnings of the program's participants at the expense of workers who don't participate and who would have gotten jobs in the absence of the program. This "crowding out" of nonparticipants by participants is especially likely if the training program were implemented in a local labor market where there were few job vacancies.

A reemployment bonus has the clear potential for a spillover or crowding-out effect. Reemployment bonuses are intended to increase the search intensity of the UI claimants who have been offered bonuses. An effective bonus offer would drive bonus-offered claimants to find job vacancies earlier (on average) than otherwise. As a result, part of the improved labor market performance of bonus-offered work-

Table 6.1 Transferability Problems and Features of the Model that Allow Them to Be Analyzed

Effect or change considered	Features of the model
Spillover effects	Multiple groups of workers/parameters characterizing workers' behavior and responses to changing incentives
Classification changes without efficiency implications	Multiple groups of workers
Behavioral changes with efficiency implications	Parameters characterizing workers' behavior and responses to changing incentives
Scale effects	Multiple groups of workers/parameters characterizing workers' behavior and responses to changing incentives
Exogenous economic changes	Parameters characterizing the labor market and constraints facing workers

ers would be at the expense of workers who were not offered bonuses. Some non-offered workers would, in effect, be crowded out of employment as a result of the bonus program and would experience longer spells of unemployment and a higher unemployment rate.[1]

Because of the difficulties in estimating crowding out in an experimental design, we have modeled the crowding out of a reemployment bonus program using an equilibrium search and matching model (Davidson and Woodbury 1993, 2000). In the model discussed in the appendix, which is based on our earlier work, the crowding-out effects of the reemployment bonus differ across various groups of job seekers. In particular, we distinguish among crowding out of job seekers who are offered the bonus but don't respond to it, job seekers who have been offered a bonus but whose bonus qualification period has expired (that is, UI-eligible job seekers whose spells of unemployment extend beyond the bonus qualification period), and job seekers who are never offered the bonus (both UI-eligible nonclaimants and UI-ineligible job seekers, such as new labor force entrants and re-entrants). We also check the sensitivity of the crowding-out estimates to variation in the

UI take-up rate and the *bonus take-up rate*—that is, to changes in the proportion of UI-eligible workers who claim their benefits and changes in the proportion of bonus-qualifiers who actually collect a bonus for which they qualify.

Spillover effects have real consequences for employment, unemployment, resource allocation, and efficiency. That is, spillovers imply that the economic prospects of those who do not participate in a program are harmed by the improved situation of program participants. For that reason, spillover effects are more serious than, for example, classification changes (such as changes in the bonus take-up rate, the proportion of bonus-qualified workers who collect a bonus), which have measured impacts but do not have economic or efficiency impacts. Spillover effects are discussed further on pp. 188–190.

Classification Changes without Efficiency Implications

A program's take-up rate may differ from the take-up rate observed in an experiment; that is, a greater percentage of individuals who are eligible to receive a benefit may choose to collect the benefit once a permanent program is implemented. These are classification changes without efficiency implications because they represent changes in the way workers classify themselves but require no change in underlying economic behavior (such as a change in job-search intensity). Although they will change the government's cost of financing a program, classification changes have no effect on economic outcomes or resource allocation.

It is well-known that less than 100 percent of the individuals who are eligible to collect benefits under social programs actually do so. For example, available estimates suggest that only between 55 and 75 percent of workers who are eligible to claim UI benefits do so, and it was seen in Chapter 3 that only one-half to two-thirds of the workers who qualified for a bonus in the Illinois, Pennsylvania, and Washington experiments actually collected a bonus.

The concern is that some workers would reclassify themselves in one of two ways if a bonus program were adopted. Consider first UI-eligible workers with short expected durations of unemployment who used to find that the costs of claiming UI outweighed the benefits. After adoption of a bonus program, these UI-eligible nonclaimants could, with no change in job-search intensity or timing of reemployment, become UI-eligible claimants and receive both UI benefits and a bonus. This would be observed as increases in the UI take-up rate (the proportion of UI-eligible workers who claim benefits), the bonus take-up rate, and the financial cost of providing benefits and bonuses to claimants. Second, once a bonus program were adopted, a higher percentage of workers who qualify for a bonus might collect one. This would be observed as increases in the bonus take-up rate and the financial cost of providing bonuses. Both of these are "classification changes" because either could occur if workers reclassified themselves; that is, if they claimed benefits or collected a bonus *without any change in job-search behavior or the timing of reemployment.*

Classification changes pose a problem for the validity of experimental estimates of the financial cost of a bonus program. If either the UI take-up rate or the bonus take-up rate increased after program adoption, the government's cost of the UI program would increase. In other words, classification changes would lead to measurable differences between the financial cost of the experiments and the financial cost of a program.

However, classification changes would not lead to differences between the employment and unemployment outcomes of an experiment and those of a bonus program. The reason, as already noted, is that no change in economic behavior—job-search intensity or timing of reemployment—would be required in order to effect these classification changes. Unlike spillover effects and the other effects considered, classification changes have only measured impacts on the government's cost of the program. They have no consequences for resource allocation and efficiency. Classification changes without efficiency implications are discussed further on pp. 191–195.

Behavioral Changes with Efficiency Implications

The responses of workers to an actual program may differ from their responses during an experiment for several reasons (which are not necessarily mutually exclusive). First, social experiments are inevitably of limited duration. If participants' planning horizons exceed the length of an experiment, then the behavior of participants during the experiment may differ from what it would be if the program were adopted. This can be thought of as a time-horizon effect. Time-horizon effects posed a concern for the income maintenance experiments of the 1960s and 1970s because participants may have been reluctant to give up jobs and adjust their labor supply in response to an experimental (and hence short-term) negative income tax system. If a negative income tax program were adopted, participants might make long-term adjustments that differed from the short-term adjustments observed during the experiment.

The time-horizon problem could be a concern in transferring the results of the reemployment bonus experiments to an actual program. For example, it is possible that bonus-offered claimants viewed the experimental bonus offer as evanescent—an offer that would be available only during the current spell of unemployment and never again. If so, then claimants might be prone to respond to and collect a bonus under the experiment, whereas they might not do so under a bonus program. As a result, the bonus effects estimated in an experiment could be larger than those in an actual program, although it is difficult to gauge by how much.

A second reason for differences between behavior during an experiment and under an actual program is the learning effect. Learning effects are changes in behavior that may occur as program participants learn more about the workings of a program. Such changes may occur as participants become more convinced of the authenticity and permanence of a program, as they become increasingly aware of the consequences of their behavior under the program, or because it takes time for participants to make adjustments and rearrangements in response to new incentives.[2]

If a program is subject to learning effects, then a short-term experiment may be an incomplete guide to what could be expected under an actual program. In general, the existence of learning effects implies that experimental results will underestimate the long-run response to a fully implemented program because, under an actual program, participants would have enough time to understand fully and respond to the incentives created by a program. There is some evidence that learning effects may have been a problem in the Illinois bonus experiment. In a follow-up survey of a random sample of UI claimants who were offered the Illinois bonus, about one-third of those who refused to participate in the experiment indicated that failure to understand or trust the experiment was the reason for refusal (Spiegelman and Woodbury 1987, Chapter 7). This was the case even though the bonus offer was simple to understand, its credibility was easily established, and participants needed little time to adapt or respond to the program.

A third reason for behavioral changes after adoption of a program would be changes in norms that occur over time after adoption of a program. Especially with an income transfer program like welfare, social norms may make it difficult for many individuals to participate, at least when a program is first adopted. It is possible that some bonus-offered claimants chose not to respond to the bonus offer because they felt some stigma attached to doing so—they would be taking a bribe to accept a job, perhaps. However, there is little evidence of such stigma in the responses to follow-up questions that were put to bonus-offered workers in Illinois (Spiegelman and Woodbury 1987, Chapter 7).

As with spillover effects, behavioral changes have consequences for employment, unemployment, and efficiency. For example, if a higher proportion of bonus-offered workers responded to a bonus by increasing their job-search intensity, then bonus-offered workers as a group would experience shorter spells of unemployment and increased employment. Such behavioral changes with efficiency implications are discussed further (pp. 192–195).

Scale Effects

There may be differences between an experiment and a program that result because a program is adopted on a different scale (either larger or smaller) than the scale on which the experiment was conducted. Scale effects could result because a program is adopted across a wider (or narrower) geographical area than in an experiment or because it is implemented for different groups of individuals (or more or fewer groups of individuals) than in an experiment. Such differences in scale may again result in differences between experimental results and the outcomes of an actual program.

Typically, the scale of an actual program is larger than that of an experiment, as would occur if bonus offers were made to all new UI claimants rather than only to randomly assigned claimants in certain geographic areas. Increased scale could affect the outcomes of a reemployment bonus program, for example, by changing the likelihood of crowding out, or by extending the bonus offer to groups of workers who had been ineligible for experimental bonus offers and whose behavioral responses differed from the groups who were tested.

However, a reemployment bonus program could also be adopted on a smaller scale than the experiments. For example, it would be feasible (and consistent with the goals of a bonus offer) to limit bonus offers to dislocated workers or workers who are believed to be potential UI exhaustees. An important feature of the Washington reemployment bonus experiment was to test whether dislocated and other workers responded differently to the bonus offer. The results suggested no important difference between the two groups (Spiegelman, O'Leary, and Kline 1992), but there could be scale effects if, by offering the bonus to a relatively small group of workers, the overall increase in job-search intensity induced by the bonus program were relatively small. A small increase in search intensity would lead to a relatively small increase in overall employment and the possibility of greater crowding out of workers who are not offered a bonus. These implications are developed further on pp. 195–198.

Exogenous Economic Changes

The economic conditions under which a program is implemented may differ from the economic conditions that prevailed during an experiment. Fully controlling for differences in economic conditions during an experiment may be difficult or impossible, but failing to do so may lead to experimental estimates that differ from the outcomes of the program.

In terms of the model used below, exogenous economic changes amount to changes in parameters that characterize the labor market. In principle, adequate data and modeling should allow us to explain differences across the experiments in Illinois, Pennsylvania, and Washington and to predict the circumstances under which the bonus will be most effective.

Results presented in Chapter 4 of this volume (Table 4.6) suggest that, in Pennsylvania and Washington, the effect of a reemployment bonus offer was greater at sites where labor market conditions were good. This finding poses a puzzle—the bonus impact was greater in Illinois than in either Pennsylvania or Washington, even though labor market conditions appear to have been worst in Illinois. The issue of labor market conditions and the efficacy of the reemployment bonus are discussed further on pp. 198–201.

Remarks on Internal Validity

The five problems discussed above all come under the heading of external validity or transferability. Other pitfalls in social experimentation involve internal validity; that is, ensuring that the comparison between the control and experimental groups is unbiased. Internal validity is prior to the questions of transferability; it is a necessary but not sufficient condition for transferability of experimental results to a program setting. The most commonly cited problem of internal validity is the so-called Hawthorne effect, which occurs if subjects respond to an unintended treatment rather than to the designed treatment. The Hawthorne effect takes its name from experiments at the Hawthorne plant of Western Electric Company (in Chicago), where changes in lighting and room color were made to determine their effects on productivity. The experimenters found that productivity improved, but they discovered that the improvements resulted from the increased attention that was paid to workers whose work spaces were changed rather than from the tested changes in lighting and color.

A Hawthorne effect could have existed in the reemployment bonus experiments if participants increased the intensity of their job search because they felt they were being watched or wanted to please those conducting the experiment, rather than in response to the bonus offer. A Hawthorne effect seems unlikely in the reemployment bonus experiments for two reasons. First, in the Illinois bonus experiment, there were actually two treatments: the claimant bonus (in which new UI claimants were offered a $500 bonus to become rapidly reemployed) and an employer bonus, in which a random sample of new UI claimants was instructed to tell each prospective employer that he or she (the prospective employer) would receive a $500 bonus for hiring the claimant within 11 weeks of the initial claim. This employer bonus showed quite small effects, whereas the bonus offer to claimants showed significant effects (Woodbury and Spiegelman 1987). If the impacts of the bonus offer to claimants were merely a Hawthorne effect, then the employer bonus should have turned up significant effects. Hence, the Illinois experiment itself provides evidence that the impacts of the bonus offer to claimants were not the result of a Hawthorne effect. Second, in both the Pennsylvania and Washington experiments, several treatments were offered, with various bonus amounts and qualification periods. As discussed in Chapter 4, the bonus treatments were related to outcomes in predictable ways that suggest that economic incentives, rather than Hawthorne effects, were at work in the experiments.

SPILLOVER EFFECTS, CLASSIFICATION CHANGES, AND BEHAVIORAL CHANGES FOLLOWING ADOPTION OF A BONUS PROGRAM

In the chapter appendix, we develop a model that provides a framework for evaluating and quantifying the differences between the outcomes of the reemployment bonus experiments and what could be expected in an actual program. The model considers four well-defined groups of workers who exhibit optimizing behavior. It includes parameters characterizing the labor market and various constraints facing workers and parameters characterizing the preferences of workers and governing their responses to changed incentives. Changes in behavior that were observed in the reemployment bonus experiments are used to calibrate the model; that is, the behavioral impacts of the bonus experiment are used to gauge important and otherwise unobservable behavioral parameters. Once the model is calibrated, it is possible to simulate how various outcomes—such as unemployment duration and employment—would be altered if groups other than bonus-offered workers were affected by a bonus program or if bonus-offered workers behaved differently in a program than during the experiment. Direct observation of these effects, were it possible, would be preferable to the modeling approach taken here. Absent direct observation, however, the model provides a framework for analyzing the transferability problem and for roughly quantifying impacts that cannot be observed in an experiment.[3]

In the model, the bonus offer increases the opportunity cost of unemployment for bonus-offered workers, and some bonus-offered workers respond by increasing the intensity of their job search. This increase in search intensity has the following implications. First, there is an increase in overall steady-state employment. That is, more of the total available jobs are filled as the bonus-offered workers who respond to the offer search harder for jobs and accept jobs that would otherwise have remained vacant. Second, reemployment probabilities and employment levels rise for bonus-offered workers who respond to the offer, and they fall for all other workers, who are beaten to vacancies and crowded out of the labor market by the more aggressive workers who respond to the bonus offer. In general, the larger the increase in overall steady-state employment, the less crowding out will occur.[4]

These impacts of the bonus offer can be thought of respectively as a *gross employment effect* and *a crowding-out effect*. Note that the gross employment effect is an increase in total employment that is driven by the increase in search effort of workers who respond to the bonus offer. The increase in employment of these responders is offset at least partially by decreases in employment of other groups of workers—the crowding-out effect.

From the standpoint of analyzing the transferability of the bonus experiments' results to an actual program, the model has three main features. First, it breaks workers into four groups: 1) UI-ineligibles, 2) UI-eligibles who claim their benefits and respond to the bonus, 3) UI-eligibles who claim their benefits and fail to respond to the bonus, and 4) UI-eligible nonclaimants (see Figure 6.A1 and the accompanying discussion in the appendix). This breakdown lets us consider the impact of the bonus on groups other than those offered the bonus (UI-ineligibles and UI-eligible nonclaimants) and on workers who, although offered the bonus, do not respond. As a result, the model provides a way of understanding spillover effects. In the case of the reemployment bonus, crowding out is the most important spillover; that is, the bonus program tends to prolong the unemployment spells and reduce the employment of workers who are not offered or do not respond to the bonus.

Second, the model allows for variation in the UI take-up rate, defined as the proportion of UI-eligible unemployed workers who claim their benefits (denoted by k in the model). A concern raised about a reemployment bonus program is that it could lead to an increased UI take-up rate, which has hovered around 65 percent for the past 20 years. Increased UI take-up would involve the reclassification of workers, increasing the government's cost of the reemployment bonus program but leaving the real economic outcomes of the program unchanged. Because the UI take-up rate is a parameter in the model, the model provides a way of showing that the real economic outcomes of a bonus program would be unchanged if the UI take-up rate were to rise.

Third, the model specifies and distinguishes between the reemployment bonus response rate (defined as the proportion of bonus-offered workers who respond to the bonus by increasing their search intensity, denoted by ρ in the model) and the reemployment bonus take-up rate (defined as the proportion of workers who qualify for a bonus who actually collect it, denoted by τ in the model). The bonus response rate cannot be observed, but inclusion of the bonus take-up rate (which is observable) in the model allows us to identify and solve for the bonus response rate. Once solved for, the bonus response rate can be varied exogenously to gauge how the outcomes of a bonus program would differ if the bonus response rate increased. This allows examination of how an important behavioral change would affect the outcomes of a bonus program.

Because we refer to the above three parameters frequently in the following discussion, their definitions are repeated here:

k—the UI take-up rate, defined as the proportion of UI-eligible unemployed workers who claim their UI benefits;

ρ—the reemployment bonus response rate, defined as the proportion of bonus-offered workers who respond to the bonus by increasing their search intensity;

τ—the reemployment bonus take-up rate, defined as the proportion of workers who qualify for a bonus who actually collect it.

Distinctions among these three parameters are important and worth highlighting. A change in the bonus response rate (ρ) represents a change in behavior that has implications for employment, unemployment, and earnings—that is, implications for real economic outcomes and efficiency. In other words, changes in ρ are behavioral changes with efficiency implications. Changes in the UI and bonus take-up rates (k and τ), on the other hand, result in measured changes only, such as changes in bonus payouts and (consequently) the government's cost of financing UI or a reemployment bonus program. In other words, changes in k and τ are classification changes without efficiency implications.

Spillover Effects

In the context of a reemployment bonus, the main spillover effect that has concerned policymakers is crowding out. Our goal is to gauge the seriousness of crowding out and to illustrate the extent to which variations in the UI take-up rate (k) and the bonus take-up rate (τ) affect estimates of crowding out. To do so, we solve the model for various values of k and τ and compare the results. The results are reported in Table 6.2.

Column 1 of Table 6.2 shows the model's predictions of how a bonus program would affect employment and the duration of unemployment, assuming that all UI-eligible workers claim benefits and all who qualify for a bonus collect it.[5] Both of these underlying assumptions are clearly unrealistic. In this case, for every job gained by UI-eligibles, 0.39 job is lost by UI-ineligibles (138/351 = 0.39). We refer to this as the *crowding-out ratio*—the ratio of employment losses suffered by groups that lose employment to employment gains of the group that benefits from the bonus offer. Note also that the average spell of unemployment of UI-ineligibles would lengthen by 0.27 week. These results suggest that, although a bonus program would entail some crowding out, the amount would be rather small.

Column 2 reports results when we assume (more realistically) that the UI take-up rate is 65 percent, and (still unrealistically) that the bonus take-up rate is 100 percent. Column 2 suggests that crowding out is now more serious: for every job gained by UI-eligible claimants, 0.60 job is lost by the losers (i.e., the crowding-out ratio is now (96 + 78)/292 = 0.60). Note that the employment losses suffered by those not offered the bonus are split about equally between UI-eligible non-claimants and UI-ineligibles.

Column 3 reports results when we again assume a UI take-up rate of 65 percent but now assume a bonus take-up rate of 55 percent (as occurred in the Illinois bonus experiment). Crowding out is now even greater: for every job gained by bonus-offered workers who respond to

Table 6.2 Changes in Employment and in Duration of Unemployment Resulting from a $500 Reemployment Bonus[a]

UI take-up rate (k) 100%		65%	65%	65%
Bonus take-up rate (τ) 100%		100%	55%	55%
Worker group	(1)	(2)	(3)	(4)
UI-eligibles	351*	196	194	328
	(−0.741)	(−0.398)	(−0.393)	(−0.482)
Claimants	—	292*	297	455
		(−0.714)	(−0.714)	(−0.877)
Respond to bonus	—	—	415*	599*
			(−1.718)	(−1.652)
Ignore bonus	—	—	−118	−144
			(0.223)	(0.286)
Nonclaimants	—	−96	−103	−127
		(0.188)	(0.204)	(0.251)
UI-ineligibles	−138	−78	−94	−115
	(0.269)	(0.152)	(0.185)	(0.228)
Net increase in employment (J)	213	118	100	213
Crowding-out ratio[b]	0.39	0.60	0.76	0.64
ρ (bonus response rate)[c]	—	—	0.488	0.55

[a] The top number in a pair of values is the change in employment per 100,000 labor-force participants; the number in parentheses is the change in unemployment duration in weeks. The group that gains from the reemployment bonus offer in each case is shown by an asterisk (*). Values are based on simulations described in the text.

[b] The crowding-out ratio is the ratio of employment losses suffered by groups that lose employment to employment gains of the group that benefits from the bonus offer.

[c] In column 3, the bonus response rate (ρ) is retrieved from the observed bonus impacts; in column 4, it is set to 0.55, the calibration from column 3 is retained, and the employment changes and changes in duration of unemployment are solved.

the bonus, 0.76 job is lost by bonus-offered workers who ignore the bonus offer, UI-eligible nonclaimants, and UI-ineligibles (that is, the crowding-out ratio is [118 + 103 + 94]/415 = 0.76). Again, the employment losses suffered by those not offered the bonus are split about equally among the three groups of losers.

Why does the crowding-out ratio progressively increase as the assumptions are made more "realistic"? Consider first column 1. In this case, we assume that all UI-eligible workers claim their benefits and respond to the bonus. This means that 40 percent of all unemployed workers increase their search effort during the first six 2-week periods of unemployment. A direct result of this increase in search effort is an increase in overall employment; that is, more of the economy's total available jobs (F) are filled—J rises and V falls. This increase in employment allows the UI-eligibles to obtain jobs with relatively little crowding out of UI-ineligibles.

The results in column 2 suggest that crowding out would be larger in the presence of a UI take-up rate of only 65 percent. Because, in this case, 35 percent of UI-eligibles do not claim their benefits, fewer workers are offered the bonus, and there is less scope for the bonus offer to alter behavior. In other words, fewer workers have increased their search effort as a result of the bonus offer. When fewer workers claim their UI benefits and respond to the bonus offer, employment increases by less as a result of the bonus offer (that is, J rises by less and V falls by less), and more of the increase in UI-eligible employment must come at the expense of other workers.

Finally, in column 3, it is again the case that 35 percent of UI-eligible workers do not claim their benefits (and hence are never offered the bonus). In addition, of the UI-eligible workers who do claim benefits and qualify for a bonus, only 55 percent collect the bonus. This implies that even fewer workers increase their search effort as a result of the bonus, and employment increases relatively little as a result. It follows that even more (over 75 percent) of the increase in employment for bonus recipients comes at the expense of other workers. The results reported in column 3 indicate that the UI-eligible claimants who do not respond to the bonus suffer the largest drop in employment. Why? Because these workers are receiving UI, they do not search as hard as UI-ineligibles. Also, they face a harder time finding a job than UI-eligible nonclaimants (because, by assumption, UI-eligible nonclaimants have higher reemployment probabilities). Thus, the workers who make the least effort to find a job are harmed the most.

Changes in the UI Take-Up Rate:
Classification Change without Efficiency Implications

Only 55 to 75 percent of the unemployed workers who are eligible to receive UI benefits actually claim them (Blank and Card 1991; Vroman 1991). Meyer (1995, pp. 108–110) argued that adoption of a bonus program could induce more UI-eligible workers to claim their benefits and hence would increase the UI take-up rate. In particular, for a worker expecting a short spell of unemployment and facing a low UI replacement rate, the existence of the bonus for rapid reemployment might make it worthwhile to claim benefits where, in the absence of a bonus, the benefits of claiming UI benefits might not outweigh the costs. Meyer referred to this as an "entry effect" because workers would in effect enter the UI program in response to a change in the program. He suggested that a bonus the size of the Illinois bonus would lead to a 7 to 12 percent increase in the UI take-up rate.[6]

We previously referred to such effects generally as classification changes without efficiency implications. This is because workers who newly chose to claim UI benefits (that is, reclassified themselves from UI-eligible nonclaimants to UI-eligible claimants) in order to take advantage of the bonus offer would behave no differently after the change than they did before. Workers who claimed UI benefits in response to the bonus would generally be workers with short expected durations of unemployment for whom the advantages of claiming benefits were previously not enough to outweigh the costs.[7] For such workers, the bonus offer tips the benefit-cost balance in favor of claiming benefits, but no change in behavior (apart from claiming benefits) is needed for these workers to receive benefits and collect a bonus—they would behave as they would have in the absence of a bonus, experiencing a short spell of unemployment.[8]

Another way of viewing this point is to compare columns 1 and 2 of Table 6.2. The net increase in employment resulting from the bonus is estimated to be 213 per 100,000 labor-force participants when the UI take-up rate is 100 percent (column 1) but only 118 per 100,000 when the UI take-up rate is 65 percent (column 2). It is tempting to argue that, if the UI take-up rate increased following adoption of a bonus program, then the benefits of the bonus program (in terms of increased employment) would rise, but that would not be correct. Workers classified as UI-eligible nonclaimants in column 2 would be reclassified as UI-eligible claimants if they claimed benefits in response to the bonus offer, but their job-search behavior would be unchanged. As a result, employment gains among UI-eligible claimants would fall, as would employment losses among UI-eligible nonclaimants. These offsetting changes would be measured changes only—there would be no real change in economic outcomes.

It follows that, although the increased UI take-up rate that would result from adopting a bonus program would increase the total payout of the UI system (weekly benefits plus bonuses), it would not affect efficiency or resource allocation. That is, it would not reduce the real economic benefits of the bonus program, which stem from employment increases that are induced by the bonus. Although the cost of the UI program would rise as a result of increased UI take-up, the increase would amount to an income transfer—a cost to the program but not to society.[9]

Changes in the Bonus Response and Take-Up Rates

Fewer than half of the individuals who are eligible to participate in social programs such as Aid to Families with Dependent Children and job training programs actually do so. Why this is true is one of the least understood aspects of social programs (Moffitt 1992a,b; Heckman and Smith 1995). Similarly, only 55 percent of the workers who qualified for a bonus in the Illinois bonus experiment chose to collect the bonus. It is difficult to explain why this should be the case, as was seen in Chapter 3. Moreover, there is no way of directly observing the proportion of workers who changed their behavior in response to the bonus offer and intensified their job search.

These points lead to one of the most difficult issues in analyzing the transferability of the bonus experiments' results to an actual policy—the possibility that the response to an actual bonus program would be greater (or less) than occurred during the experimental demonstrations. Changes in response, which we define as changes in the proportion of workers who show a behavioral response to the bonus offer, could occur with the adoption of a reemployment bonus program for a variety of reasons. If there are learning effects associated with a bonus offer—for example, it takes time for some UI claimants to understand or trust the bonus offer, as suggested by the available survey evidence—then response to a bonus program might be greater than response to the experiments. In our discussion of transferability problems in the first section of this chapter, these problems came under the heading of behavioral changes with efficiency implications because in the context of our model they will take the form of a change in a behavioral parameter, ρ, defined as the proportion of workers who respond to the bonus by increasing their job search intensity.

As already noted, the model includes the bonus take-up rate (τ, the proportion of bonus qualifiers who collect a bonus) as a parameter. Unlike ρ (the bonus response rate), τ can be observed. Inclusion of the bonus take-up rate in the model allows us to identify the bonus response rate. To see this, note first that Equation 27 in the appendix defines τ as the ratio of a) those who responded to and collected the bonus to b) those who qualified for a bonus by receiving 11 or fewer weeks of UI benefits. Next, recall that about 55 percent of the workers who qualified for the $500 reemployment bonus in Illinois actually collected it. This observation allows us to impose an additional constraint on the model that identifies the bonus response rate.

Column 3 of Table 6.2 shows the results of setting the bonus take-up rate (τ) equal to 55 percent (rather than 100 percent as in columns 1 and 2) and then solving the model to obtain an estimate of ρ. The estimate is about 49 percent—that is, roughly half of the UI claimants who were offered the $500 bonus in the Illinois experiment actually changed their behavior as a result of the bonus offer. This is an estimate of the proportion of workers who responded to the bonus offer whether or not they succeeded in shortening their spell of unemployment enough to qualify for the bonus. The estimate also accounts for (that is, excludes) workers who collected a bonus without responding—that is, workers who would have been unemployed for less than 11 weeks in any event and for whom the $500 bonus was a windfall.[10]

Column 3 also yields an estimate of the average reduction in unemployment duration of the workers who responded to the bonus. This estimated reduction is 1.7 weeks, more than twice the 0.7-week reduction for all workers who were offered the bonus. Bonus-offered workers who ignored the bonus offer had slightly longer spells of unemployment, according to the model.

The model can also be used to gain insight into what would happen if the bonus response rate were to rise after adoption of a bonus program. To do so, the bonus response rate (ρ) is treated as a parameter and imposed exogenously rather than solved for as in column 3. In column 4, a bonus response rate of 55 percent is imposed—about 6 percentage points (or 10 percent) higher than our estimate of ρ from column 3. The higher bonus response rate significantly changes program outcomes. With a higher response rate, the employment increases of claimants who respond to the bonus are much larger (599 per 100,000 rather than 415 per 100,000), although in absolute terms the crowding out of other groups of workers is also greater. In relative terms, though, crowding out is less when the bonus response rate is higher; the crowding-out ratio is 0.64 in column 4 versus 0.76 in column 3.

Note also that, with the 10 percent increase in the bonus response rate, the net increase in jobs more than doubles from 100 per 100,000 to 213 per 100,000. These gains occur because, when the response to the bonus is larger, job vacancies are filled more quickly and steady-state employment increases. All of these gains go to UI claimants who respond to the bonus.

Note that existing data provide no way of estimating how (or whether) either the bonus take-up rate (τ) or the bonus response rate (ρ) would change if a bonus program were adopted. Nevertheless, some observations can be made about what would occur if either τ or ρ changed following adoption of a bonus program. First, a change in the τ is a classification change without efficiency implications. An increased bonus take-up rate implies that more of the workers who qualify for the bonus actually collect it. It implies no change in the job-search intensity or timing of reemployment of bonus-offered workers and hence has no effect on "real" program outcomes, such as employment or crowding out. An increase in the bonus take-up rate increases the payout of bonuses to UI claimants, leads to additional income transfers, and increases the UI system's costs. In other words, increases in the bonus take-up rate are like the increases in the UI take-up rate (k)—they have implications for the finances of the bonus program but no implications for efficiency or resource allocation.

In contrast, an increase in the bonus response rate is a behavioral change with efficiency implications; that is, an increase in ρ changes real program outcomes. An increased response to the bonus leads to larger increases in net employment and reduced crowding out (compare columns 3 and 4 in Table 6.2). In other words, the results suggest that increases in the bonus response rate would improve the functioning of the program by leading to both greater employment gains and reduced crowding out.

DISLOCATED WORKERS AND EXOGENOUS ECONOMIC FACTORS

Limiting a Bonus Program to Dislocated Workers

If a bonus program were implemented, one likely option would be to offer bonuses only to specific groups of workers, such as dislocated workers (that is, workers who had seniority of at least three years with the employer who laid them off). Indeed, administrative rules proposed by the Clinton Administration in 1994 enabled state employment security agencies to offer a reemployment bonus to workers who meet the state's "profiling" criteria—that is, to workers predicted to have a high probability of exhausting their UI benefits.[11]

Implementing a bonus program on such a restricted basis poses a potentially serious problem for transferring the results of the bonus experiments to actual policy. In all three of the bonus experiments, bonuses were offered to most new UI claimants. To restrict a bonus program to dislocated workers would imply significant changes in the type of workers eligible to participate in the program, since dislocated workers tend to be older and earn higher wages than the average UI claimant. Also, restricting a bonus program to dislocated workers would mean implementing the program on a smaller scale than occurred during the experiments.[12]

A variant of the model developed in the previous section can provide insight into whether a bonus program that was available only to dislocated workers would yield different results than were observed in the reemployment bonus experiments. That is, it is possible to model both the change in the population of workers who would be offered the bonus and the change in the scale of the program (relative to the experiment) by adding appropriate subgroups to the model and assuming the bonus is offered only to a specific (and relatively small) group of workers.

To consider dislocated workers, we use a model similar to that developed in the appendix, but with one main difference. Rather than assume that the labor market has a single sector, we assume the existence of two employment sectors—high wage and low wage. Worker dislocation is treated by assuming that the economy experiences a one-time shock that causes part of the high-wage sector to shut down. Dislocated workers in the model are former employees of the high-wage sector who must now seek low-wage employment. In contrast, high-wage workers who experience a regular layoff search for (and eventually find) a high-wage job. Hence, in this model, there are three groups of UI-eligible claimants: 1) low-wage UI-eligible claimants, 2) high-wage UI-eligible claimants, and 3) dislocated UI-eligible claimants.[13]

In this modified model, the bonus offer to dislocated workers increases the opportunity cost of unemployment for dislocated workers and results in increased search effort on their part. For example, in a model in which half of all UI-eligible claimants are high-wage workers and 15 percent of all initial claimants for UI are dislocated, the search effort of dislocated workers increases by approximately 30 percent. This increase in search effort of dislocated workers has the same employment and crowding-out effects that were discussed on pp. 185–186. However, the employment effect is smaller than when the bonus is offered to all UI claimants because the group being offered the bonus—dislocated workers—is a relatively small portion of the labor force. The model's results suggest that the crowding-out effects of a bonus program for dislocated workers would be far greater than the crowding-out effects of a bonus program for most UI claimants precisely because of this smaller employment effect.

Table 6.3 shows the impacts of a reemployment bonus targeted on dislocated workers (column 1) and comparable results from a bonus offer to all UI claimants (column 2). In both sets of results, we assume that 60 percent of all unemployed workers are ineligible for UI ($q = 0.6$) and that 65 percent of UI-eligible workers claim their benefits ($k = 0.65$). The results in column 1 are based on the assumptions that half of all workers are high-wage workers and that 17.6 percent of low-wage UI-eligible claimants were dislocated from the high-wage

Table 6.3 Changes in Employment and in Duration of Unemployment Resulting from a $500 Reemployment Bonus Offered Only to Dislocated Workers[a]

Worker group	(1)[b]	(2)[b]
UI-eligible claimants	202	292*
	(–0.116)	(–0.714)
Dislocated	447*	—
	(–0.894)	
High wage	–93	—
	(0.016)	
Low wage	–152	—
	(0.025)	
UI-eligible nonclaimants	–93	–96
	(0.015)	(0.188)
UI-ineligibles	–105	–78
	(0.017)	(0.152)
Net increase in employment (J)	4	118

SOURCE: Figures in column 1 come from Davidson and Woodbury (2000, Tables 7A and 7B). Figures in column 2 are repeated from Column 2 of Table 6.2.

[a] The top number in a pair of values is the change in employment per 100,000 labor-force participants; the number in parentheses is the change in unemployment duration in weeks. The group that gains from the reemployment bonus offer in each case is shown by an asterisk (*).

[b] In column 1, the bonus offer is made to dislocated workers only. In column 2, the offer is made to all UI claimants.

sector. As we have shown in Davidson and Woodbury (2000, Tables 7A and 7B), the results in column 1 are robust to significant variation in both the percentage of the labor market that is high wage and the percentage of workers who are dislocated. Note that we have not divided dislocated workers into those who respond to the bonus offer and those who do not respond. This could be done at a cost of considerable added complexity, but the main points made presently would not change.

The main result is that a reemployment bonus targeted on dislocated workers would increase employment of dislocated workers (by 447 per 100,000 labor force participants) and decrease their unemployment duration (by about 0.9 week), but these gains for dislocated workers come almost entirely at the expense of other groups of workers, all of whom suffer employment reductions as a result of the bonus offer to dislocated workers. The net increase in employment resulting from a bonus offered only to dislocated workers is just 4 jobs per 100,000 in the labor force, as compared with a net gain of 118 per 100,000 when the bonus is offered to all UI claimants. Crowding out is virtually complete in the case of a bonus program targeted on dislocated workers (the crowding-out ratio equals 0.99).

Crowding out is nearly complete in this case because the employment gains that result from offering a bonus to a small percentage of unemployed workers (in this case, dislocated workers) are correspondingly small. Recall that, in this model, employment gains occur through increases in the search intensity of workers who are offered an inducement (such as a bonus) to search harder. When search intensity increases, vacancies disappear and more of the total available jobs in the economy are filled. If only a few workers are offered a bonus, employment rises only modestly.[14]

If the crowding-out effects of the bonus to dislocated workers are as large as our results suggest, then such a bonus fails miserably the Pareto criterion. However, for three reasons, we would not conclude that a bonus program for dislocated workers should be ruled out. First, worker dislocation results from structural changes in the economy that presumably benefit the majority of workers and society at the expense of dislocated workers. It is the burden of structural change, which itself fails the Pareto criterion, that the reemployment bonus is intended to redress. Second, as discussed in detail elsewhere (Davidson and Woodbury 2000, section III.E), the crowding-out results outlined above are quite sensitive to the assumption that full employment (or the total number of available jobs, F) is fixed and exogenous. Specifically, we find that if employers responded to a bonus for dislocated workers by increasing labor demand by just 0.025 to 0.03 percent, there would be no crowding out of nondislocated workers.

Exogenous Economic Factors and Differences among the Illinois, Pennsylvania, and Washington Experiments

Chapter 4 showed that the reemployment bonus experiments in Illinois, Pennsylvania, and Washington produced varied results. In Illinois, a $500 cash bonus offer for finding reemployment within 11 weeks of claiming unemployment benefits resulted in a reduction of the expected duration of unemployment of 0.7 week for claimants eligible only for state regular benefits (that is, ineligible for FSC). In the Pennsylvania and Washington experiments, similar bonus offers reduced the expected duration of unemployment by 0.6 and by 0.34 week, respectively. Also, in the Illinois experiment, the impact of the bonus offer varied greatly depending on the potential duration of UI benefits. For workers eligible for 38 weeks of benefits as a result of Federal Supplemental Compensation (FSC), the bonus offer reduced the expected duration of unemployment by 1.75 weeks, whereas for otherwise similar workers eligible only for state regular benefits, it reduced unemployment duration by only 0.7 week (Davidson and Woodbury 1991).

The model developed in this chapter can provide some limited insight into why the bonus offers in Illinois, Pennsylvania, and Washington had such varied impacts. The exogenous economic factors that determine the efficacy of a bonus offer can be divided into supply and demand factors. On the supply side, we have anything that influences the job-search behavior of unemployed workers. The size of the bonus offer (and qualification period), the level and potential duration of UI benefits, and the expected reemployment wage all influence the search intensity of jobless workers. These supply factors provide at least a partial explanation of why the bonus offer had such a large impact on FSC-eligible workers in Illinois. When the potential duration of UI benefits is extended from 26 to 38 weeks (other things equal), as it was by the FSC program, optimal search intensity of UI recipients falls (that is, expected utility maximizing search intensity is reduced). This follows because an increase in the potential duration of UI benefits reduces the opportunity cost of being unemployed. If the marginal cost of search intensity increases with search intensity (that is, the opportunity cost of leisure is increasing), then in the absence of a bonus program, FSC-eligible workers would search less hard and face a lower marginal cost of search than workers who were eligible for only 26 weeks of benefits. Because FSC-eligible workers face a lower marginal cost of search, a bonus offer should induce a larger increase in their search intensity. The larger bonus-induced increase in search intensity of the FSC-eligibles implies a larger bonus impact for these workers.[15]

On the demand side of the model, we have the job separation rate (s) and the total number of available jobs (F). Low separation rates (s) and rising availability of jobs (F) are both consistent with lower equilibrium unemployment rates, but low separation rates and rising availability of jobs have opposite implications for the effectiveness of a bonus program. When s is low, jobs do not turnover rapidly, so there are few vacancies (that is, unemployment is low because expected job duration is high). With few vacancies, it is difficult to find a job. So when s is low, a bonus offer will have a relatively small impact (Davidson and Woodbury 1993, Tables 1 through 4). On the other hand, when F grows, unemployment falls because there are a growing number of vacancies; so, jobs are easy to find and the increase in search effort induced by the bonus program should lead to a large reduction in unemployment duration (see again Davidson and Woodbury 1993, Tables 1 through 4).

So how can the differences across and within the Illinois, Pennsylvania, and Washington bonus experiments be explained? Across states, the bonus response was larger in Illinois, where the unemployment rate was high, than it was in Pennsylvania and Washington, where the unemployment rate was much lower. A possible explanation is that the Illinois experiment was conducted during the early stages of the 1980s recovery, whereas the Pennsylvania and Washington experiments took place after the recovery had matured. In Illinois, then, the separation rate (s) was falling from a high level and the number of available jobs (F) was growing as the recovery progressed. The high but falling separation rate would be consistent with a large but declining bonus impact, and the ready availability of jobs would be consistent with a large bonus impact. In Pennsylvania and Washington, on the other hand, separation rates were low and the number of available jobs, although high, was no longer growing rapidly. The low separation rate and slow growth of available jobs would both be consistent with a smaller bonus impact.

Within all three experiments, the bonus response was larger in areas with low unemployment. A plausible explanation is that differences in local unemployment rates are due to the massing of vacancies rather than to differences in local turnover rates. That is, within Illinois, Pennsylvania, or Washington, differences in unemployment rates would result more from variation in the availability of jobs (F) across local labor markets than from variation in the separation rate (s). If so, then we would expect a larger bonus impact in local labor markets with low unemployment rates because low local unemployment rates reflect ready availability of jobs (rather than low turnover rates).

Although these explanations of the differences within and across the three experiments are connected to a consistent labor market model, they must be viewed as speculative in the absence of local labor market data on separation rates and job vacancies.

SUMMARY AND CONCLUSIONS

Designers of social experiments often pay little attention to whether the results of an experiment will be "externally valid" or transferable to a program setting. Clearly, the reason for devoting public funds to social experiments is to learn what would be the actual effects of programs that might be adopted. To ignore the transferability of an experiment is to invite experimental results that may say little about what policymakers want and need to know.

This chapter has examined the pitfalls in applying the results of the reemployment bonus experiments to what might be expected under a reemployment bonus program. The first section provides a model-based catalog of the problems that impede direct application of the results of an experiment to an actual program: spillover effects, classification changes without efficiency implications (including increases in the UI and bonus take-up rates), behavioral changes with efficiency implications (including changes in the bonus response rate), scale effects (including targeting a program on a specific group), and exogenous economic changes.

In the second section, we apply a model that is fully described in the chapter appendix to the five issues that are most important to transferring the results of the bonus experiments to a program setting. We examine the crowding-out effects of the bonus and find that increasingly realistic assumptions about the UI take-up rate and the bonus response rate suggest increasing degrees of crowding out. For example, if all UI-eligible workers claim benefits and respond to the bonus, then for each job gained by bonus-offered claimants, only 0.39 worker who was not offered the bonus is crowded out of employment (we refer to this as a crowding-out ratio of 0.39). But, if we assume more realistically that only 65 percent of UI-eligible workers claim benefits and only 49 percent of the bonus-offered workers respond to the offer, the crowding-out ratio rises to 0.76. That is, the estimate of the crowding-out effect of the bonus program nearly doubles when we make realistic assumptions about the UI take-up rate and the bonus response rate. The reason for this increase in crowding out is that a reduced take-up of UI and less response to the bonus offer imply that fewer workers increase their search intensity as a result of the bonus offer. It follows that the net increase in employment resulting from the bonus offer is less, and the scope for crowding out is greater.

Pages 191–192 provide a fuller explanation of how an increase in the UI take-up rate would increase the government's cost of financing a bonus program but would have no implications for employment, unemployment, or the timing of reemployment. Accordingly, we refer to it as a classification change without efficiency implications. We also suggest that an increase in the UI take-up rate should not, in itself, be viewed as an adverse outcome of a bonus program.

On pages 192–195, we provide an estimate of the bonus response rate (ρ), which cannot be observed directly, but which can be solved for in the model. The estimate suggests that about half of all bonus-offered claimants responded to the bonus offer by increasing the intensity of their job search. Also, we estimate that these "bonus responders" shortened their unemployment spells by about 1.7 weeks on average, compared with an average reduction of 0.7 weeks among all workers who were offered the bonus. We also obtain results suggesting that a modest increase in the bonus response rate of about 10 percent (that is, from 49 percent to 55 percent) would greatly improve the outcomes of a bonus program: the net increase in jobs resulting from the bonus program would roughly double and the crowding-out ratio would drop from 0.76 to 0.64.

We also provide estimates of the likely impacts of a bonus program that targets dislocated workers (pp. 195–198). The results suggest that a bonus program for dislocated workers would increase the employment and reduce the duration of unemployment (by 0.9 week per spell) of dislocated workers, but these gains for dislocated workers would be almost wholly at the expense of other (nondislocated) workers (crowding-out ratio = 0.99). The reason for this virtually complete crowding-out is that the net increase in employment resulting from a bonus program for dislocated workers would be negligible because dislocated workers are a relatively small group. That is, because a bonus program for dislocated workers would induce only a small group of workers to increase their job-search intensity, the resulting employment increases would be correspondingly small.

Finally, we attempt an explanation of the differences in observed bonus impacts across and within the Illinois, Pennsylvania, and Washington bonus experiments (pp. 198–201). First, similar bonus offers produced larger effects in Illinois (where the unemployment rate was high) than in Pennsylvania or Washington (where the unemployment rates were low). Second, within each state, better labor market conditions (lower unemployment rates in a local labor market) were associated with larger bonus impacts. We explain these two apparently conflicting observations by referring to the model and noting that a low job separation rate (s) and growing number of available jobs (F) are consistent with a low unemployment rate, but a high job separation rate (s) and a growing number of available jobs (F) are consistent with a large bonus impact. We speculate that the relatively large bonus effect in Illinois was due to the high (albeit falling) separation rate and growing availability of jobs during the Illinois experiment, which occurred during the most robust part of the expansion of the 1980s. Both the Pennsylvania and Washington experiments were conducted later in the expansion, when the separation rate would have been low and job growth relatively slow. Both conditions would be consistent with relatively small bonus effects. Also, we speculate that the inverse relation between the size of the bonus effect and the unemployment rate within each of the experiments is a result of variation in the availability of job vacancies across the experimental sites. That is, growth in the availability of jobs would be the main reason for the relatively large bonus effects that occurred in local areas where the unemployment rate was low.

Notes

1. In fact, crowding out could compromise the internal validity as well as the transferability of experimental results. In the bonus experiments, if the reemployment prospects of control group members were harmed by the increased search intensity of bonus-offered claimants, then the experimental results would overstate the effect of the bonus program. Because the number of bonus-offered claimants was small in relation to the labor markets in which bonus-offered workers were searching, and because there was no incentive for employers to hire bonus-offered claimants rather than other applicants, it seems unlikely that crowding out would have compromised the internal validity of the bonus experiments.

2. Learning effects and time-horizon effects, although related, are distinct. For example, an experiment could be long enough for participants to be convinced of the experiment's legitimacy, to understand the consequences of their behavior, and to have all the time needed to make adjustments. If their planning horizons exceed the experiment's duration, however, time-horizon problems could arise. Learning effects may also occur as a result of changes in the behavior of program administrators.

3. The model imposes three simplifying assumptions that need to be recognized. First, the total number of jobs available in the economy (or the demand for labor) is considered fixed; that is, there is no attempt to model employers' demand for labor. This could be an important shortcoming if a policy change could have a significant impact on labor demand. Second, the size of the labor force (L) is exogenous; that is, we do not model the labor force participation decision, although one could do so. Third, the wage rate is exogenous in the models we use below, although again one could endogenize the wage rate if thee were reasons for doing so. In an early version of the model, we did endogenize the wage in a bargaining framework (Davidson and Woodbury 1990).

4. There is also a third, relatively subtle effect: as the reemployment probabilities of workers who are not offered the bonus (or do not respond) change, their optimal search effort changes. As it becomes more difficult for the workers who are not offered the bonus (or do not respond) to find jobs, their search effort adjusts. We refer to this as the rivalry effect but do not discuss it in detail here because it turns out to be extremely small (see Davidson and Woodbury 2000).

5. With both take-up rates equal to 100 percent, the model is identical to the one used in Davidson and Woodbury (1993). The results reported in Table 6.2, column 1 are the same as in Table 2, column 4 of that paper.

6. Meyer (1995) also suggested three additional reasons for increased UI take-up in response to a bonus program. First, he wrote that voluntary job changers would claim UI benefits and prolong their jobless spells in order to receive the bonus (p. 109). However, since voluntary separations with reemployment within 3 months (the longest bonus qualification period that has been considered) are not eligible for UI, these workers would not be eligible for either UI or a bonus.

Second, Meyer was concerned about the significant number of dislocated workers who arrange a new job without an intervening spell of unemployment. The concern is that, with a bonus program, these workers would arrange for the new job to start a week or two after the old job ends, in order to receive a week of UI benefits and collect a bonus. This would be a clear abuse of the system because these workers could have obtained work earlier but chose not to. In effect, these workers would not satisfy the work-search test for UI—they would not be able, available, and searching for work—and hence should not be eligible for UI or a bonus.

Third, he wrote that firms would alter their temporary layoff behavior in response to implementation of a bonus (pp. 109–110). However, since recalled individuals would not receive a bonus by design, temporary layoff behavior would not be influenced by the presence of a bonus. (Meyer pointed out that about one-third of layoffs that start out as temporary end up as permanent, but the purpose of temporary layoff with recall is to keep the temporarily laid-off workers—workers with specific skills who the employer wants to rehire when demand recovers—from taking alternative employment. In cases where the employer's expectations were wrong, and the workers are not recalled, the bonus qualification period would have expired.)

The first two points above do raise issues of enforcement and fraud prevention. The existence of a bonus program would increase the importance of ensuring that workers who quit voluntarily did not receive benefits (and, possibly, a bonus). Also, the UI agency would need to verify that a worker who applied for a bonus had not arranged to delay a new job start so as to receive UI benefits and a bonus. Employers would generally be willing to cooperate in this kind of enforcement, since their payroll taxes are experience rates (that is, linked to the extent to which laid-off workers receive UI benefits). Clearly, these are real costs of administering a bonus program that require consideration.

7. This is consistent with existing evidence on take-up of UI. See, for example, Bland and Card (1991), Vroman (1991), and Anderson and Meyer (1994).

8. It is possible that some UI-eligible nonclaimants with an expected duration of unemployment of slightly longer than the qualification period might claim benefits and increase their job-search intensity in order to qualify for the bonus. This increased search intensity would imply an added real economic benefit of increased UI take-up, in return to the bonus expense. In contrast, it would make little sense for a UI-eligible nonclaimant with a long expected duration of unemployment (for example, a professional worker facing a low UI replacement rate) to become a claimant after adoption of a bonus program, since the bonus offer would not change the payoff to claiming UI benefits. (If the payoff to claiming were changed by the bonus offer and this worker did claim benefits, then the implication would be that the bonus offer would raise job-search intensity and have real economic benefits.)

9. There would be a social cost of the added transfers if the taxes levied to finance them distorted economic incentives in some way. The UI payroll tax may well

create such incentives (see, for example, the review by Topel 1990), but the amount of the transfers in question is not great in this case.

10. The estimate of 0.49 is similar to the proportion of bonus-offered workers in Illinois who found reemployment within 11 weeks and filed a Notice of Hire, which was 0.56 (Spiegelman and Woodbury 1987, Chapter 7). In Illinois, workers were asked to submit a Notice of Hire at the time of reemployment if they wanted to collect a bonus. The Notice of Hire was mainly a monitoring device that helped the experimenters to track the progress of the experiment and ensure that the bonus budget would not be exceeded. It also may have some behavioral content, however, as suggested by the correspondence between the proportion submitting a Notice of Hire and the estimated ρ.

11. The correspondence between workers who meet likely profiling criteria and dislocated workers is incomplete. In the model, dislocated workers are those who have lost high-wage jobs and have little expectation of returning to such jobs. Hence, they have long expected durations of unemployment and would meet most conceivable profiling criteria.

12. Nevertheless, Spiegelman, O'Leary, and Kline (1992) found no difference between the bonus responses of dislocated and nondislocated workers in the Washington Reemployment Bonus experiment.

13. For a full description of the model, see Davidson and Woodbury (2000).

14. Recall that the bonus offer can increase employment even though full employment (or the total number of available jobs, F) is fixed in the model. Because $F = V + J$ (total available jobs equal the sum of vacancies and jobs that are filled), inducements to search harder cause V to fall and J to rise.

15. By similar reasoning, workers who receive large weekly benefits and those who expect lower wages after reemployment would be expected to search less hard than workers who receive small weekly benefits or who face high wages after reemployment. Accordingly, the impacts of a bonus offer should increase with the weekly benefit amount and decrease with expected wages after reemployment.

Appendix: A Model for Transferring Experimental Results to an External Setting

This appendix provides a statement of the model that underlies the estimates given in Chapter 6. Following a discussion of our reasons for choosing the model we use, three sections offer a narrative development of the model. The final section is a full statement of the model's equations and notation.

The model we use is patterned after the "trade frictions" models of Diamond (1982), Mortensen (1982), and Pissarides (1984, 1990), among others. In such models, the number of contacts between workers and firms is determined by search effort, a matching (or search) technology, and equilibrium conditions stating that in steady state, the rate of job creation must equal the rate at which jobs break-up. In most models of this kind, job offers are never rejected (but see Diamond and Maskin [1979] for an exception).

The trade frictions approach we take contrasts with the approach to job search used more frequently in labor economics, in which unemployed workers choose a reservation wage and receive job offers that they are free to accept or reject. Job offers arrive randomly at an average rate (λ, say) and the wage offers come from a stationary cumulative distribution function $F(w)$. The rate of offer arrival and the distribution of wage offers are both exogenous, so that no attempt is made to model the firm's side of the labor market or to characterize the full labor market equilibrium. Because they consider only labor supply, models that rely on the reservation wage are commonly referred to as "partial-partial" models. In such models, unemployment is tied to the reservation wage and the rate of job rejection, whereas in the trade frictions approach, unemployment is determined by search effort and the matching technology.

We have two main reasons for choosing the trade frictions approach. First, it is relatively easy to incorporate institutional details of the UI system into a trade frictions model because this approach offers a natural way to model the progress of job search over time and to model changes in incentives that occur over the course of a spell of insured unemployment. The reemployment bonus and the UI system in which it is embedded both generate exogenous changes in search incentives that occur at discrete times during the unemployment spell, and it is essential that these be captured in our model. Atkinson et al. (1984) and Atkinson and Micklewright (1991) have also noted the difficulty of incorporating institutional detail in partial-partial models.

Second, it is very difficult to implement the partial-partial approach empirically because it places severe demands on our knowledge of the labor market—for example, knowledge of the wage-offer distribution, $F(w)$. In particular, quantitative predictions of partial-partial models are highly sensitive to the wage-offer distribution and other underlying parameters. (See Marshall and Zarkin [1987] for a discussion of the importance of distinguishing the unobservable wage-offer distribution from the observable wage distribution.) Although in the trade frictions approach, different assumptions about underlying parameters (both observable and unobservable) generate different quantitative predictions, we show below that it is possible to estimate the underlying unobservable parameters. We find that the model's implications are quite robust to variations in those parameters.

ASSUMPTIONS, DEFINITIONS, AND NOTATION

This section gives a description of the variables and notation included in the full model, focusing on its main features. In describing the model, we make frequent reference to Figures 6A.1 and 6A.2, which depict the groups of workers treated in the model and the labor market flows analyzed in the model.

We begin by dividing all workers into four classes:

1) Employed workers—denoted by J.
2) Unemployed UI-ineligible workers—U_i. This group (about 60 percent of unemployed workers) includes mainly new entrants and re-entrants to the labor force and workers who have too little work experience during the last year or so to make them eligible for UI. The group also includes workers who are ineligible for UI benefits because they voluntarily quit their previous job or were terminated for cause.
3) Unemployed UI-eligible nonclaimants—U_k. These job seekers are eligible for UI benefits but choose not to claim them. This group appears to have grown dramatically over the past 15 years, and it has been the subject of considerable research and debate (Blank and Card 1991; Vroman 1991).
4) Unemployed UI-eligible claimants—$U_{j,\,t}$ and $U_{j,\,x}$. Four groups of UI-eligible claimants are considered in the model (see the upper left quadrant of Figure 6A.1). First, there are UI eligibles who respond to the bonus offer by increasing their search intensity and qualify for the bonus by gaining reemployment within 11 weeks. We denote these responders who qualify for the bonus by $U_{r,\,t}$ ($t \leq 6$).[1] Second, there are UI-eligibles who fail to respond to the bonus offer (that is, do not increase search effort) but qualify for the bonus nonetheless by gaining reemployment within 11 weeks. We denote this group by $U_{nr,\,t}$ ($t \leq 6$). Third, there are UI eligibles who respond to the bonus but fail to qualify because they don't gain reemployment within 11 weeks. We denote this group by $U_{r,\,t}$ ($t > 6$). (A subcategory of this third group is made up of workers who

respond to the bonus but fail to qualify for the bonus and ultimately exhaust their UI benefits. We denote these workers by $U_{r,x}$.) Finally, there are UI eligibles who neither respond to the bonus offer nor find reemployment within 11 weeks, denoted by $U_{nr,\,t}$ ($t > 6$). (A subcategory of this last group is made up of workers who don't respond to the bonus and ultimately exhaust their UI benefits, denoted by $U_{nr,x}$.) The latter three categories of workers are depicted and summarized in Figure 6A.1.

Three issues relating to unemployed workers who are UI-eligible and claim their benefits (class 4 above) deserve further mention. First, note that all UI-eligible claimants are offered a cash bonus for rapid reemployment. To actually qualify for the bonus, a UI-eligible claimant must gain reemployment within 11 weeks of filing his or her UI claim. (In practice, a worker also needed to hold the job for four months in order to qualify for the bonus.)

Second, in modeling the reemployment bonus, we want to pay attention to two issues. The first is that the response to the reemployment bonus program was less than 100 percent, in that not all workers who were offered the bonus responded to the offer by increasing their search intensity. We denote the proportion of bonus-offered workers who did respond to the bonus offer by ρ; this *bonus response rate* cannot be observed, but can be solved for in the model. In Figure 6A.1, ρ equals the number of claimants in the upper two quadrants of UI-eligible claimants divided by all UI-eligible claimants. The second issue is

Figure 6A.1 Groups of Unemployed Workers Considered in the Model

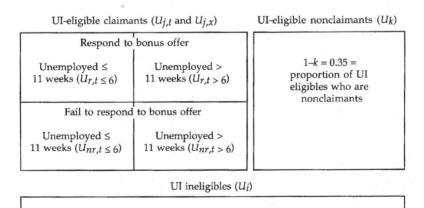

that not all workers who qualified for the bonus collected it. That is, the *bonus take-up rate* was less than 100 percent, as discussed in Chapter 3. We denote the bonus take-up rate, which can be observed, by τ, and set $\tau = 0.55$ based on the Illinois experiment (see Woodbury and Spiegelman 1987, Table 7). The parameter τ is not shown in Figure 6A.1, but equals the number of bonus recipients divided by the number of claimants in two left quadrants of UI-eligible claimants. (Note that it is possible for a worker to collect a bonus without responding to the bonus incentive.) As will be seen below, the ability to observe the bonus take-up rate allows us to identify the bonus response rate.

Third, workers who have exhausted their entitlement to UI benefits are an important subgroup of UI-eligibles. We use $U_{j,x}$ (where $j = r$ for workers who respond to the bonus and $j = nr$ for workers who fail to respond) to denote the number of eligible claimants with $t > 14$. That is, we assume that UI claimants exhaust their benefit entitlement after a continuous spell of 28 weeks (14 two-week periods) of unemployment.[2]

It is also important to remark further on UI-eligible nonclaimants (class 3 above). Blank and Card (1991) found that only 65 to 75 percent of the unemployed workers who are eligible for UI benefits actually claim those benefits; Vroman (1991) obtained an even lower estimate of about 55 percent. Accordingly, we use k to denote the *UI take-up rate* and set $k = 0.65$. Thus, we make the appropriate assumption that only 65 percent of all UI-eligible workers claim their UI benefits. Also, we assume that the search behavior of UI-eligible nonclaimants is unaffected by changes in UI policy, such as changes in benefit amounts or the introduction of a bonus. This should be a relatively uncontroversial assumption, since it is unlikely that a worker who fails to claim UI benefits would behave as if he or she were receiving a weekly benefit.

Finally, we assume that workers who do not collect bonuses for which they qualify behave as if they were never offered a bonus. This assumption is more questionable, since it is possible that a bonus-offered worker might increase search intensity with the intention of collecting a bonus but never follow through.

EQUATIONS OF THE MODEL

The model consists of five sets of equations: accounting identities, steady-state conditions, reemployment probabilities, expected lifetime income, and level of search effort. For reference, these equations are written out on pp. 216–219. Figure 6A.2 depicts the flows of workers through various labor market states that are modeled. Stocks of workers in different states are shown as rectangles and the arrows indicate the transition rates of workers from one state to another.

Figure 6A.2 Labor Market Flows in the Model

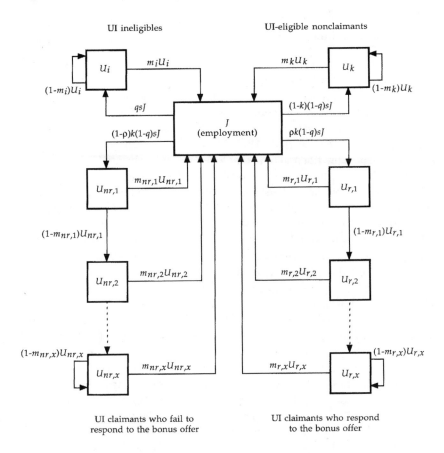

UI ineligibles

UI-eligible nonclaimants

UI claimants who fail to
respond to the bonus offer

UI claimants who respond
to the bonus offer

Accounting identities

Let F denote the total number of jobs available in the economy and let V represent the number of vacancies in the steady-state equilibrium. Since all jobs are either filled or vacant, the first identity is $F = J + V$ (Equation 1, p. 216). The second identity states that all workers must be either employed or unemployed. Letting L denote the total number of workers and U total unemployment, the second identity is $L = J + U$ (Equation 2). The third identity simply

· states that total unemployment equals the sum of the various subgroups of unemployed (Equation 3).

Steady-state conditions

The steady-state equations (p. 216) equate the flows into and out of each employment state. If these equations are satisfied, then total unemployment and its composition remain constant over time. For example, consider the flow of workers into state U_i—UI-ineligible unemployment. We use s to denote the *separation rate*—the fraction of jobs from which workers separate (voluntarily or involuntarily) in each period. Thus, sJ workers lose their job in each period. If we let q denote the fraction of unemployed workers who are UI-ineligible ($q = 0.65$), then qsJ is the flow of workers into UI-ineligible unemployment, and $(1 - q)sJ$ is the flow of workers into UI-eligible unemployment. (This latter group is divided into UI-eligible nonclaimants, UI claimants who respond to the bonus offer, and UI claimants who fail to respond to the bonus offer.) To calculate the flow out of UI-ineligibility (state U_i), let m_i denote the reemployment probability for any UI-ineligible worker. Then $m_i U_i$ unemployed UI-ineligible workers find jobs in any given period, and this represents the flow out of state U_i. In a steady-state equilibrium, U_i must remain constant over time. Therefore, we must have $qsJ = m_i U_i$ (Equation 4).

Consider next the three groups of UI-eligible workers. Again, the total flow of workers into UI-eligible unemployment is $(1 - q)sJ$. Since the proportion of UI-eligibles who claim benefits equals k, the proportion of UI-eligibles who do not claim benefits equals $1 - k$. Accordingly, the flow of workers into UI-eligible nonclaimant status (state U_k) is $(1 - k)(1 - q)sJ$ (see again Figure 6A.2). This flow must equal the flow of workers out of state U_k. Since the reemployment probability of UI-eligible nonclaimants is m_k, the flow out of U_k equals $m_k U_k$, and the steady-state condition is $(1 - k)(1 - q)sJ = m_k U_k$ (Equation 5).

Next, some UI claimants (a proportion ρ) respond to the bonus, whereas others $(1 - \rho)$ do not. As a result, the number of newly unemployed workers who respond to the bonus each period is $(1 - \rho)k(1 - q)sJ$, and the number of newly unemployed workers who do not respond to the bonus is $\rho k(1 - q)sJ$. These are the flows into states $U_{r,1}$ and $U_{nr,1}$. In steady-state, all workers in states $U_{r,1}$ and $U_{nr,1}$ at the beginning of a period flow out by the end of the period. Workers in state $U_{r,1}$ flow either back to J or into $U_{r,2}$, and workers in state $U_{nr,1}$ flow into either back to J or into $U_{nr,2}$. Hence, the flow out of $U_{r,1}$ in each period $[m_{r,1}U_{r,1} + (1 - m_{r,1})U_{r,1}]$ equals $U_{r,1}$, and the flow out of $U_{nr,1}$ in each period $[m_{nr,1}U_{nr,1} + (1 - m_{nr,1})U_{nr,1}]$ equals $U_{nr,1}$. It follows that the steady-state conditions for these two states are $(1 - \rho)k(1 - q)sJ = U_{r,1}$ and $\rho k \times (1 - q)sJ = U_{nr,1}$ (Equations 6 and 7).

The last two steady-state equations (8 and 9) are the analogous steady-state equations for all of the remaining states of unemployment.

Reemployment probabilities

Equations 10 through 14 define the probability of reemployment for any given unemployed worker as a function of the search intensity of both the given worker and all other workers, and the number of vacancies. We denote the reemployment probabilities by m (for match probability, with appropriate subscripts). Each reemployment probability is in turn a product of three other probabilities: the probability of a worker contacting a firm (this is the worker's job-search intensity), the probability that a contacted firm has a job vacancy, and the probability that the worker gets a job offer, conditional on applying to a firm that has a vacancy. For example, let p_k denote the probability that a UI-eligible nonclaimant contacts a firm in the tth period of search (or the number of firms contacted, if $p_k > 1$). (The terms $p_{j,t}$ and p_i refer to similar probabilities of UI-eligible claimants [with $j = r$ for claimants who respond to the bonus and $j = nr$ for claimants who fail to respond to the bonus] and UI-ineligibles, respectively.) Again, these contact probabilities are a measure of a worker's search intensity. Next, assuming that workers choose firms at random, the probability that any given firm has a vacancy is V/T. Finally, if we let λ denote the average number of applications filed per firm, then the probability that a worker gets a job conditional on applying at a firm with a vacancy is $(1 - e^{-\lambda})/\lambda$ (see Davidson and Woodbury 1993 for details). So the probability of an unemployed UI-eligible claimant in the tth period of search finding a job is given by the product $m_{j,t} = p_{j,t}(V/T)[(1 - e^{-\lambda}/\lambda)]$. There is an analogous reemployment probability equation for each state of unemployment (Equations 10 through 14).

The probability of reemployment increases with search effort, but increasing search effort is costly. We assume that the cost of search effort is given by a cost function—cp^z—where z (> 1) and c are search cost parameters. More precisely, z denotes the elasticity of search costs with respect to search effort and c is a constant that transforms the number of firm contacts (p) into cost units. The form of the cost function implies that search cost increases with search intensity at an increasing rate. We assume that c differs between UI-eligible and UI-ineligible workers but that z is the same for all groups of workers.

Expected lifetime income and level of search effort

The fourth and fifth sets of equations are used to calculate the optimal search effort of unemployed workers. In Equations 15 through 22, we calculate the expected lifetime income of workers in each possible state of unemployment

214

and employment. Then, in Equations 23 through 26, we calculate the level of search effort that maximizes these expected lifetime incomes.

Expected lifetime income is calculated by considering both the current and future prospects faced by the worker. For example, let $V_{r,t}$ denote the expected lifetime income for a UI claimant (one who responds to the bonus) in the tth period of unemployment, V_w denote the expected lifetime income for an employed UI-eligible worker, w the wage, B the bonus amount, and x the per-period UI benefit. This UI claimant in the tth period of search receives $x - c(p_{r,t})z$ (that is, UI benefits less the cost of search). With probability $m_{r,t}$ this worker finds a job and can expect to earn $V_{r,w}$ in the future, and if $t < 6$, this worker may also collect a bonus. With probability $1 - m_{r,t}$ the worker remains unemployed and can expect to earn $V_{r,t} + 1$ in the future. Therefore,

$$V_{r,t} = x - c(p_{r,t})^z + [m_{r,t}(V_{r,w} + B) + (1 - m_{r,t})V_{r,t} + 1]/(1 + r).$$

Note that future income is discounted at interest rate r. For $t > 6$, $V_{r,t}$ takes the same form as above, except that the worker cannot collect a bonus upon finding a job. An analogous condition describes the expected lifetime income for workers in every other state of unemployment and employment (again, see Equations 15 through 22).

Finally, for each unemployed worker, search effort is chosen to maximize expected lifetime income. Therefore, there is an equation defining optimal search effort for each possible state of unemployment, with one exception. The exception is for UI-eligible nonclaimants. The most likely reason that some UI-eligible workers do not file for UI benefits is that they do not expect to be unemployed for a significant length of time—that is, they expect to be able to find jobs relatively easily and with little effort. For these workers, the cost of claiming benefits may well outweigh the value of the benefits that would be received. Therefore, we treat these workers differently, assigning them high reemployment probabilities and ignoring their search decision. Provided that their reemployment probabilities are set high enough (so that their expected duration of unemployment is roughly half the expected duration faced by UI-eligible claimants), our results are not sensitive to the assumption that their reemployment probability is high.[3]

MODEL SOLUTION

To examine the impact of the reemployment bonus program on groups of workers other than those offered the bonus, we first solve the model with the bonus amount set to zero ($B = 0$), then solve it again with the bonus amount set to $500 ($B = 500$), and compare the results. In solving the model, we make use of the data that were gathered for the Illinois reemployment bonus experiment for as many of the model's variables and parameters as possible and use secondary data sources where necessary (for a discussion, see Davidson and Woodbury 2000). Also, we use the behavioral responses that were observed to the Illinois reemployment bonus in calibrating the model. The Illinois experiment was used to calibrate the model because the treatment impacts for FSC-ineligible workers were essentially similar to the average impacts in the Pennsylvania and Washington experiments (Davidson and Woodbury 1996). The details of this approach to solving the model follow.

The key endogenous variables in the model are employment (J), the number of each type of unemployed worker in each state of unemployment (the U terms), the reemployment probabilities for unemployed workers in each state of unemployment (the m terms), the search effort of unemployed workers in each state of unemployment (the p terms), and the proportion of UI-eligible claimants who respond to the bonus (ρ). The key parameters are the wage (w), the interest rate (r), the size of the bonus (B), the level of unemployment benefits (x), total jobs available (F), the total number of workers (L), the job separation rate (s), the fraction of unemployed workers who are ineligible for UI benefits (q), the UI take-up rate (k), and the search cost parameters (z and c). Except for the search cost parameters, estimates of all of these parameters can be obtained either from the data collected to analyze the Illinois experiment or from other sources.

To obtain estimates of the search cost parameters, we follow the procedure developed in earlier work (Davidson and Woodbury 1993). First, we note that in the absence of a reemployment bonus, the expected duration of unemployment for UI claimants was 22.4 weeks (this was the average unemployment duration for the control group in the Illinois experiment). We then arbitrarily choose a value of z and solve the model to find the value of c that is consistent with the model predicting the expected duration of unemployment (22.4 weeks) that was observed for UI claimants who were not offered a reemployment bonus (that is, for whom $B = 0$). This gives us a pair (z,c) for every z. Next, we solve the model again, but with $B = 500$ (the Illinois bonus offer) for each (z,c) pair and observe the reduction in the expected duration of unemployment for UI claimants that is predicted by the model. We then choose the pair (z,c) that generates a prediction that is consistent with the outcome observed in the Illinois experiment.[4]

The model developed and used here resembles models we have used previously to examine the crowding-out effects of reemployment bonuses and effects of wage-rate subsidies paid to dislocated workers (Davidson and Woodbury 1993, 2000). Two extensions are embodied in the model used here. First, the introduction of additional groups of workers, such as UI-eligible nonclaimants and UI claimants who fail to respond to the bonus offer, allows us to

216

consider spillover effects, classification changes, behavioral changes, and scale effects that could not be considered in a simpler model. Second, introducing the UI take-up rate (k) and the bonus take-up rate (τ) allows us to make appropriate assumptions about these rates, both of which are less than 100 percent. We show on pp. 195–203 that these extensions lead to markedly different predictions about the outcomes of adopting a reemployment bonus program. The introduction of τ is especially useful, because it allows us to identify the proportion of bonus-offered workers who responded to the bonus by increasing their search effort (ρ), which cannot be observed directly.

COMPLETE STATEMENT OF THE MODEL

Identities

(1) $F = J + V$

(2) $L = J + U$

(3) $U = \Sigma_{j=r,nr}\Sigma_{t=1,14}U_{j,t} + U_{r,x} + U_{nr,x} + U_k + U_i$

Steady-State Conditions

(4) $qsJ = m_iU_i$

(5) $(1-k)(1-q)sJ = m_kU_k$

(6) $\rho k(1-q)sJ = U_{r,1}$

(7) $(1-\rho)k(1-q)sJ = U_{nr,1}$

(8) $(1-m_{j,t-1})U_{j,t-1} = U_{j,t}$ for $j = r,nr$ $(t = 2, \ldots, 14)$

(9) $(1-m_{j,14})U_{j,14} = m_{j,x}U_{j,x}$ for $j = r,nr$

Reemployment Probabilities

(10) $m_i = p_i(V/F)[(1-e^{-\lambda})/\lambda]$

(11) $m_k = p_k(V/F)[(1-e^{-\lambda})/\lambda]$

(12) $m_{j,t} = p_{j,t}(V/F)[(1-e^{-\lambda})/\lambda]$ for $j = r,nr$ $(t = 2, \ldots, 14)$

(13) $m_{j,x} = p_{j,x}(V/F)[(1-e^{-\lambda})/\lambda]$ for $j = r,nr$

(14) $\lambda = (1/F)[p_iU_i + p_kU_k + \Sigma_{j=r,nr}\Sigma_{t=1,14}\, p_{j,t}U_{j,t} + p_{r,x}U_{r,x} + p_{nr,x}U_{nr,x}]$

Expected Lifetime Utility

(15) $V_i = -c_i(p_i)z + [m_iV_{i,w} + (1 - m_i)V_i]/(1 + r)$

(16) $V_{r,t} = x - c(p_{r,t})^z + [m_{r,t}(V_{r,w} + B) + (1 - m_{r,t})V_{r,t+1}]/(1 + r)$ for $t = 1, \ldots, 6$

(17) $V_{r,t} = x - c(p_{r,t})^z + [m_{r,t}V_{r,w} + (1 - m_{r,t})V_{r,t+1}]/(1 + r)$ for $t = 7, \ldots, 13$

(18) $V_{nr,t} = x - c(p_{nr,t})^z + [m_{nr,t}V_{nr,w} + (1 - m_{nr,t})V_{nr,t+1}]/(1 + r)$ for $t = 1, \ldots, 13$

(19) $V_{j,14} = x - c(p_{j,14})^z + [m_{j,14}V_{j,w} + (1 - m_{j,14})V_{j,x}]/(1 + r)$ for $j = r,nr$

(20) $V_{j,x} = -c(p_{j,x})^z + [m_{j,x}V_{j,w} + (1 - m_{j,x})V_{j,x}]/(1 + r)$ for $j = r,nr$

(21) $V_{i,w} = w + [sV_i + (1 - s)V_{i,w}]/(1 + r)$

(22) $V_{j,w} = w + [sV_{j,1} + (1 - s)V_{j,w}]/(1 + r)$ for $j = r,nr$

Optimal Search Effort

(23) $p_i = \arg\max V_i$

(24) $p_{j,t} = \arg\max V_{j,t}$ for $j = r,nr$ ($t = 1, \ldots, 14$)

(25) $p_{j,x} = \arg\max V_{j,x}$ for $j = r,nr$

(26) $p_k = p_{nr,x}$

Observed Bonus Take-Up Rate

(27) $\tau = \Sigma_{t=1,6}m_{r,t}U_{r,t} / [\Sigma_{t=1,6}m_{r,t}U_{r,t} + \Sigma_{t=1,6}m_{nr,t}U_{nr,t}]$

Summary of Notation

L = the size of the labor force

J = steady-state employment

U = steady-state unemployment

V = steady-state job vacancies

F = the total number of jobs available

subscripts: r = UI-eligible claimants who respond to the bonus

nr = UI-eligible claimants who do not respond to the bonus

x = UI-eligible claimants who have exhausted their benefits

i = UI-ineligible unemployed workers

k = UI-eligible nonclaimants

t = the period of search

w = employed workers

U_i = the number of UI-ineligible workers seeking employment

U_k = the number of UI-eligible non-claimants seeking employment

$U_{j,t}$ = the number of type j UI-eligible workers in their tth period of search $(j = r,nr)$

$U_{j,x}$ = the number of type j UI-eligible workers who have exhausted their UI benefits $(j = r,nr)$

q = the proportion of unemployed workers who are ineligible for UI

s = the job-separation rate

k = the proportion of UI-eligible workers who claim their benefits (that is, participate in the UI program)

ρ = the proportion of UI-eligible claimants who respond to the bonus

m_i = the reemployment probability for UI-ineligible workers

m_k = the reemployment probability for UI-eligible nonclaimants

$m_{j,t}$ = the reemployment probability for a type j UI-eligible claimant in the tth period of search $(j = r,nr)$

$m_{j,x}$ = the reemployment probability for a type j UI-eligible claimant who has exhausted UI benefits $(j = r,nr)$

λ = the average number of job applications received per firm

p_i = the search intensity of UI-ineligible workers (that is, the probability that a UI-ineligible worker contacts a firm, or if greater than 1, the number of firms contacted)

p_k = the search intensity of UI-eligible nonclaimants

$p_{j,t}$ = the search intensity of a type j UI-eligible claimant in the tth period of search $(j = r,nr)$

$p_{j,x}$ = the search intensity of a type j UI-eligible claimant who has exhausted UI benefits $(j = r,nr)$

V_i = expected lifetime utility of a UI-ineligible unemployed worker

$V_{j,t}$ = expected lifetime utility of a type j UI-eligible claimant in the tth period of search $(j = r,nr)$

$V_{j,x}$ = expected lifetime utility of a type j UI-eligible claimant who has exhausted UI benefits $(j = r,nr)$

$V_{j,w}$ = expected lifetime utility of an employed type j UI-eligible worker $(j = r,nr)$

$V_{i,w}$ = expected lifetime utility of an employed UI-ineligible worker

x = UI benefit per period

c, c_i = search cost parameters

z = the elasticity of search costs with respect to search effort

r = the interest rate

B = the reemployment bonus amount

w = the wage

τ = the observed bonus take-up rate (that is, of UI claimants who qualify for the reemployment bonus, the proportion who actually collect it)

Appendix Notes

1. In the model, a worker qualifies for bonus if $t \leq 6$, because we measure time in two-week intervals.
2. The assumption of continuous unemployment is not wholly correct because about 10 percent of UI recipients experience multiple spells of unemployment in a benefit year. Nevertheless, a single spell of unemployment characterizes most of the insured unemployed, so we maintain the assumption.
3. In other words, a lower reemployment probability could be assigned without substantially changing the results. The main point is that these workers don't respond to the reemployment bonus offer, so the bonus program raises employment by less than it would otherwise.
4. A different procedure was used to estimate c_i the cost parameter for UI-ineligibles because the expected duration for UI-ineligibles is not observable. See Davidson and Woodbury (1993, pp. 587–588) for details.

References

Aigner, Dennis J. 1985. "The Residential Electricity Time-of-Use Pricing Experiments: What Have We Learned?" In *Social Experimentation*, Jerry A. Hausman and David A. Wise, eds. Chicago, Illinois: University of Chicago Press and National Bureau of Economic Research, pp. 11–53.

Anderson, Patricia M., and Bruce D. Meyer. 1994. "Unemployment Insurance Benefits and Take-up Rates." Working paper no. 4787, National Bureau of Economic Research, Cambridge, Massachusetts.

Atkinson, Anthony B., and John Micklewright. 1991. "Unemployment Compensation and Labour Market Transitions: A Critical Review." *Journal of Economic Literature* 29(December): 1679–1727.

Atkinson, A.B., J. Gomulka, J. Micklewright, and N. Rau. 1984. "Unemployment Benefit, Duration, and Incentives in Britain: How Robust Is the Evidence?" *Journal of Public Economics* 23: 3–26.

Blank, Rebecca M., and David E. Card. 1991. "Recent Trends in Insured and Uninsured Unemployment: Is There an Explanation?" *Quarterly Journal of Economics* 106(November): 1157–1189.

Davidson, Carl, and Stephen A. Woodbury. 1990. "The Displacement Effect of Reemployment Bonus Programs." Working paper 90-02, W.E. Upjohn Institute for Employment Research, Kalamazoo, Michigan.

Davidson, Carl, and Stephen A. Woodbury. 1991. "Effects of a Reemployment Bonus under Differing Benefit Entitlements, or Why the Illinois Experiment Worked." Manuscript, Department of Economics, Michigan

State University and W.E. Upjohn Institute for Employment Research, Kalamazoo, Michigan.

Davidson, Carl, and Stephen A. Woodbury. 1993. "The Displacement Effect of Reemployment Bonus Programs." *Journal of Labor Economics* 11(October): 575–605.

Davidson, Carl, and Stephen A. Woodbury. 1996. "Unemployment Insurance and Unemployment: Implications of the Reemployment Bonus Experiments." Working paper 96-44, W.E. Upjohn Institute for Employment Research, Kalamazoo, Michigan.

Davidson, Carl, and Stephen A. Woodbury. 2000. "Wage Subsidies for Dislocated Workers." *Research in Employment Policy* 2: 141–184.

Diamond, Peter A. 1982. "Wage Determination and Efficiency in Search Equilibrium." *Review of Economic Studies* 49(April): 217–228.

Diamond, Peter A., and Eric Maskin. 1979. "An Equilibrium Analysis of Search and Breach of Contract, I: Steady States." *Bell Journal of Economics* 10(Spring): 282–316.

Garfinkel, Irwin, Charles F. Manski, and Charles Michalopoulos. 1992. "Micro Experiments and Macro Effects." In *Evaluating Welfare and Training Programs*, Charles F. Manski and Irwin Garfinkel, eds. Cambridge, Massachusetts: Harvard University Press, pp. 253–273.

Heckman, James J., and Jeffrey A. Smith. 1995. "Understanding Participation in the JTPA System: Evidence on Cream-Skimming." Chapter 8 of "Performance Standards in a Government Bureaucracy: Analytic Essays on the JTPA Performance Standards System." Manuscript, Department of Economics, University of Chicago.

Marshall, Robert C., and Gary A. Zarkin. 1987. "The Effect of Job Tenure on Wage Offers." *Journal of Labor Economics* 5(July): 301–324.

Meyer, Bruce D. 1995. "Lessons from the U.S. Unemployment Insurance Experiments." *Journal of Economic Literature* 33(March): 93–131.

Moffitt, Robert. 1992a. "Evaluation Methods for Program Entry Effects." In *Evaluating Welfare and Training Programs*, Charles F. Manski and Irwin Garfinkel, eds. Cambridge, Massachusetts: Harvard University Press, pp. 231–252.

Moffitt, Robert. 1992b. "Incentive Effects of the U.S. Welfare System." *Journal of Economic Literature* 30(March): 1–61.

Mortensen, Dale T. 1982. "Property Rights and Efficiency in Mating, Racing, and Related Games." *American Economic Review* 72: 968–979.

Pissarides, Christopher. 1984. "Efficient Job Rejection." *Economic Journal* 94(Supplement): 97–108.

Pissarides, Christopher. 1990. *Equilibrium Unemployment Theory*. Oxford: Basil Blackwell.

222

Spiegelman, Robert G., Christopher J. O'Leary, and Kenneth J. Kline. 1992. *The Washington Reemployment Bonus Experiment: Final Report.* Unemployment Insurance Occasional Paper 92-6, Washington, D.C.: U.S. Department of Labor, Employment and Training Administration, Unemployment Insurance Service.

Spiegelman, Robert G., and Stephen A. Woodbury. 1987. *The Illinois Unemployment Insurance Incentive Experiments.* Final report to the Illinois Department of Employment Security. Kalamazoo, Michigan: W.E. Upjohn Institute for Employment Research.

Spiegelman, Robert G., and Stephen A. Woodbury. 1990. "Controlled Experiments and the Unemployment Insurance System." In *Unemployment Insurance: The Second Half-Century*, W. Lee Hansen and James F. Byers, eds. Madison, Wisconsin: University of Wisconsin Press, pp. 355–392.

Topel, Robert. 1990. "Financing Unemployment Insurance: History, Incentives, and Reform." In *Unemployment Insurance: The Second Half-Century*, W. Lee Hansen and James F. Byers, eds. Madison, Wisconsin: University of Wisconsin Press, pp. 108–135.

Vroman, Wayne. 1991. *The Decline in Unemployment Insurance Claims Activity in the 1980s.* Unemployment Insurance Occasional Paper 91-2, Washington, D.C.: U.S. Department of Labor, Employment and Training Administration, Unemployment Insurance Service.

Woodbury, Stephen A., and Robert G. Spiegelman. 1987. "Bonuses to Workers and Employers to Reduce Unemployment: Randomized Trials in Illinois." *American Economic Review* 77(September): 513–530.

7

A Benefit-Cost Analysis
of a Bonus Offer Program

Robert G. Spiegelman

INTRODUCTION AND METHODOLOGY

An experiment is run at considerable expense for the purpose of providing information to guide the government in decisions to launch or modify programs. A major advantage of an experiment is that, despite its expense, it is much cheaper than the alternative of inaugurating an expensive program and then discovering that it doesn't work. The second advantage is that an experiment can generate more reliable estimates of program effect than other modes of analysis. To provide policy guidance, the effects of an experiment must be translated into an estimate of the benefits that can be expected to accrue to a program that replicates these experiments.

The process of assessing the positive and negative effects of a program is called benefit-cost analysis (BCA) and involves adding up benefits and costs and providing a present value estimate of the difference, called net benefits. It can be said with some assurance that no program should be launched that doesn't generate net benefits (i.e., net positive effects). However, this statement is not as simple as it seems, since the answer as to whether or not a program generates net benefits depends upon the perspective of the interested party. A benefit to one group may be a cost to another, and neither a benefit nor a cost to a third group. Thus, it will be necessary to compute net benefits from several perspectives.

For an unemployment insurance (UI) bonus offer program, there are five decision-making groups that one should consider: society as a whole, government as a whole, employers, claimants, and the UI system. The ultimate test of a program should be whether or not the program generates net benefits to society as a whole. According to the "Kaldor compensation criteria" as defined in Kaldor (1939), any project that generates positive net benefits to society should be undertaken, since winners (those obtaining the benefits) can pay off losers (those bearing the costs) and leave a net surplus. Since society is concerned about the distribution of income as well as its total size, it is probably unjustified to ignore distributional effects in the calculation of social benefits (see Okun 1981, p. 276). However, we have no basis for explicitly assigning monetary values to distributional changes. At a minimum it may be stated that no program should be undertaken that doesn't meet the criteria of generating net benefits to society.

Within society, the groups most directly affected by a bonus offer are employers and claimants. In an important sense the employer group is represented by the UI Trust Fund, and a program that benefits the trust fund (i.e., results in lower payments out of the fund) is beneficial to employers. Claimants need not be separately considered either. Because the program is totally voluntary, it may be assumed that claimants would not participate unless they perceived a net benefit.

Government as a whole, and the UI system in particular, are the agencies that must implement the program, and they will not do so unless there are net benefits from their perspective. Government is a net beneficiary if the program generates directly or indirectly more revenues than costs. The UI system is the front line agency. The ostensible purpose of a bonus offer program is to reduce the amount of insured unemployment. From the perspective of the UI system, a net benefit arises if the reduction in UI compensation payments exceeds direct costs of the program. If it does not directly benefit from the program, but the government as a whole does, then a transfer of funds among government agencies can be carried out.

The essential structure of benefit-cost analysis from the perspectives of society, government, and the UI system is described more fully in the sections to follow.

Society

For there to be net benefit to society as a whole, there must be an increase in real income greater than the real costs incurred to produce that income. Net benefits to society is the sum of all benefits and costs to the individuals who comprise the society. As shown in Table 7.1,

Table 7.1 Reemployment Bonus Benefits and Costs by Perspective

Parameter	Society	Government	UI Trust Fund
Increased output	+		
Value of home time lost	−		
Increased tax receipts		+	
Decreased UI benefit payments		+	+
Bonus payments		−	−
UI administrative costs	−	−	−

real gains to society occur due to increases in the value of output, best represented in this program by the increases in earnings of those responding to the bonus offer by obtaining jobs more quickly.

The real gains, however, are only the net increase in earnings. The additional income due to the more rapid reemployment of participating claimants may be considered the gross increase. To calculate net increase, several deductions should be made. These include loss in wages due to poorer paying jobs (if any), lost income due to displacement of nonparticipants, and any loss in earnings due to entry effects (such loss will only occur if the entry effect results in workers leaving jobs earlier than they otherwise would). In addition, many economists would claim that the benefits to the individual who returns to work more quickly are less than the additional income by the value of the home time that is foregone (see Gordon 1973, pp. 133–206). This issue is discussed further below.

The societal costs are the costs of administering the program. These are the only costs that represent utilization of real resources in the first round. Leaving aside the direct benefits or costs of distributional changes, transfer payments (such as UI compensation and bonus payments) net out to zero in the first round, since they are benefits to one group of members (transfer recipients) and costs to another group (taxpayers). However, the second round effects of additional transfer payments may not be so benign. It is argued by many that increasing government size has deleterious effects on real income. If the net benefits to government are negative, this implies a shift in resources from taxpayers to transfer recipients. Such a transfer would have income consequences—which might be positive or negative—that shouldn't be ignored. In this analysis, second round effects are ignored, because the bonuses are small relative to total UI payments, and most program options considered here have benefit/cost ratios for the government as a whole close to 1.

Government

Government as a total, not distinguishing either the level of government or any of its functions, represents the whole public body that collects taxes and dispenses public services. Any income taxes generated as a result of additional earnings represents a benefit to government. Any reductions in transfer payments from any of its insurance or welfare programs that result directly or indirectly from increased employment of constituents are also benefits. Thus, a reduction in UI compensation paid is a direct benefit to government. Costs to the government include any costs directly or indirectly associated with government programs that must increase because of the bonus offer. Thus, bonus payments are a direct cost, as is the cost of administering the bonus offer program.

The UI System

We are concerned about the net benefits to the UI system, because it is the agency of the government that would administer the bonus offer program. If such a program does not generate net benefits to this agency, then the program would not be implemented, regardless of its benefits to larger entities, without a conscious transfer of resources. Although the experimental bonus payments were not made from the UI funds, it is logical to assume that bonuses would be paid from the UI Trust Fund in a regular bonus offer program. Thus, costs to the UI system are bonus payments and administrative costs, while benefits are the savings in UI compensation payments to claimants.

IDENTIFICATION OF BENEFITS FOR A UI BONUS OFFER PROGRAM

As previously stated, benefits are defined in terms of the decision-maker's perspective. Under a UI bonus program, increases in output (or real income) are benefits to society. Increased tax revenues represent benefits to government, and reductions in UI compensation payments are benefits to the UI system and government as a whole. Each of these benefits are described in the following sections.

Output (Earnings)

For a bonus offer program, increases in earnings of those responding to the bonus offer represent increases in output, if there are no offsetting losses in output from displacement or entry effects. These earnings changes are a result of net increases in employment that derive from the more rapid return to work, adjusted for any changes in wage rates.

For the bonus experiments, earnings change has two components. The first component is a short-run increase in earnings due to more rapid reemployment after filing for UI benefits. The second component represents earning changes over a longer period of time due to the new job. If earnings on the new (post-unemployment) job differ from earnings on the pre-unemployment job, then there is a change in the rate of earnings that might be attributable to the bonus. These earnings changes are attributed to the experimental treatment if the post-unemployment wages of bonus-offered claimants and controls differ. As discussed in Chapter 5, if job search had been optimal prior to the bonus offer, then taking jobs more quickly could imply taking less satisfactory jobs. This would be expected to show up in participants taking jobs paying lower wages than those being paid to control group members. The overriding evidence presented in Chapter 5 is that the experimental subjects did not take lower paying jobs.

For there to be positive societal benefits from a bonus program, it is essential that there be net positive effects on earnings, since earnings is our measure of societal output. The results of the experiment, as shown in Chapter 5, however, do not encourage us to expect such positive effects. Table 5.3 shows that none of the Pennsylvania or Washington programs have impacts on earnings that are statistically significant. Only the single Illinois treatment shows statistically significant positive impacts on earnings. Nevertheless, we make estimates of net benefits utilizing the expected value of the impacts, and six of the 10 Pennsylvania and Washington treatment groups have an estimated impact on earnings that is positive.

Reduction in benefits due to entry effects, displacement, or lost value of home activity are outside of the experimentally induced effects and are introduced here in the form of sensitivity tests to show the effects of including reasonable estimates of values of these parameters in the calculation.

Tax Revenues

Any increases in earned income as a result of the bonus offer can be expected to generate increases in tax revenues collected by federal, state, or local governments. These revenues are general to the governmental level and do not automatically accrue to any particular agency, unless they are user fees, which are not considered in this study. No effort is made in this study to precisely estimate income tax burdens, and no estimate is made of other tax payments that may indirectly result from high earnings, such as sales taxes. Most of the bonus recipients would be expected to be in the low (15 percent) federal tax bracket. Adding 7.65 percent for FICA and a small amount for state taxes brings the estimated tax return to about 25 percent of the marginal increase in earned income.

Change in UI Compensation

A direct effect of the bonus offer is to reduce UI compensation that results from the earlier termination of benefit receipts by participating claimants. These estimates are directly measured by differences in UI compensation to experimentals and controls, as described in Chapter 4. Remember, these estimates are for changes in compensation averaged over the entire assigned population; they are not confined to the population of respondents or claimants who collect bonuses. There are several estimates of this difference. For the BCA, we chose to use the adjusted means calculations for Table 4.2 in Chapter 4 to estimate UI compensation savings in the programs modeled directly on the experimental treatments.

IDENTIFICATION OF COSTS FOR
A UI BONUS OFFER PROGRAM

The same issues of identification and association exist for costs as for benefits. Social costs accrue if real resources are used. To the extent that bonus payments exceed the savings in UI compensation payments, there are transfers of resources from taxpayers or lenders to bonus recipients. Distributional effects aside, these do not represent first-round social costs. They would represent costs in future rounds if the redistribution of income resulted in lower real product. Only the costs incurred to administer the program utilize resources in the first round, and thereby represent first-round costs from all three perspectives. If there were more substantial distributional costs, their effects on real output in subsequent rounds would need to be addressed.

Since displacement of nonparticipants (see Chapter 6) reduces the earnings accruing to society, they must be considered a cost, offsetting part (or all) of the benefits derived from additional earnings of participants. In addition, any entry effects of the bonus offer generate additional bonus payments and additional payment of UI compensation, and they therefore represent additional costs to the UI system and the government. Entry effects generate social costs only if the greater use of the UI system is accompanied by a decrease in earned income.

Lastly, the loss of value of home activity needs to be considered. Robert Gordon carefully considered this issue in the context of estimating the revenue costs from job refusal. He estimated the ratio of value of home time to previous after tax wage to be 0.206 (Gordon 1973, Table A-1). This is equivalent to about 15 percent of pretax earnings. In calculating net benefits to society, earnings gains will be offset by the estimated value of lost home time that will occur because of the more rapid reemployment of program participants.

Administrative Costs

The relevant costs are those of an anticipated ongoing program, not the costs of running the experiment or the costs of starting up a new program. Administering the experiment had high costs associated with the research and with an effort to telescope learning time for claimants to bring their program knowledge up to a point roughly equivalent to that which could be expected in an ongoing program two to three years after start-up. The 5- to 10-minute enrollment interviews were several times longer than would be expected in an ongoing program. The additional time was used to assure that the claimants received and processed the information about the program. For instance, a single-page information sheet was given to the claimant, then read to the claimant by the interviewer, who then asked the claimant several questions to guarantee comprehension. In a real program, the interviewer might simply mention the bonus, hand the claimant the explanatory sheet, and tell the claimant to be sure to read it. Administrators in Washington estimate that two minutes per interview would be sufficient. The central staff devoted to the bonus offer would be considerably smaller than that used to operate the experimental program. It might consist of an administrator and one or two assistants, whose time would be taken in processing and auditing bonus claims, assuring that information sheets are available to the local offices, and occasionally training interviewers. Other costs include the costs of communicating disallowances to claimants and operating an appeals process. The estimates of staffing and costs to administer a simple bonus offer program are quite small, totaling only $3 in 1988 dollars, based on estimates made by the staff of the Department of Human Services in the state of Washington (Table 9-3 in Spiegelman, O'Leary, and Kline 1992)[1] and reproduced as Appendix Table 7A.1 herein. The table shows in detail the derivation of the cost estimates.

Bonus Payments

For the cost calculation, bonus payments are averaged over the total experimental population, just as is the change in UI compensation. Thus, if 10 percent of the eligible claimants each are paid a $500 bonus, the average cost of the bonus is $50 per claimant. Chapter 3 provides estimates of the proportion of the eligible population who collected bonuses. These proportions are multiplied by the average dollar value of bonuses paid within each treatment group to provide the estimate of the bonus cost per claimant.

Displacement Costs

Another cost that may or may not arise from the bonus offer program is the loss of earnings by nonparticipants who are displaced from jobs by participants, as described in Chapter 6.

Entry Effects

As discussed in Chapter 6, entry effects are the increases in UI filings caused by the bonus offer. This effect will increase both bonus payments and UI compensation.

AGGREGATION OF THE EFFECTS AND INTERPRETATION OF THE RESULTS

The last step in BCA is the aggregation of benefits and costs. Two methods of calculation are used. First, net benefits are calculated simply as the difference between all benefits (B) and all costs (C) (i.e., $B - C$). The second method is to calculate a benefit/cost ratio (i.e., B/C).[2] For society as a whole, net benefits is the most appropriate measure. Even if one doesn't accept the Kaldor compensation criterion (mentioned above) that would result in the acceptance of all projects that generate positive net benefits, it is true that society is not budget constrained and therefore can consider any project generating net benefits. However, governmental agencies operating within budget constraints would tend to use the B/C ratio, choosing those projects with the highest ratios first, and so on down the line of projects with ratios greater than one until the appropriate budget is exhausted. Both calculations are reported here.

Benefit-Cost Analysis of Bonus Offer
Program Alternatives from Three Perspectives

The BCA is conducted for 11 alternative bonus offer programs that replicate the bonus offer treatments in the three experiments. For each program, the BCA is conducted from the perspective of the UI system, the government as a whole, and total society. Each of the benefit and cost components that are used in various combinations to compute net benefits from each of the perspectives are described in the section below.

Tables 7.2 through 7.4 show the benefit-cost comparisons for the six Washington, four Pennsylvania (the declining bonus offer treatment in Pennsylvania is omitted), and one Illinois bonus offer programs.

For many of the program options, societal net benefits are quite large, with B/C ratios in some instances—particularly for the high bonus offer programs—approaching 100 to 1. Large net social benefits and very high B/C ratios occur primarily because the denominator in the ratio is occupied exclusively by administrative costs, which are very low for a bonus offer program. These estimates are based on expected values. If statistical properties were included, the confidence in these estimates would be shown to be quite low. The earnings estimates are particularly weak, because earnings impacts were statistically significant only in the single Illinois offer. The next section, where B/C calculations are made for a set of hypothetical offers making use of the combined data from all of the experiments, the results are much stronger and the impact on UI benefits statistically significant, thereby increasing our confidence in the results to some extent.

The earnings estimates, where they are positive due to increased employment, may overstate net benefits to society because they do not take into account reduced utility for loss of home time (Gordon 1973) and do not show any earnings offset because of displacement of nonparticipants. They also do not take into account the potential entry effect that would result from bonus offers encouraging more job leaving or more layoffs. The displacement and entry effects are discussed below.

For Washington, only the high bonus offers generate net benefits (Table 7.2). Earning effects for low and medium-sized bonus offers were usually negative, although the difference from controls was not statistically significant (see Table 5.3, pp. 159–160).

Illinois shows positive social benefits for its only bonus offer (Table 7.3), which conforms roughly to the mid-level offer in Washington and is somewhat larger than the low bonus offer in Pennsylvania. The Illinois results are consistent with the findings for the long/low-bonus-offer treatment in Pennsylvania but not with Washington, which showed negative social benefits for low- and middle-sized bonuses.

The second perspective is that of total government, including both state and federal. Benefits to government mirror those to the UI system (the third perspective), with the added benefit of tax revenues generated by the additional earnings of participants. With regard to benefits accruing to the government as a whole or the UI system specifically, there are mixed results.

In Pennsylvania, positive net benefits accrue to the government in three of the four programs (Table 7.4). The short qualification/low bonus offer generated negative benefits to the government as a whole, because of the large (though not statistically significant) negative impact on earnings. However, this program generated positive benefits for the UI system, because reduction in UI payments more than covered bonus and administrative costs. Only the short duration/high bonus offer generated positive net benefits to both the government as a whole and the UI system.

In Washington, small positive net benefits accrue to the government only for the long qualification/low bonus and the short qualification/high bonus treatments (see Table 7.2). The other four offers all generated negative net governmental benefits. The small negative number for the long qualification/high bonus offer was the result of the large bonus payments outweighing the positive effects on earnings. For the UI system, positive net benefits were generated by the long qualification/low bonus offer. We tend to discount this result because it is inconsistent with that from all other treatments.

Only in Illinois do we find positive and large net benefits accruing to the government in general or the UI system in particular. Even for the UI system, the program generates a benefit cost ratio of 2.7/1, higher than that generated by any program option—even with higher bonus offers—in Pennsylvania or Washington. Thus, if the results of the Illinois program prevailed, every $1 spent on the bonus program would result in more than $2 in reduced UI compensation payment.

Table 7.2 Benefit-Cost Analysis for Washington Treatments, Four Quarters of Earnings ($ are per eligible claimant; ratios are for total program)

Variable	Short/Low	Short/Med.	Short/High	Long/Low	Long/Med.	Long/High
Change in earnings[a] ($)	−239	−141	155	−197	−193	296
Change in tax receipts[b] ($)	−60	−35	39	−49	−48	74
Change in UI benefit payments[c] ($)	−22	28	117	112	44	135
Administrative costs[d] ($)	3	3	3	3	3	3
Bonus payments[e] ($)	29	80	142	46	114	215
Net benefits[f] ($)						
Society	−242	−144	152	−200	−196	293
Government	−114	−90	11	14	−121	−9
UI system	−54	−55	−28	63	−73	−83
Benefit/cost ratio[g]						
Society	negative	negative	51/1	negative	negative	99/1
Government	negative	negative	1.1/1	1.3/1	negative	0.96/1
UI system	negative	0.33/1	0.8/1	2.3/1	0.4/1	0.6/1

[a] Equivalent to earnings increase, calculated as quarterly earnings reported for the treatment group in the quarter of filing plus the quarterly earnings in the subsequent three quarters (from Table 5.3, Chapter 5).

[b] Estimated to be 25% of earnings.

[c] From Table 4.2, Chapter 4. A reduction in benefit payments is shown by a positive value in a cell.

[d] See Table 7A.1, p. 247.

[e] From Spiegelman, O'Leary, and Kline (1992), Table 9-2A, p. 191.

[f] The benefits and costs from the three perspectives are defined as follows:

 Society: benefits = increased earnings

     costs = administrative expenses

 Government: benefits = change in UI compensation + change in tax revenues

       costs = bonus payments + administrative expenses

 UI system: benefits = change in UI compensation

      costs = bonus payments + administrative expenses.

[g] The benefit/cost ratios from the three perspectives are calculated as follows:

 Society: (Δearnings)/admin. expense

 Government: (ΔUI comp. + Δtax rev.)/(bonus pay + admin. expense)

 UI system: (ΔUI comp.)/(bonus pay + admin. expense).

**Table 7.3 Benefit-Cost Analysis for Illinois Treatments,
Four Quarters of Earnings ($ per eligible claimant)**

Variable	Total	FSC-elig.	FSC-inelig.
Change in earnings[a] ($)	250		
Change in tax receipts[b] ($)	63		
Change in UI benefit payments[c] ($)	150	228	57
Administrative costs[d] ($)	3	3	3
Bonus payments[e] ($)	68	79	55
Net benefits[f] ($)			
Society	247		
Government	142		
UI system	79	146	−1
Benefit/cost ratio[g]			
Society	83/1		
Government	3.0/1		
UI system	2.1/1	2.8/1	1/1

[a] Equivalent to earnings increase, calculated as follows: quarterly earnings reported for the treatment group in the quarter of filing plus the quarterly earnings in the subsequent three quarters.

[b] Estimated to be 25% of earnings.

[c] From Table 4.2, Chapter 4.

[d] From Table 7A.1, p. 247.

[e] From Spiegelman and Woodbury (1987), Table 5.1, and Davidson and Woodbury (1991).

[f] The benefits and costs from the three perspectives are defined as follows:
    Society: benefits = increased earnings
           costs = administrative expenses
    Government: benefits = change in UI compensation + change in tax revenues
           costs = bonus payments + administrative expenses.
    UI system: benefits = change in UI compensation
           costs = bonus payments + administrative expenses.

[g] The benefit/cost ratios from the three perspectives are calculated as follows:
    Society: (Δearnings)/admin. expense
    Government: (ΔUI comp. + Δtax rev.)/(bonus pay + admin. expense)
    UI system: (ΔUI comp.)/(bonus pay + admin. expense).

Table 7.4 Benefit-Cost Analysis for Pennsylvania Treatments, Four Quarters of Earnings ($ per eligible claimant)

Variable	Short/Low	Short/High	Long/Low	Long/High
Change in earnings[a] ($)	−269	133	166	175
Change in tax receipts[b] ($)	−67	33	42	44
Change in UI benefit payments[c] ($)	99	99	67	133
Administrative costs[d] ($)	3	3	3	3
Bonus payments[e] ($)	39	60	95	151
Net benefits[f] ($)				
Society	−272	130	163	172
Government	−10	69	11	23
UI system	57	36	−31	−21
Benefit/cost ratio[g]				
Society	negative	44/1	55/1	15/1
Government	0.76/1	2.1/1	1.1/1	1.1/1
UI system	2.35/1	1.6/1	0.7/1	0.9/1

[a] Equivalent to earnings increase, calculated as follows: quarterly earnings reported for the treatment group in the quarter of filing plus the quarterly earnings in the subsequent three quarters.

[b] Estimated to be 25% of earnings.

[c] From Table 4.2, Chapter 4.

[d] From Table 7A.1. p. 247.

[e] From Corson et al. (1992), Tables IX/2–IX.5.

[f] The benefits and costs from the three perspectives are defined as follows:
       Society: benefits = increased earnings
             costs = administrative expenses
    Government: benefits = change in UI compensation + change in tax revenues
             costs = bonus payments + administrative expenses
    UI system: benefits = change in UI compensation
             costs = bonus payments + administrative expenses.

[g] The benefit/cost ratios from the three perspectives are calculated as follows:
       Society: (Δearnings)/admin. expense
    Government: (ΔUI comp. + Δtax rev.)/(bonus pay + admin. expense)
     UI system: (ΔUI comp.)/(bonus pay + admin. expense).

It was the substantial positive net benefits generated for the UI system in Illinois that encouraged the U.S. Department of Labor to undertake additional experiments with the goal of selecting an optimal program. The favorable Illinois results were not replicated in Pennsylvania or Washington, however, leaving us with the preponderance of evidence leaning to a conclusion that none of the observed levels of bonus offers are likely to generate net benefits to the UI system. However, the high bonus offers did generate positive societal benefits in both Pennsylvania and Washington, and overall governmental benefits in Pennsylvania. This opens the possibility of undertaking the program by either incurring some of the costs outside of the UI system (i.e., paying bonuses from general revenues) or by transferring funds into the UI system to partially pay the bonus costs.

These results are, however, likely to be optimistic, since they do not yet include the negative corrections for spillover effects as the experiment moves into a full program (see discussion in Chapter 6 and the benefit-cost corrections below).

Benefit-Cost Analysis for Four Hypothetical Programs

Four hypothetical programs were tested using fixed dollar bonuses of $500 and $1000 and fixed qualification periods of 6 and 12 weeks. The combined data from the Pennsylvania and Washington experiments were used to determine the effects of these four programs (as reported in Decker and O'Leary 1992). These results provide a somewhat different perspective than the results of the tested treatments that use weekly benefit amount (WBA) multipliers to generate the bonus offer. As noted in the sections above and as seen in Tables 7.2 and 7.4, the high bonus multipliers generate the largest social benefits and usually the larger governmental benefits.

The striking result from combining the data from the two experiments is that all four options produce positive net social benefits. Furthermore, government as a whole benefits from three of the four treatment alternatives, and even the UI system benefits from the low bonus offer (Table 7.5). In the hypothetical treatment, it is still true that the high bonus treatments generated the highest social benefits—because bonus payments are not social costs and administrative costs are indifferent to the size of the bonus offer. However, net benefits to

Table 7.5 Benefit-Cost Analysis for Hypothetical Treatments, Four Quarters of Earnings ($ per eligible claimant)

Variable	6 weeks		12 weeks	
	$500	$1,000	$500	$1,000
Change in earnings[a] ($)	75	217	8	150
Change in tax receipts[b] ($)	19	54	2	38
Change in UI benefit payments[c] ($)	69	105	101	137
Administrative costs[d] ($)	3	3	3	3
Bonus payments[e] ($)	45	129	72	183
Net benefits[f] ($)				
Society	72	214	5	147
Government	40	27	28	−11
UI system	21	−27	2	−49
Benefit/cost ratio[g]				
Society	24/1	71/1	1.7/1	49/1
Government	1.8/1	1.2/1	1.4/1	0.9/1
UI system	1.4/1	0.8/1	1.3/1	0.71/1

[a] Earning increase is positive. Earnings are the earnings in the quarter of filing plus the quarterly earnings in the subsequent three quarters. Source: Decker and O'Leary (1992), Table IV.7, p. 72.

[b] Estimated to be 25% of earnings.

[c] A reduction in UI benefit payments is positive. Source: Decker and O'Leary (1992), T.III.5, p. 52.

[d] From Spiegelman, O'Leary, and Kline (1992), Table 9-3.

[e] From Spiegelman, O'Leary, and Kline (1992), T.II.4, p. 32.

[f] The benefits and costs from the three perspectives are defined as follows:

      Society: benefits = increased earnings

            costs = administrative expenses

   Government: benefits = change in UI compensation + change in tax revenues

            costs = bonus payments + administrative expenses

     UI system: benefits = change in UI compensation

            costs = bonus payments + administrative expenses.

[g] The benefit/cost ratios from the three perspectives are calculated as follows:

      Society: (Δearnings)/admin. expense

   Government: (ΔUI comp. + Δtax rev.)/(bonus pay + admin. expense)

     UI system: (ΔUI comp.)/(bonus pay + admin. expense).

the government as a whole and to the UI system are larger for the low bonus offer treatments. The results are not particularly sensitive to the length of the qualification period. The low bonus offer dominates because the larger reduction in UI compensation payments caused by the higher bonus offer is totally negated by the higher cost of bonus payments. In fact, these results suggest that a bonus offer of about $500, with a relatively short qualification period, is optimal from the governmental point of view, generating positive benefits to the government as a whole and to the UI system. The more socially beneficial high bonuses would require some transfer of funds (or additional taxes) to the UI system in order to compensate for their losses to government.

ADJUSTMENT TO BENEFIT-COST ESTIMATIONS IN THE MOVE FROM EXPERIMENT TO PROGRAM

In Chapter 6, the issue of how the results of the bonus experiments can be transferred to an actual reemployment bonus program is discussed. Two of the issues addressed in that chapter are of particular importance to an estimate of the net benefits to be derived from the implementation of a bonus offer program. These are the take-up rates for both UI and the bonus, and secondly, the crowding-out effect of bonus participation.

The UI take-up rates refer to the proportion of unemployed eligible for UI benefits who actually file and receive such benefits. As noted in Chapter 6, this proportion in the three states conducting the experiments was about 65 percent. It may be expected that a bonus offer increases the utility of filing UI claims for eligibles who might not otherwise bother. We will attempt to estimate the effect on the net benefit calculation if the UI participation rate among eligible unemployed increases from 65 to 75 percent. A 15 percent increase in the UI take-up rate is consistent with the estimates by Meyer (1995) in his critique of the bonus experiments.[3] In addition, a 75 percent participation rate is on the high side for most government programs.

The second participation issue is that of the bonus program itself. In Chapter 3, it was estimated that only 55 percent of those eligible to receive bonuses actually collect them. We attempt to determine the effect on net benefits if this proportion increases to 75 percent.

"Crowding out" is what we call the tendency for bonus program participants to take jobs that would otherwise by occupied by nonparticipants. This issue, addressed in Chapter 6, will increase the unemployment rate of these nonparticipants and therefore impose a cost on both society and the government that is not taken into account in the benefit calculation for the experiment. Using the crowding-out parameters estimated in Chapter 6, we will estimate the effect on net benefits.

The Effects on Net Benefits of Increased Take-Up

Our estimates of the effect on net benefits of increasing the UI take-up rate from 65 to 75 percent is shown in column 2 of Table 7.6. We start with the assumption that this increase in UI take-up has no efficiency implications; that is, there is no change in employment or earnings. It is simply that unemployed persons file for benefits to which they are already entitled and do not change their job search behavior as a consequence. If such additional filing is accompanied by decreased exit or increased entry into unemployment, then there will be additional negative impacts on net benefits. However, considering only the additional UI take-up without efficiency changes, there is still a significant negative impact on net benefits derived by government or the UI system. As seen in Table 7.6, column 2, increasing the UI take-up rate from 65 to 75 percent reduces the positive changes in UI payments from $69 to $30 and increases the bonus payment costs from $45 to $52 per experimental participant (including nonresponders and responders who do not collect a bonus). The impact on UI payments from additional take-up is calculated using the formula derived by Meyer (1995, Table 7-6). As a result, the positive net benefits from a $500 bonus offer with a six-week qualification period turn negative for the government as a whole and the UI system.

If the bonus take-up rate increases from 55 to 75 percent without any changes in the UI take-up rate, the bonus cost naturally increases, and the net benefits to government and the UI system decline (as shown in Table 7.6, column 3), but the net benefits to these two constituencies remain positive. Naturally, if both take-up rates increase to 75 percent, the negative effects are larger than either separately (see column 4) and

Table 7.6 Benefit/Cost of Hypothetical Treatment (6 weeks/$500) with Additional UI and Bonus Take-Up

Parameter				
UI take-up rate (%)	65	75	65	75
Bonus take-up rate (%)	55	55	75	75
Variable				
Change in earnings[a] ($)	75	75	75	75
Change in tax receipts[b] ($)	19	19	19	19
Change in UI payment ($)	69[c]	30[d]	69	30
Administrative cost[e] ($)	3	4	3	4
Bonus payments ($)	45[f]	52[g]	61[h]	70[i]
Net benefits[j] ($)				
Society	72	71	72	71
Government	40	–7	24	–25
UI system	21	–26	5	–40

[a] The positive change in earnings is the same as in Table 7.5. It is the earnings change generated by the response to the bonus offer. Source: Decker and O'Leary (1992), Table IV.7, p. 72.

[b] As in Table 7.5, tax receipts to all government is estimated at 25% of earnings gain.

[c] Positive change in UI payment for columns 1 and 3 are the same as in Table 7.5. Source: Decker and O'Leary (1992), T.III.5, p. 52.

[d] Positive change in UI payments for columns 2 and 4, responding to the projected increase in UI take-up rate, is calculated using the formula in Meyer (1995). The formula is change in UI payment (new) = change in UI payment (old) – (av. WBA × av. weeks of benefit receipt for recipients terminating benefits before 6 weeks × change in ratio of new to old UI take-up rate). The average WBA is calculated as the average for the control group in the three states of the ratio of dollars of UI compensation to insured weeks shown in Table 4.1. The average weeks of benefit receipt for recipients terminating benefits is derived using the average of the UI hazard rates for spell lengths less than 6 weeks for the controls in the three states shown in Table 4.5. The calculation is: $69 - (\$145 \times 1.75 \times 0.154) = 30$.

[e] From Spiegelman, O'Leary, and Kline (1992), Table 9.3.

[f] From Table 7.5, column 1.

[g] $45 × ratio of new to old UI take-up rate (i.e., $45 × 75%/65% = $45 × 1.154 = $52).

[h] $45× ratio of new to old bonus take-up rate (i.e., $45 × 75%/55% = $45 × 1.36 = $61).

[i] $45 × ratio of new to old UI take-up rate × ratio of new to old bonus take-up rate (i.e., $45 × 1.154 × 1.36 = $70).

[j] Formulas for calculating net benefits are shown in footnote to Table 7.5.

result in negative net benefits to government and the UI system. However, none of these changes in take-up affect benefits to society, since we have hypothesized that these changes would take place without any changes in unemployment and therefore without any earnings impacts. Thus, it is still true that by raising additional taxes to pay the bonuses, society would be better off, even if both UI and bonus take-up rates increase as shown in Table 7.6.

The Effects on Net Benefits of Crowding Out

Crowding out is the term used in Chapter 6 to describe the reduced employment probabilities of unemployed workers who do not respond to the bonus offer. They are either claimants who ignore the bonus offer or nonclaimants who may or may not be eligible for UI. Using column 4 in Table 6.2, we estimate the effect on earnings of crowding out. For the BCA, we estimate the crowding out ratio differently from that in Table 6.2. Since the negative effect on earnings of those UI claimants who do not respond to the bonus have already been included in the earnings impacts reported in Chapter 5 and the previous sections of Chapter 7, the numerator of the crowding-out ratio need only include those workers who are not in the experimental population (i.e., the UI eligible nonclaimants and the UI-ineligibles). Thus, the corrected crowding-out ratio (based on the numbers reported on line 3 of Table 6.2) is (103 + 94)/297 = 0.65. Since this ratio is based on changes in employment, it is necessary to weight each of the employment impact numbers by appropriate rate of annual earnings. We see below that this correction causes the ratio to fall to 0.5, calculated as follows:

$$(103 \times 5100 + 94 \times 7000)/(415 \times 8200 - 118 \times 8800) = 0.50.$$

The increased earnings of $75 in column 1 of Tables 7.5 and 7.6 is reduced to $37.50 due to crowding out. The change in tax receipts is appropriately changed for Table 7.7. Otherwise, the change in UI payments, administrative costs and bonus payments are as shown in Table 7.6. As a result of crowding out, all the net benefits are lower than reported in Table 7.6 due to the reduced positive effects on earnings.

Table 7.7 Benefit/Cost of Hypothetical Treatment (6 weeks/$500) with Additional UI and Bonus Take-Up and Crowding Out

Parameter		
UI take-up rate (%)	65	75
Bonus take-up rate (%)	55	75
Variable		
Benefits ($)		
Increased earnings[a]	37.50	37.50
Tax receipts	9.38	9.38
UI benefit payments	69	30
Costs ($)		
Administrative costs	3	4
Bonus payments[b]	45	70
Net benefits ($)		
Society	34.50	33.50
Government	30.38	−34.62
UI system	0	−44

[a] See text for the calculations. The earnings impact from Table 7.6, $75, is multiplied by 1 minus the crowding-out ratio of 0.50.
[b] Bonus payment from columns 1 and 4, Table 7.6.

CONCLUSIONS

The benefit-cost analysis certainly does not provide unambiguous support for a bonus offer program. Based on the Washington and Pennsylvania results, societal benefits are strongly positive for the high bonus program. This finding is influenced by the very low costs of administering the program, and these are the only costs that effect society as a whole. The changes in UI compensation and the bonus payments represent transfer payments and do not enter the benefit-cost calculation for society as a whole. These benefits and costs do enter the calculus for governmental benefits and, in that arena, the bonus offer rarely generates positive benefits to the UI system, as the decreases in UI compensation are usually outgunned by higher bonus costs. This undoubtedly reflects the payments of bonuses to a large number of UI recipients who would return to work quickly without the incentive of a bonus offer. However, the addition of tax revenues from increased earnings does bring about positive overall governmental benefits in 6 of the 11 program offers (6 in Washington, 4 in Pennsylvania and 1 in Illinois).

By combining all the data in the construction of hypothetical treatments (namely 6- and 12-week qualification periods and $500 and $1000 bonuses), the results show large social benefits to high bonuses, and positive benefits to government in three out of four programs, and to the UI system in two of the four programs. This is more encouraging.

A problem arises, however, when we recognize that only half of claimants eligible to receive bonuses actually collect them and when we attempt to correct for entry and crowding-out effects. These effects clearly reduce any net positive benefits from the offer program. However, encouragement might be taken from the fact that, using the combined data and one hypothetical treatment (six-week qualification period and $500 bonus), even allowing for a 50 percent increase in bonus take-up, 15 percent increase in entry into UI, and a crowding-out effect due to the reduced employment of those not offered or eligible for a bonus, there is still positive net benefits to society as a whole for this bonus offer program.

Notes

1. This estimate compares with a cost of $31 per claimant estimated in Pennsylvania. This large difference arises for several reasons. First, while the Pennsylvania estimate deducted costs associated solely with experimental operations, all other demonstration costs were included in the estimates. Second, these costs included sizable costs for central and local office Job Service personnel who were used to make the bonus offer. Third, all costs were also assumed to be variable and no assumptions concerning economies of scale were imposed on the estimates. If, instead, it is assumed that UI staff rather than Job Service staff will provide information on the bonus offer as part of the claims process and if it is assumed that central office supervisory costs are fixed, administrative costs in Pennsylvania equal approximately $11 per claimant.
2. In order to add together and compare benefits and costs that occur over time, or that occur in different years, it is necessary to discount future effects. In the BCA for a bonus offer, most, if not all, the benefits and costs occur in a single year. A

possible exception would be the longer run earnings effects of accepting less than optimal jobs in order to become reemployed sooner. It might take several years to regain full earning potential. A key issue in discounting is the selection of the discount rate. The long-term Treasury Bond rate is often used and is certainly appropriate for three perspectives considered in this analysis.

3. Meyer (1995) estimated that a $500 bonus offer with a 10-week qualification period could be expected to increase UI take-up by at least 7 to 12 percent. He claimed that this is an underestimate, making our 15 percent increase reasonable.

References

Corson, Walter, Paul Decker, Shari Dunstan, and Stuart Kerachsky. 1992. *Pennsylvania Reemployment Bonus Demonstration: Final Report.* Unemployment Insurance Occasional Paper 92-1, Washington, D.C.: U.S. Department of Labor, Employment and Training Administration.

Davidson, Carl, and Stephen A. Woodbury. 1991. "Effects of a Reemployment Bonus under Differing Benefit Entitlements, or Why the Illinois Experiment Worked." Unpublished manuscript, Department of Economics, Michigan State University, and W.E. Upjohn Institute for Employment Research.

Decker, Paul T., and Christopher J. O'Leary. 1992. *An Analysis of Pooled Evidence from the Pennsylvania and Washington Reemployment Bonus Demonstrations.* Unemployment Insurance Occasional Paper 92-7, Washington, D.C.: U.S. Department of Labor.

Gordon, Robert J. 1973. "The Welfare Cost of Higher Unemployment." *Brookings Papers on Economic Activity* no. 1, Table A-1, p. 181.

Kaldor, N. 1939. "Welfare Propositions in Economics." *Economic Journal* 49: 549–552.

Meyer, Bruce. 1995. "Lessons from the U.S. Unemployment Insurance Experiments." *Journal of Economic Literature* 33: 108–109.

Okun, Arthur. 1981. *Prices and Quantities: A Macroeconomic Analysis.* Washington, D.C.: The Brookings Institution

Spiegelman, Robert G., and Stephen A. Woodbury. 1987. *The Illinois Unemployment Insurance Incentive Experiments: Final Report.* Kalamazoo, Michigan: W. E. Upjohn Institute for Employment Research, February.

Spiegelman, Robert G., Christopher J. O'Leary, and Kenneth J. Kline. 1992. *The Washington Reemployment Bonus Experiment: Final Report.* Unemployment Insurance Occasional Paper 92-6, Washington, D.C.: U.S. Department of Labor.

Appendix Table 7A.1 Administrative Costs for an Ongoing Bonus Offer Program

Central office cost (1988 $)	
1 program administrator and 1 clerical assistant	45,900
Fringe benefits at 28.3%	12,990
Nonpersonnel services at 16% of salary	7,344
Administrative, staff and technical cost at 16.35%	7,505
	73,739
Total new intra-state claims, FY90	227,484
Central office cost per new claim	0.32

Job service center costs[a]	Time per operation	Units per claim	$ per claim
Additional time for the initial claim	2 minutes	1	0.64
Processing bonus payments	4.5 minutes[b]	0.129[c]	0.19
Allowance	27 minutes[d]	0.129[c]	1.11
Denials	27 minutes[d]	0.029[e]	0.25
Appeals			
Lower level	34 minutes		
Higher level	20 minutes[f]	0.002[g]	0.01
			2.20
Total cost per claimant			2.52
Total cost per eligible claimant (add 16%)			2.92

[a] Costs per minute: JSC Specialist II at 1,776 per month, plus fringe benefits at 28.3%, nonpersonnel services at 16%, and AST costs at 16.35% of salary = $1,776 × 1.6065 = $3,705 per month/9600 minutes per month = $0.32 per minute.

[b] Allowed time for processing a Continued Claim Form.

[c] Ratio of total bonuses to initial claims in experiment, i.e., 1,816/14,080 (see Table 3.1, Chapter 3).

[d] Time allowed for a nonseparation denial or allowance.

[e] Ratio of NOH and bonus denials to initial claims in experiment, i.e., (278 + 130) ÷ 14,080 (see Table 3.1, Chapter 3).

[f] Time allowed for lower and higher level appeals.

[g] Proportion of nonseparation appeals to initial claims: 0.06 × 0.029 (lower) + 0.01 × 0.029 (higher) = 0.07 × 0.029 = 0.002.

8
Summary and Policy Implications

Philip K. Robins

The previous chapters have presented findings from three unemployment insurance (UI) bonus experiments conducted in the United States during the 1980s. This chapter summarizes the findings, provides an assessment of what they seem to imply for the viability of a national system of UI bonuses, and compares a bonus system to other possible UI reform measures.

SUMMARY OF RESULTS

Background of Experiments

The UI bonus experiments were conceived just after unemployment in the United States had reached a post–World War II high. In 1982 and 1983, for example, the civilian unemployment rate was nearly 10 percent (Council of Economic Advisers 1999). During the 1960s, the unemployment rate averaged under 5 percent and during the 1970s, it averaged just over 6 percent.

High unemployment, coupled with a growing consensus among academics and policy analysts that the UI program exacerbated unemployment by reducing the incentive to become reemployed, prompted policymakers to search for alternative ways to help lower unemployment. Offering a bonus was a novel idea. It was thought that a bonus, if structured properly, could partially offset the financial disincentives of the UI system and reduce unemployment.

Economic theory provided an unambiguous prediction about the impact of a bonus on the length of an unemployment spell. Basic job-search theory implies that if a time-limited offer of a bonus is extended to UI recipients, a number of them would respond by finding employment more quickly than they would if there had been no bonus. The reduced unemployment would be the result of the combined effects of more intensive job searches and a greater incentive on the part of the unemployed to accept jobs that are offered (because of a lower reservation wage).

From the policymaker's perspective, the source of the reduced unemployment is important. If the reduced unemployment comes about as the result of lower reservation wages, then the bonus may induce workers to accept lower-paying jobs. On the other hand, if job-search intensity increases, workers may find jobs that pay at least as much as they would in the absence of a bonus offer.

The key policy questions that arose then were 1) by how much would a bonus reduce unemployment, 2) by how much would the reduced unemployment lead to lower UI payments, 3) would the reduced unemployment be associated with lower or higher paying jobs, 4) to what extent would the cost of the bonus be offset by reduced UI benefits, and 5) would the U.S. economy be better or worse off by the enactment of a bonus program?

These were critical questions that seemed well suited to being answered definitively by a carefully conceived and operated social experiment. In 1984, the Illinois bonus experiment was launched. It was followed in 1988 by the Pennsylvania and Washington bonus experiments.[1]

Features and Main Findings

Table 8.1 summarizes the features and main findings from the Illinois, Pennsylvania, and Washington experiments.[2] The Illinois experiment tested a single treatment.[3] Unemployment insurance recipients were offered a bonus of $500 if they found a job within 11 weeks of filing for benefits and if they held the job for at least 4 months. The experiment in Pennsylvania tested four treatments.[4] Unemployment insurance recipients were offered bonuses ranging from $105 to $1,596 if they found a job within 6 or 12 weeks of filing for benefits and held the job for at least 16 weeks. The experiment in Washington tested six treatments. Unemployment insurance recipients were offered bonuses ranging from $110 to $1,254 if they found a job within 3 to 13 weeks and held the job for at least 4 months.

Table 8.1 Summary of Findings from the UI Bonus Experiments[a]

	Illinois, 1984–1985	Pennsylvania, 1988–1990	Washington, 1988–1989
Number of sites	22	12	21
Sample size	8,138	12,226	15,534
Treatment	4,186	8,834	12,452
Control	3,952	3,392	3,082
Average weekly UI benefit and range ($)	135 (51–161)	185 (35–266)	153 (55–209)
Average replacement rate[b] (%)	36	43	39
Number of bonus treatments	1	4	6
Average bonus offer and range ($)	500 –	778 (105–1,596)	574 (110–1,254)
Average qualification period and range	11 weeks –	9.8 weeks (6–12 weeks)	8.4 weeks (3–13 weeks)
Reemployment period	4 months	16 weeks	4 months
Percent leaving UI by qualification date	43	57	56
Percent fully qualifying for bonus	30	34	31
Percent receiving bonus	14	11	15
Average bonus payment[c] ($)	68	98	95
Average impact on benefit weeks, regression-adjusted	−1.04* (−1.46** FSC-elig.; −0.65* FSC-inelig.)	−0.58**	−0.40*
Average impact on annual benefit amount[c] ($)	−150	−102	−63
Average impact on probability of employment, quarter 3	0.021	−0.014	0.00
Average impact on annual earnings[c] ($)	250*	93	−88

Table 8.1 (continued)

	Illinois, 1984–1985	Pennsylvania, 1988–1990	Washington, 1988–1989
Net annual benefit per claimant[d] ($)			
Claimant	105	66	–33
UI system	78	1	–36
Government	142	24	–57
Society	247	90	–91

[a] For impacts, * = statistically significant at the 10% level; ** = statistically significant at the 5% level.
[b] Average UI benefit/average wage.
[c] Taken from Chapter 7, Tables 7.2, 7.3, and 7.4. For the Pennsylvania and Washington experiments, values are weighted averages across treatment groups.
[d] Claimant net benefits are earnings impact minus reduced UI benefits plus bonus payment minus estimated taxes. UI system net benefits are reduced UI benefit minus bonus payment minus administrative cost of bonus program. Government net benefits are UI system net benefits plus increased taxes. Society benefits are earnings impact minus administrative cost of bonus program. Administrative cost is assumed to be $3 per claimant and taxes are assumed to be 25% of earnings impact.

Each bonus experiment had what seemed to be relatively large sample sizes, ranging from 8,138 in Illinois to 15,534 in Washington. However, as will be discussed below, unless a "parameterized" model is used to estimate impacts, the sample sizes in Pennsylvania and Washington were not really large enough to detect modest *differential* impacts among the various bonus treatments.[5]

The UI programs in the three states provided weekly benefits that replaced, on average, nearly 40 percent of weekly wages. The bonuses represented between two and six times the weekly UI benefit amount (WBA). On the surface, then, the bonuses appeared to have the potential to provide a significant financial incentive. However, the bonuses would have to reduce unemployment by at least 2 to 6 weeks among those who took up the bonus, otherwise they would not be cost-effective from the perspective of the UI trust fund. Because a number of recipients received "windfall" benefits (that is, they received a bonus without reducing their unemployment), the reduction in unemployment *among those who responded to the offer* would have to be greater than 2 to 6 weeks for the bonus to be cost-effective.

As Table 8.1 indicates, between 43 and 57 percent of the treatment group members left UI by the qualification date and, of those, between half and three-quarters fully qualified for the bonus. However, the proportion of claimants receiving bonuses was very low in all three experiments, ranging from 11 to 15 percent of eligible treatment group members. Surprisingly, almost half of those who fully qualified for the bonus failed to claim it. In Illinois, roughly three-quarters of those that fully qualified for the bonus claimed it, while in Washington and Pennsylvania approximately one-half of those fully eligible for the bonus claimed it. Such a large number of "no-shows" increases the cost-effectiveness of the bonus, but the take-up rate by eligible claimants in a full-scale national program would probably be higher than that experienced in the experiment. The administrators of the experiments have not provided any explanation why so many individuals failed to claim the bonus. Certainly the transaction costs involved in filing a claim would appear to be low relative to the payoff.

Although in some sense each of the 11 treatments in the 3 experiments can be viewed as independent programs, the average experimental effect in each experiment can be loosely considered the result of a treatment that is the weighted average of the bonus offers and qualification periods in each experiment. For the most part, it is this "average treatment" that will be the major focus of attention in what follows.

Each experiment significantly reduced the number of weeks claimants received UI benefits, with Illinois having the largest impact of just over one week and Pennsylvania and Washington reducing UI benefit receipt by close to one-half week. If the Federal Supplemental Compensation (FSC-eligible) treatment group is excluded from the Illinois calculations, the reductions in UI receipt become similar across all experiments, ranging from 0.40 week in Washington to 0.65 week in Illinois. Although it is not entirely clear why those eligible for FSC benefits would be more likely to respond to the bonus, one explanation is presented in Chapter 6 (see p. 199). In short, because FSC-eligibility reduces search effort, the marginal cost of increased search is lower, and the bonus can have an increased impact.

The Pennsylvania and Washington experiments tested more than one treatment in order to measure the sensitivity of the impact to the bonus amount. The Pennsylvania experiment tested two bonus amounts and two qualification periods. The Washington experiment

Figure 8.1 Results of the Washington and Pennsylvania Experiments

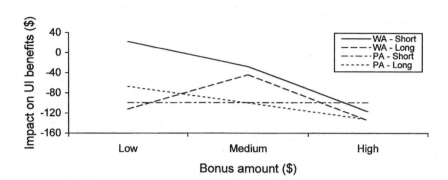

tested three bonus amounts and two qualification periods. Figure 8.1 shows the relationship between the bonus amount in each experiment and the impact on UI benefits for each qualification period. This figure indicates that only in the case of the short qualification period in the Washington experiment and the long qualification period in the Pennsylvania experiment does their appear to be a pattern of increasing negative impact on UI benefit amount with the size of the bonus. However, with the exception of the short qualification period in the Washington experiment, the differences in impacts across treatments are not generally very large and are not statistically significant. Thus, one must conclude that the Pennsylvania and Washington experiments were not very successful in measuring the sensitivity of the impact to the bonus amount.

Because so few members of the treatment group received a bonus, the bonus amount per treatment group member averaged only $68 in Illinois, $98 in Pennsylvania, and $95 in Washington. The average reduction in UI benefits exceeded the average bonuses (including administrative costs) in Illinois and equaled the average bonus in Pennsylvania, making the bonus cost-effective from the perspective of the UI trust fund in Illinois and cost-neutral in Pennsylvania. Only the Washington experiment was not cost-effective from the perspective of the UI trust fund.

While seemingly cost-effective in Illinois, a higher take-up rate would have reversed this conclusion. As indicated above, it is not known why the take-up rate was so low in Illinois (as well as in the other two experiments). If bonuses are to remain a serious policy alternative, future research needs to investigate and understand the reasons for the low take-up rate.

In addition to reducing UI benefits, the bonuses also increased earnings in Illinois and Pennsylvania, but they decreased earnings in Washington. Because there was no significant change in the probability of being employed in any of the experiments, the increased earnings in Illinois and Pennsylvania implies that the claimants were probably not taking lower paying jobs in order to receive the bonus. Wage rates may have been somewhat reduced in Washington.

In Illinois and Pennsylvania, the claimants experienced net benefits from the program. The net benefits arose because of both the bonus payments plus the increased earnings (net of taxes). In Washington, the net benefits to claimants were slightly negative because earnings and UI benefits fell by more than the bonus payments.

The Illinois and Pennsylvania experiments also conferred net benefits on society. The positive net societal benefits arose because of the increased earnings. Because the Washington experiment decreased claimant earnings, net benefits to society were negative.

Generalizing the Experimental Findings

Chapter 6 described three major concerns that arise in generalizing the experimental findings to a national program. First, there is the possibility that the availability of a bonus would induce more individuals to apply for UI benefits. At the time of the experiments, approximately 65 percent of those eligible for UI were applying for benefits. It would seem likely that the percentage of eligible persons that apply for UI would be greater under a national program. Second, as has been indicated, the take-up rate among persons that were fully eligible for a bonus was only about 50 percent. Again, it is likely that the take-up rate would be higher under a national program, perhaps because of greater information about the bonuses, less stigma attached to receiving them, and belief in the credibility of the issuing agent. Finally, there is the possibility that bonus recipients would "crowd out" other workers from jobs that the others would have taken.

Accounting for each of these concerns affects the net benefits of the program. In some cases, net benefits increase, while in others they decrease. Table 8.2 shows how net benefits change from each of the four perspectives (claimant, UI system, government, and society), after accounting for these concerns. The first row of Table 8.2 shows the net benefits under a hypothetical program having a bonus of $500, a qualification period of six weeks, a UI take-up rate of 65 percent, a bonus take-up rate of 50 percent, and no crowding out. These conditions approximate the average conditions prevailing in the three UI experiments. Under these conditions, net benefits from all four perspectives are positive.

Increasing the UI take-up rate to 75 percent increases the net benefits to the claimant but decreases the net benefits to the UI system and the government, making them negative. Because there is no change in real output, net benefits to society only change slightly due to higher administrative costs. Increasing the bonus take-up rate further increases the net benefits to the claimants and further decreases the net benefits to the UI system and the government. Finally, allowing for a crowding-out ratio of 40 percent reduces net benefits from all perspectives except the UI system.

Of course, it is not known with certainty whether these changes, which were estimated using a simulation model, would occur under a

Table 8.2 Net Annual Benefits per Claimant under a Hypothetical National Program ($)

Parameter	Claimant	UI system	Government	Society
Base program[a]	32	21	40	72
Increase UI take-up rate to 75%	78	−26	7	71
Increase bonus take-up rate to 75%	96	−40	−25	71
Increase crowding-out ratio to 0.40	68	−44	−35	34

NOTE: Taken from results from the Pooled Experimental Samples in Chapter 7, except for claimant benefit calculation. Each successive row represents a change from the previous row.
[a] Bonus = $500, qualification period = 6 weeks, UI take-up rate = 65%, bonus take-up rate = 50%, crowding out ratio = 0.

national program. Nonetheless, the experimental findings strongly suggest that a national bonus program similar to the ones tested in the three UI experiments would not be cost-effective from the perspectives of the UI Trust Fund or the government. However, claimants and society are predicted to experience net benefits from the program, even after accounting for "macro-effects."

ASSESSING THE EXPERIMENTS

There are at least two ways in which to assess the UI experiments. First, one needs to determine whether they achieved their objective of providing definitive information about the impacts of a UI bonus system. Second, if the impacts are judged as definitive, one needs to form a conclusion about whether bonuses are a good idea for national policy. Regardless of whether or not they are a good idea for national policy, the experiments may be judged as successful if they provided definitive answers to the questions originally posed.

From the standpoint of standards for social policy research, the experiments were quite successful. As described in Chapter 2, the experiments were generally carried out as originally designed and the use of randomized treatments ensured that the results had internal validity. Furthermore, the findings were generally consistent across the experiments; however, there were some differences in the findings that might limit their generalizability. UI benefits were significantly decreased in all three experiments by similar amounts, but average earnings rose in Illinois and Pennsylvania and fell in Washington (although the Pennsylvania and Washington earnings impacts were not statistically significant). None of the experiments significantly affected employment, although the estimated impact was positive in Illinois, negative in Pennsylvania, and zero in Washington. Overall, however, the differences across experiments were not large enough to be statistically significant. Financial incentives appeared to work the way economists and policy analysts predicted they would, but the impacts were not nearly as large as advocates of a bonus would have hoped for.

In addition to some inconsistencies across the experiments, they were also not entirely successful in pinpointing the differential impacts of alternative program features, such as the size of the bonus and the length of the qualification period. Given the success of the Illinois experiment (which tested only a single bonus treatment), the Pennsylvania and Washington experiments were designed to confirm the Illinois results and to provide estimates of the sensitivity of impacts to various program features. The Pennsylvania experiment tested four treatments and the Washington experiment tested six treatments, both varying the size of the bonus offer and the length of the qualification period.[6]

Within each experiment, there were no statistically significant differences across treatments. In a continuous variable model in which weeks of UI was regressed on the bonus amount and the length of the qualification period (plus other control variables), the estimated impacts were not statistically significant at conventional levels, although both were of the expected negative sign (see Chapter 4, Table 4.3). When the Pennsylvania and Washington samples were pooled, the impact of the bonus amount was statistically significant at the 10 percent level. When all three experimental samples were pooled, the length of the qualification period became statistically significant at the 5 percent level, but the impact of the bonus amount was not statistically significant.

What can the lack of significant differences across treatments be attributed to? It appears that the sample sizes were not large enough to detect differences of the order of magnitude that actually occurred. Of course, it could not have been known beforehand what the impacts would turn out to be, but it appears not enough attention was paid to identifying differential impacts across treatments. In retrospect, it might have been better to have tested fewer treatments in Pennsylvania and Washington, with greater differences in bonus amounts and qualification periods to have possibly generated larger differential impacts. However, parameterizing the bonus and qualification options was always considered an acceptable alternative format that generally requires smaller sample sizes across treatments, although functional form in a parameterized model is an important issue that needs to be resolved before determining sample size requirements.

Despite these shortcomings, the experimental approach appears to have generated credible and definitive findings relative to other evaluation methods. As noted by Linkz (1999), policymakers were generally convinced by the experimental findings, found them simple to comprehend, and concluded that the experimental design was the only one that would have produced credible results. The only real limitation of the experimental approach was that it took some time for the results to be generated and disseminated and by the time they became available (the late 1980s and early 1990s), the policy agenda had changed somewhat, with welfare reform overshadowing UI reform and fiscal conservatism gripping Congress. By the time the results became fully available, UI bonuses had become a much less feasible policy option. Worker profiling had taken center stage as the policy of choice, and the experiments did not provide any direct evidence on how worker profiling would work with a system of bonuses (although, as I indicate below, more recent work has used the experimental data to simulate the effects of worker profiling in a system with bonuses).

ALTERNATIVE POLICIES

The results presented in this book have suggested that the UI bonus schemes tested in the Illinois, Pennsylvania, and Washington experiments were only marginally cost-effective from the perspective of the UI Trust Fund and the overall government budget. If a relatively unrestricted bonus scheme does not achieve the kinds of objectives that were originally hoped for, the natural question arises as to whether there are alternative policies for encouraging reemployment among UI recipients that may be more cost-effective. In this section, I discuss five alternatives that have been proposed since the UI bonus experiments were undertaken. Three of these—an earnings supplement, stricter sanctioning of work-search requirements, and stricter work-search requirements—have also been evaluated using a randomized experiment. The other two—worker profiling and Unemployment Insurance Savings Accounts (UISAs)—have been evaluated using non-experimental methods.

An Earnings Supplement

One alternative to bonuses is to provide an earnings supplement to UI recipients who are willing to take a pay cut to become reemployed more quickly. The objective of a UI supplement scheme is to cushion any income losses suffered as a result of the pay cut. In order to minimize windfall, the supplements should be provided only to individuals who would otherwise not have become reemployed. Displaced workers (persons who have lost stable, long-term, and often well-paying jobs due to technology, increased international competition, or shifting market demand) and repeat users of UI are groups for whom an earnings supplement might be effective.

Permanent job displacement is a problem throughout North America and Europe.[7] In Canada, between 1981 and 1991, more than one million persons were permanently laid off from jobs. Unemployment insurance in Canada (now officially referred to as Employment Insurance) is the largest source of government assistance to displaced workers. The UI system in Canada is more generous than it is in the United States. It replaces close to 55 percent of wages for most workers and pays benefits for up to 50 weeks. As in the United States, much has been written about the potential for the Canadian UI system to prolong unemployment. Because of this, and because of the high cost of the UI program in Canada, policymakers there have been exploring new kinds of reemployment policies.

Given the limited success of the UI bonus experiments, Canadian policymakers were reluctant to test a similar kind of program. Instead, they proposed and tested an alternative—an earnings supplement. An earnings supplement is designed to make up part of the earnings loss suffered by displaced workers who are able to find reemployment more quickly but at wages lower than what they had previously experienced. In 1995, the Canadian government funded an experimental evaluation of an earnings supplement program for displaced workers and repeat users receiving UI. The experimental program, termed the Earnings Supplement Project (ESP), was carried out on close to 6,000 persons (half of which were assigned to a control group and half to a treatment group) in five Canadian cities.[8]

The features and findings of the ESP are presented in Table 8.3.[9] To be eligible for the supplement, UI recipients had to find a full-time job (30 hours or more of work per week) within 6 months of filing for UI benefits. This job could not be with their most recent employer at their previous work location. If an eligible job were found, the individual could receive a weekly payment equal to 75 percent of the difference between the previously weekly insurable wage and the new wage, with a maximum supplement equal to Can$250 per week.[10] Thus, if the individual found a job that payed the same, or more, than the previous job no supplement would be paid.

Individuals were eligible for the supplement for up to two years. Unlike the U.S. bonus experiments, there was no required preemployment period—individuals became eligible to receive the supplement immediately after finding a full-time job.

As Table 8.3 indicates, the average supplement recipient was paid more than Can$8,700, averaging about Can$137 per week. Like the proportion of the treatment group collecting a bonus in the U.S. experiments, however, the proportion of the ESP treatment group receiving a supplement was extremely low—only 21 percent of the treatment group received the supplement (compared with between 11 and 15 percent of the treatment group that received a bonus in the U.S. experiments).[11] The percentage leaving UI by the qualification date (26 weeks after filing for UI benefits) was similar to the percentage in the U.S. experiments (48 percent compared with between 43 and 57 percent) and the percentages fully qualifying for the supplement were also similar (28 percent compared with between 30 and 34 percent). Furthermore, unlike the U.S. bonus experiments, the ESP supplement had no perceivable impact on UI receipt. In fact, the treatment group actually stayed on UI slightly longer and received slightly more UI than the control group. Although the treatment group had a 0.023 higher employment rate than the control group (similar to the impact in the Illinois bonus experiment), average earnings were lower, although not significantly so. Thus, unlike the U.S. bonus experiments, some ESP recipients were induced to find lower paying jobs and overall employment was not increased by enough to result in an overall increase in average earnings during the first five quarters of the program.

Because of the lack of an impact on UI benefit receipt, ESP was not cost-effective from the perspective of either the UI system or the government. Additionally, because claimant earnings fell, ESP had negative net benefits for society. Only claimants benefited from the

Table 8.3 Summary of Findings from the Canadian UI Earnings Supplement Project (ESP) Experiment[a]

Years operated	1995–1997
Number of sites	5
Sample size	5,912
Treatment	2,960
Control	2,952
Average weekly UI benefit (Can$)	308
Average UI replacement rate[b] (%)	55
Number of treatments	1
Weekly supplement	$250 or 75% of lost earnings, whichever is less
Maximum number of weeks supplement could be paid	104
Average supplement paid over 104 weeks (Can$)	8,705
Average number of weeks supplement was paid	64
Average weekly supplement (Can$)	137
Qualification period to get full-time job (≥30 hours)	26 weeks
Reemployment period	none required
Percent leaving UI by qualification date	48
Percent employed full-time by qualification date	42
Percent qualifying for supplement	28
Percent receiving supplement	21
Average impact on UI benefit weeks, quarters 1–2	0.2
Average impact on UI benefit amount, quarters 1–5 (Can$)	90
Average supplement paid, quarters 1–5 (Can$)	1,165
Impact on probability of employment, quarters 1–2	0.023*
Impact on earnings, quarters 1–5 (Can$)	−682
Net annual benefit per claimant[c] (Can$)	
Claimant	592
UI system	−1,072
Government	−1,208
Society	−617

Table 8.3 (continued)

SOURCE: Adapted from Bloom et al. (1999).
[a] For impacts, * = statistically significant at the 10% level.
[b] Weekly UI benefit / weekly wage.
[c] Based on Tables 7.1 and 7.4 of Bloom et al. (1999). Claimant net benefits are earnings impact plus plus UI benefit impact plus supplement payment minus estimated
tax change. UI system net benefits are minus UI benefit impact minus supplement
payment minus administrative cost of supplement program. Government net benefits
are UI system net benefits plus estimated tax change. Society benefits are earnings
impact minus administrative cost of supplement program. Administrative cost is $89
per claimant over quarters 1–5 and taxes are assumed to be 25% of earnings impact.

program, but by less than their supplement payments (because of the decreased earnings). Hence, ESP served primarily to transfer income from taxpayers to UI recipients, but not in a cost-effective manner. From the perspective of public policy, an earnings supplement that partially replaces lost earnings appears to be much more costly and much less effective than a one-time bonus.

Stricter Sanctioning

In recent years, U.S. social policy has been increasingly using sanctions, rather than financial incentives, to promote work effort. Sanctioning consists of penalizing recipients who do not comply with program regulations. The greater emphasis on sanctioning has been a response to claims that recipients of social transfers are abusing the system.

In the UI program, sanctioning takes the form of reducing benefits (possibly to zero) for persons who do not comply with the work-search requirements. Surprisingly, little is known about the impacts of stricter sanctioning in the UI program. Recently, Ashenfelter, Ashmore, and Deschênes (2000) reported the results of four randomized experiments that took place during the mid 1980s and tested the effects of stricter enforcement and verification of work-search requirements in the UI program.[12]

The UI sanctioning experiments contained several treatments. One treatment gave claimants an expanded initial eligibility questionnaire and emphasized the UI work requirement, including being notified that work search is subject to verification and that the claimant might be disqualified if the requirement wasn't being met. In addition, at the initial visit to the UI office, the claimant completed a work history form which was used later to review the accuracy of the monetary determination of eligibility. A portion of claimants receiving the first treatment was given a second treatment consisting of an actual verification of job contacts. The evaluators compared claimants receiving the second treatment with those in the treatment group that were not subject to the verification procedures to infer the impact of the verification procedures.

Table 8.4 presents the results of the experimental evaluation. In no case did the verification procedure significantly affect qualification rates or UI recipiency rates or benefit amounts.[13] The authors concluded that sanctions are not cost-effective.

Stricter Work Search Requirements

In contrast to stricter sanctioning of existing work-search requirements, another possible UI policy would be to increase the work-search requirements themselves. In 1986, an experiment was undertaken in Tacoma, Washington, that tested several treatments of differing work-search requirements. The design and findings from this experiment are reported in Johnson and Klepinger (1994).

The Tacoma experiment had four treatments, as indicated in Table 8.5. Treatment A eliminated the work-search requirements entirely. Treatment B had the standard work-search requirements and, hence, served as the control group for the experiment. Treatment C provided individualized requirements, by tailoring them to individual circumstances, and increased the requirements and provided services for claimants who didn't find work within a reasonable period of time. Treatment D combined intensive job-search assistance with employability development planning.

Prior to the experiment, members of each treatment group had similar characteristics. They received, on average, a weekly UI benefit of about $146, which replaced about 63 percent of their pre-UI earnings.

Impacts of the experiment are also presented in Table 8.5. As indicated by the relative impacts of treatment A, the results strongly suggest that existing work-search requirements reduce UI benefits paid,

Table 8.4 Summary of Findings from U.S. UI Sanctioning Experiments

Years operated	1984–1985
Number of sites	4
Sample size	3,877
Treatment[a]	1,966
Control	1,921
Average weekly UI benefit entitlement[b] ($)	116
Average replacement rate[c] (%)	51
Impact of work search verification on[d]	
Temporary disqualification rate	0.007
Average weekly benefits	0.85
Observed claim duration (weeks)	−0.23

SOURCE: Data from Ashenfelter, Ashmore, and Deschênes (2000).

[a] There were two treatment groups. Members of the first treatment group had their work search verified in addition to a number of other verifications of initial and continuing eligibility, while members of the second treatment group were subjected to the additional verifications of eligibility but not the verification of work-search verification. The authors used differences between the two treatment groups to isolate the impact of the work-search verification component.

[b] Measured over the treatment and control groups.

[c] In three of the four sites for which earnings data were available. The rate equals the average UI benefit entitlement/average earnings.

[d] Derived from a comparison of mean outcomes of the first treatment group with the second treatment group. None of the impacts are statistically significant at the 10% level or lower.

weeks receiving UI benefits, and the percent exhausting benefits, but have no impact on employment or earnings (the lack of a negative impact on earnings may be viewed as a positive finding because it implies that work-search requirements lead to a greater intensity of search rather than a reduction in the reservation wage).

Increasing work-search requirements beyond their present levels, however, had only a modest impact. Treatment C had no significant impact on any of the UI outcomes and only modestly increases the employment rate by 1.7 percentage points. Treatment D reduced weeks of UI receipt by about one-half week and had no impact on earnings. Johnson and Klepinger indicated that Treatment D is cost-effec-

Table 8.5 Summary of Findings from the Washington Alternative Work-Search Experiment, 1986–1988[a]

Variable	Treatment A[b]	Treatment B[b]	Treatment C[b]	Treatment D[b]
Sample size	2,246	1,964	2,533	2,871
Average weekly UI benefit ($)	147	145	147	145
Average replacement rate[c] (%)	63	63	63	63
Services received (% of sample)				
Eligibility review interview	0.4	24.6	33.2	19.3
Job-search workshop	0.0	0.1	0.1	15.2
Job referral	14.8	17.9	16.9	15.7
Job placement	5.7	6.8	7.2	6.0
Job counseling	1.3	1.3	1.2	1.6
Impact relative to status quo (Treatment B)[d]				
Total UI benefits paid ($)	265**	–	5	–68
Weeks of UI benefits received	3.34**	–	0.17	–0.47*
Percent exhausting benefits	12.5**	–	0.5	–0.3
Percent employed	–0.9	–	1.7***	1.3
Hours of work	–6	–	2	22
Hourly wage rate[e]	0.12	–	–0.13	–0.01
Total earnings ($)	–23	–	–24	292

SOURCE: Data from Johnson and Klepinger (1994).

[a] * = Statistically significant at the 10% level; ** = statistically significant at the 5% level; *** = statistically significant at the 1% level.

[b] Treatment A: no work-search requirement;
Treatment B: status quo (at least three contacts per week);
Treatment C: Individualized requirements, Varying contracts per week (up to five);
Treatment D: Intensive job-search assistance and employability development planning.

[c] Average UI benefit/average earnings.

[d] Impacts are regression-adjusted. For UI variables, the impact is measured over the full benefit year. For the employment and earnings variables, the impacts are measured over the full two years after applying for benefits.

[e] Hourly wage rate impacts are selectivity-corrected.

tive, but this inference is based on a statistically insignificant reduction of $68 in UI benefits paid.

Worker Profiling

Since the mid 1990s, in response to congressional legislation, states have been implementing Worker Profiling and Reemployment Services (WPRS) systems (see, e.g., Eberts and O'Leary 1996). These systems actively help UI recipients shorten time out of work by identifying UI recipients who are most likely to exhaust benefits and referring them to required reemployment services.

Under the WPRS, UI recipients most likely to exhaust benefits are identified using a statistical methodology that assigns a probability of exhaustion to each UI recipient eligible for profiling. The probabilities are derived from a regression model that links the effects of personal characteristics and economic factors to the probability of exhaustion.

O'Leary, Decker, and Wandner (1997) argued that worker profiling can be used in a bonus program to potentially improve net benefits to the UI system. By restricting bonuses to claimants most likely to exhaust benefits, they maintain that windfall bonuses will be lower and impacts on UI benefit receipt rates and benefit amounts will be higher. Although there is no experimental evidence demonstrating that there would be an improvement in net benefits under a UI bonus program with worker profiling, O'Leary, Decker, and Wandner simulated the effects of worker profiling in the Pennsylvania and Washington UI bonus experiments.

A summary of their simulation results is presented in Table 8.6. They examine two types of profiling schemes. One would limit benefits to the top 50 percent of claimants most likely to exhaust benefits. The other would limit benefits to the top 25 percent of claimants most likely to exhaust benefits. In both cases, UI benefits were reduced by more in the profiled group. In addition, despite higher bonus amounts for the profiled group, net benefits to the UI system were higher. Perhaps surprisingly, the more restrictive profiling scheme (those limiting the bonus to the top 25 percent of claimants most likely to exhaust benefits) yielded lower net benefits than the less restrictive profiling scheme (those limiting the bonus to the top 50 percent of claimants most likely to exhaust benefits). However, the differences between the

**Table 8.6 Simulated Net Benefits under Worker Profiling,
Pennsylvania and Washington UI Experiments[a] ($)**

Variable	Pennsylvania	Washington
Impact on UI benefits paid[b]		
Bottom 50%	−70	31
Top 50%	−172*	−117*
Difference	−102	−148
Bottom 75%	−109	13
Top 25%	−129	−118
Difference	−20	−131
Average bonus paid		
Bottom 50%	86	67
Top 50%	103	142
Difference	17	75
Bottom 75%	92	85
Top 25%	104	166
Difference	12	81
Net benefit per claimant from perspective of UI system		
No worker profiling	−13	−76
Worker profiling, top 50%	36	−28
Worker profiling, top 25%	−8	−51

SOURCE: Data from O'Leary, Decker, and Wandner (1997).
[a] * = Statistically significant at the 10% level.
[b] For combined treatments using the authors' profiling models.

two types of profiling schemes were small and the differences between profiled and nonprofiled claimants in either scheme were not statistically significant. The authors concluded that a low bonus amount (perhaps three times the WBA) and a long qualification period (perhaps 12 weeks) targeted to the top half of claimants most likely to exhaust UI benefits would be the most cost-effective type of bonus profiling scheme. They estimated that such a scheme would save the UI Trust Fund about $50 per offer.

While profiling appears to make a bonus program more cost-effective, the improvement is minimal. Moreover, the existing results on profiled bonuses are based on nonexperimental simulations and may not occur under an actual program. In addition, the statistical models used to predict exhaustion rates tend to have low explanatory power and may not be accurately defining the optimal target group. Finally, in the presence of profiling, it is possible that claimants will alter their behavior to be more likely to meet the criteria used to select bonus-eligible claimants. If this occurs, the profiling procedure will become an even less accurate tool for identifying the group least likely to be receiving windfall benefits from a bonus program.

Unemployment Insurance Savings Accounts

A more radical proposal to encourage reemployment among UI recipients is the use of Unemployment Insurance Savings Accounts (UISA). As proposed by Feldstein and Altman (1998), all working persons would be required to save a fraction of their wages (up to 4 percent) in special government accounts. The funds in these accounts would earn the market rate of interest and could be drawn upon if the people were to become unemployed. In the event that the funds are exhausted, the government would lend these people money, again at the market rate of interest. If the person retires or dies with a positive balance in the account, it would be converted into retirement income or bequeathed to heirs. Negative balances would be forgiven.

By using personal wealth to subsidize unemployment, Feldstein and Altman argued that reemployment would be encouraged. Only persons who expect to retire or die with negative balances would face the same adverse reemployment incentives as under the present UI system.

Using historical data from the Panel Study of Income Dynamics, Feldstein and Altman simulated the performance of such a system. They found that only 5 percent of employees would retire or die with negative balances. They also estimated that UISAs would save the UI trust fund about half the benefits being paid under the current system. They suggest the savings could be used to reduce payroll taxes.

While such a system has intuitive appeal, about half the benefits would be paid to individuals with negative balances at retirement. This raises serious questions regarding the equity of such a system, although the current system also raises questions of equity. Furthermore, it is possible that the percentage of persons with negative balances at retirement could be even larger than suggested by the historical data, if there are adverse behavioral impacts (people borrowing money by increasing unemployment to build up negative balances at retirement). Without an actual field test of system of UISAs, it is difficult to draw any firm conclusions about its likely impacts.

CONCLUSIONS

The UI bonus experiments achieved their objective of providing credible estimates of the likely impacts of a UI bonus system. The experimental results indicate that bonuses are unlikely to have major impacts on unemployment and may only be marginally cost-effective.

The results are generally consistent across the experiments, although the magnitude of impacts varied. Impacts on benefit weeks were remarkably similar across the experiments (ranging from –0.40 to –0.65 week, excluding the FSC sample in Illinois), but the impacts on earnings were quite different (ranging from $250 in Illinois to –$88 in Washington). The Illinois experiment had the most positive impacts, leading to positive net benefits on all segments of society. The Pennsylvania experiment also yielded positive net benefits, but they were smaller than in Illinois. The Washington experiment yielded negative net benefits on all segments of society, although a few positive results did emerge for specific treatments. Despite the general similarity across experiments in average bonus amounts and qualification periods, the differences in net benefits across experiments are somewhat perplexing. Davidson and Woodbury hypothesize in Chapter 6 that differences in macroeconomic conditions across the three experimental sites (namely differences in job separation rates and growth rates in available jobs) could be responsible for the differences in net benefits across the sites.

The Illinois experiment had only one treatment and was not designed to test the sensitivity of responses to different treatment levels. The Pennsylvania and Washington experiments had several treatments and were specifically designed to test the sensitivity of responses to different treatment levels. However, the Pennsylvania and Washington experiments were not entirely successful in measuring the sensitivity of responses to different treatment levels. While the sample sizes for the entire experiments were adequate to measure experimental-control differences, the sample sizes for the individual treatments were probably not large enough to measure moderate differences in response across treatments.

Nonetheless, the evidence appears conclusive that bonuses are not the panacea originally envisioned. Allowing for macro effects that could not be measured by the experiments (higher UI take-up rate, higher bonus take-up rate, and crowding out) makes the evidence even less supportive of the bonus option.

Alternatives to bonuses have been proposed, but none appears to yield more desirable effects. Earnings supplements, tighter sanctioning, and increasing work-search requirements beyond their present levels all appear to be ineffective reforms. While some have suggested that worker profiling would improve net benefits, the evidence so far suggests that it is unlikely profiling would lead to consistently positive net benefits, although subsequent refinement of this technique may yield more positive results. However, the ability to identify key target groups is a difficult problem limiting the development of effective profiling models. Finally, the impacts of more radical reforms such as Unemployment Insurance Savings Accounts are largely speculative and may prove so inequitable that they would not be politically palatable.

The search for reform in the UI system is not as intense today as it has been in the past, largely because the economy has been healthy and unemployment has been much lower. Nonetheless, the search continues because the adverse work incentives still exist within the system and the economy might worsen in the future. As new approaches are developed, the evidence from this book strongly suggests that if at all possible, randomized experimental evaluations of such approaches should be undertaken. I believe randomized experiments provide the most effective way of gathering definitive evidence about the likely effects of a particular programmatic change and should be favored over non-experimental evaluation techniques. However, the worst possible action would be to adopt a new approach without any scientific evaluation at all.

Notes

1. There was a fourth UI bonus experiment conducted in New Jersey in 1986 and 1987. The New Jersey experiment had three treatments: job-search assistance, job-search assistance plus training or relocation, and job-search assistance plus a reemployment bonus. The New Jersey experiment is not considered in this book because the bonus offers were made only after seven weeks of insured unemployment, and hence could not be replicated in a real national program where information about the bonus would be available from the beginning of an insured unemployment spell. For details about the New Jersey experiment and its results, see U.S. Department of Labor (1989) and Meyer (1995).

2. The dollar amounts reported in Table 8.1 and subsequent tables pertain to the years in which the studies were conducted. If the reader wishes to convert the study year amounts to present-day dollars (say, for the year 2000), the study year amounts would be multiplied by the ratio of a price index in the year 2000 to the price index in the study year. If the study was conducted over more than one year, an average price index over the study years may be used as an approximation. One commonly used price index is the Consumer Price Index, or CPI. For example, in the case of the Illinois experiment, the study period was 1984 to 1985. The CPI for the year 2000 (1982–1984 = 100) was 172.2. The average CPI over the years 1984 to 1985 was 105.7. Thus the average weekly UI benefit in Illinois of $135 reported in Table 8.1 would be the equivalent of $200 in year-2000 dollars ($135 × 172.2/105.7). To convert Pennsylvania and Washington dollar amounts to year-2000 dollars, one would use the year 2000 CPI and the average CPI in Pennsylvania over the years 1988 to 1990 (which was 124.3) and the average CPI in Washington over the years 1988 to 1989 (which was 121.2). Similar calculations can be made for the other dollar amounts reported in this chapter.

3. As has been noted, Illinois also had a second experiment where bonuses were offered to employers, but extremely low participation precluded it from having any significant impacts. The employer experiment was not considered in this book because it differed from the experiments in Pennsylvania and Washington.

4. More than one treatment was tested in the Pennsylvania and Washington experiments because the success of the Illinois experiment encouraged policymakers to seek ways of finding the most cost-effective structure for a national bonus program. The Pennsylvania experiment tested a declining bonus offer (like in the New Jersey experiment) but, because it cannot be easily compared to a fixed bonus offer, it is not considered in this book.

5. The sample sizes for the Pennsylvania and Washington experiments were not determined on the basis of measuring differential impacts among the various treatments but rather were determined on the basis of measuring treatment-control impacts. By a parameterized model, it is meant that a response surface is estimated in which the treatments are quantified into a small number of continuous variables (like bonus amount or qualification period) rather than by a series of discrete dummy variables representing treatments. Thus, it was implicitly assumed

by the designers of the Pennsylvania and Washington experiments that differential impacts among the treatments would be estimated using a parsimonious response surface model. See, for example, Table 4.3 in Chapter 4.

6. There was no attempt to vary the preemployment period, which was set at four months in all three experiments.

7. See Lauzon (1995) for a discussion of the problem in Canada, Ross and Smith (1993) for a discussion of the problem in the United States, and OECD (1990) for a discussion of the problem in Europe.

8. The five cities were Saskatoon, Saskatchewan; Granby, Quebec; Winnipeg, Manitoba; Oshawa, Ontario; and Toronto, Ontario.

9. The information in this table was taken from Bloom et al. (1999). It only pertains to the program for displaced workers.

10. At an exchange rate of 0.75 Canadian dollars per U.S. dollar, the maximum supplement in U.S. dollars would be about $187.50.

11. The low percentage of treatment group members receiving a supplement in ESP may be due to the fact that UI recipients are unwilling to jeopardize long-run job prospects by taking a short-term lower-paying job. By taking a lower-paying job, claimants would have to reduce job-search behavior and might miss out on finding a new job more comparable to the predisplacement job.

12. The four experiments took place in Hartford, Connecticut; Worcester, Massachusetts; Nashville, Tennessee; and Falls Church, Virginia.

13. Other components of the treatment also did not have statistically significant impacts.

References

Ashenfelter, Orley, David Ashmore, and Olivier Deschênes. 2000. "Do Unemployment Insurance Recipients Actively Seek Work? Evidence from Randomized Trials in Four U.S. States." Princeton University, unpublished manuscript.

Bloom, Howard, Saul Schwartz, Susanna Lui-Gurr, Suk-Won Lee, Wendy Bancroft, and Jason Peng. 1999. *Testing a Re-Employment Incentive for Displaced Workers: The Earnings Supplement Project.* Ottawa: Social Research and Demonstration Corporation.

Council of Economic Advisers. 1999. *Economic Report of the President.* Washington, D.C.: U.S. Government Printing Office.

Eberts, Randall W., and Christopher J. O'Leary. 1996. "Profiling Unemployment Insurance Beneficiaries." *Employment Research* 3(2): 1, 3–4. W.E. Upjohn Institute for Employment Research, Kalamazoo, Michigan.

Feldstein, Martin, and David Altman. 1998. "Unemployment Insurance Savings Accounts." Working paper no. 6860, National Bureau of Economic Research, Cambridge, Massachusetts.

Johnson, Terry R., and Daniel H. Klepinger. 1994. "Experimental Evidence on Unemployment Insurance Work-Search Policies." *Journal of Human Resources* 29(3): 695–717.

Lauzon, Darren. 1995. *Worker Displacement—Trends, Characteristics, and Policy Responses.* Ottawa, Canada: Human Resources Development Canada.

Linkz, Donna. 1999. "The Unemployment Insurance Bonus Experiments." Unpublished manuscript, Catonsville Community College, Baltimore, Maryland.

Meyer, Bruce D. 1995. "Lessons from the U.S. Unemployment Insurance Experiments." *Journal of Economic Literature* 3 (1): 93 –131.

O'Leary, Christopher J., Paul Decker, and Stephen Wandner. 1997. "Reemployment Bonuses and Profiling." Working paper no. 98-051, W.E. Upjohn Institute for Employment Research, Kalamazoo, Michigan.

OECD. 1990. *Labor Market Policies for the 1990s.* Organisation for Economic Co-operation and Development, Paris, France.

Ross, Murray N., and Ralph E. Smith. 1993. *Displaced Workers: Trends in the 1980s and Implications for the Future.* Washington, D.C.: U.S. Congressional Budget Office.

United States Department of Labor. 1989. *The New Jersey Unemployment Insurance Reemployment Demonstration Project.* Unemployment Insurance Occasional Paper 89-3, Washington D.C.: United States Government Printing Office.

Glossary

UNEMPLOYMENT INSURANCE TERMS

Benefit Year

A 12-month period, generally starting with the Sunday of the week in which a claim is filed, during which time unemployment insurance (UI) benefits are payable. At the end of that period, a new benefit year must be established by earning a sufficient income to reestablish UI benefit entitlement.

Compensable Duration

The number of weeks that benefits are payable during the benefit year. In some states, it is a fixed number of weeks (e.g., in Illinois, 26). In other states, it is a variable number of weeks determined by the claimant's UI benefit entitlement divided by his or her weekly benefit amount (WBA).

Filing for Unemployment Insurance

The process by which an unemployed worker establishes a claim for payment of UI benefits. A prospective claimant files a claim to establish a benefit year.

Full Referral Union

A union that operates a hiring hall and takes full responsibility for placing its members in jobs. A claimant who is a member of such a union is work-search exempt.

Monetary Eligibility

The determination on the part of the UI agency that the claimant has sufficient earnings in the base period to be eligible to receive at least the minimum benefits.

Nonmonetary Eligibility

The determination on the part of the UI agency that the claimant is "able and available for work," a necessary condition for benefit payment, and does not have a separation issue (i.e., did not voluntarily quit a job or was not fired for cause).

Registration with Employment Service

Claimants are required to register with the Employment Service (ES; often called the Job Service) as part of the requirement that they must be seeking work to draw benefits. The Employment Service is the agency of the state government responsible for monitoring work search requirements for UI and in general providing a job-matching service for employers and job seekers.

Standby

A claimant who has been temporarily laid off of a job and whose employer has stated in writing that it is the intent to recall that claimant within 60 days of layoff. A claimant on standby is work-search exempt.

UI Benefit Entitlement

The total benefits that a claimant could draw over his or her benefit year. The entitlement is determined in each state as a specified fraction of the claimant's earnings during a given period, called the base period.

Waiting Week

Most states (including all three states that ran the experiments described in this book) require that claimants forgo payment during the first week of the benefit year, after which the period of compensable duration begins. After serving the waiting week and the first compensable week, the claimant files for the first compensable week's benefits.

Weekly Benefit Amount

The maximum benefit payable in a compensable week. The WBA is set as a fixed proportion of a claimant's full-time weekly wage, with both minimum and maximum amounts set by each state.

Work-Search Exempt

A claimant status in which the claimant is eligible to receive UI benefit payments without meeting the work-search requirements.

BONUS EXPERIMENT TERMS

Assignment to the Experiment

A random process of allocating eligible members of a population to experimental groups (called treatments). It is usually accomplished by giving each eligible member of the population a number, which has been selected by a random process, and then allocating those numbers to the different experimental groups, including the control group.

Agreement to Participate

Used in Illinois only, it is the conscious decision to enroll in the experiment, expressed by signing an agreement to participate.

Bonus Voucher

The form that the claimant submits to the administrating agency requesting payment of the bonus. The form states that the claimant believes he or she has met all the requirements for the bonus.

Eligibility for the Bonus Program

Designation of a set of characteristics that define an individual who is eligible to be enrolled in the experiment. Some characteristics, such as filing an initial claim for UI benefits, are universal across the three experiments. Other characteristics, such as registering with the ES or not being on standby, are conditions of eligibility selected by some (but not all three) experiments.

Notice of Hire (NOH)

A form submitted by the claimant stating that he or she had become fully employed by the end of the qualification period and had met other conditions for bonus eligibility, such as not being recalled to a previous job (in Pennsylvania and Washington).

Qualification Period

The length of time from the date of enrollment into the experiment to the date by which the participating claimant must obtain a full-time job in order to be eligible for a bonus.

Reemployment Period

The length of time after obtaining a qualifying job that the participating claimant must remain fully employed in order to receive a bonus.

Cited Author Index

The italic letters *f*, *n*, or *t* following a page number indicate that the cited name is within a figure, note, or table, respectively, on that page.

Aigner, Dennis J., 176, 220
Altman, David, 269, 273
Anderson, Patricia M., 22, 173, 173*n*14, 205n7, 220
Ashenfelter, Orley, 11, 21, 263, 265*t*, 273
Ashmore, David, 11, 21, 263, 265*t*, 273
Atkinson, Anthony B., 207, 220

Bailey, Martin N., 5, 21
Bancroft, Wendy, 273
Benus, Jacob, 12, 21
Blank, Rebecca M., 191, 205*n*7, 208, 210, 220
Blaustein, Saul, 3, 4, 21
Bloom, Howard, 263*n*, 273, 273*n*9
Burgess, Paul L., 6, 9, 20*n*4, 21
Burtless, Gary, 4, 5, 6, 21
Byers, James F., 21, 222

Card, David E., 191, 205*n*7, 208, 210, 220
Classen, Kathleen P., 6, 22
Cohen, Jacob, 40, 43, 44, 72*n*19, 74
Conlisk, J., 72*n*14, 74
Corson, Walter, 8, 9, 10, 20*n*6, 20*n*11, 22, 46, 58*t*, 67*t*, 71*n*11, 74, 108, 144*n*6, 145, 153, 172*n*2, 173, 174, 237*t*, 246

Davidson, Carl, 7, 22, 106, 145, 176, 178, 197, 198, 199, 200, 204*n*3, 204*n*4, 204*n*5, 206*n*13, 213, 215, 220, 220*n*4, 221, 236*t*, 246
Decker, Paul T., 6, 22, 74, 143*n*1, 145, 153, 172*n*3, 173, 173*n*8, 174, 238, 239*t*, 242*t*, 246, 267, 268*t*, 274
Deschênes, Olivier, 11, 21, 263, 265*t*, 273

Diamond, Peter A., 207, 221
Dunstan, Shari Miller, 22, 74, 145, 174, 246

Eberts, Randall W., 267, 273
Ehrenberg, Ronald G., 20*n*4, 22
Eliason-Kisker, Ellen, 9, 22

Fair, Jerilyn, 25, 74
Feldstein, Martin, 5, 22, 269, 273
Fisher, R.A., 25, 74
Freeman, Howard E., 40, 74

Garfinkel, Irwin, 74, 176, 221
Gomulka, J., 220
Gordon, Anne R., 22, 174
Gordon, Robert J., 225, 229, 232, 246
Grover, Neelima, 12, 21
Gueron, Judith, 71*n*8, 74

Hansen, W. Lee, 21, 222
Hausman, Jerry, 40, 69*n*1, 74, 220
Heckman, James J., 192, 221
Hershey, Alan, 8, 22
Hicks, Charles R., 25, 74
Holen, Arlene, 20*n*4, 22
Homrighausen, John, 22

Johnson, Terry R., 10, 11, 20*n*6, 22, 264, 265, 266*t*, 274

Kaldor, N., 246
Kerachsky, Stuart, 8, 9, 22, 48, 51, 73*n*23, 74, 145, 174, 246
Kershaw, David, 25, 74
Kiefer, Nicholas M., 144*n*13, 146
Kingston, Jerry L., 6, 9, 20*n*4, 21
Klepinger, Daniel H., 10, 11, 20*n*6, 22, 264, 265, 266*t*, 274

279

SUBJECT INDEX

The italic letters *f, n,* or *t* following a page number indicate that the subject information is in a figure, note, or a table, respectively, on that page.

Adjusted treatment impacts, 112–116
    differences between experimental
        and control groups, 114*t*–115*t*
Administrative costs, 72*n*15, 230
    for ongoing bonus offer program,
        247*t*
    See also Costs
Age
    in control groups, 55*t*
    partial bonus qualification and, 84,
        90
Allocation model, 73*n*23
    in Pennsylvania sample design, 46
Assignment, to experiments, 62–64
Automated job matching, 9

B/C ratios. *See* Benefit-cost analysis
Backdated claims, 33–34
Base period, for unemployment
    compensation, 4
Base period earnings (BPE)
    adjusted treatment impacts and,
        112–116
    as partial qualification variable, 85
BCA. *See* Benefit-cost analysis
Behavioral changes, with efficiency
    implications, 177, 180–182
Benefit(s)
    in control groups, 55*t*
    exhausted, 4
    reduction of, 228
    See also Benefit-cost analysis
Benefit-cost analysis (BCA), 19,
    223–245
    adjustment to estimations in move
        from experiment to program,
        240–243

aggregation of effects and
    interpretation of results,
    231–238
for four hypothetical programs,
    238–240, 239*t*
Benefit groups, target efficiency and, 77
Benefit payments, sample design for, 41
Benefit year, 4
Benefits Rights Interview (BRI), 11
Biases, examining treatment impacts by
    population subgroup and, 136
Bonus
    characteristics as partial qualification
        variable, 85
    collection of, 192
    continuous variables model of
        impacts, 116–121
    declining, 143*n*3
    explaining variations in qualification,
        receipt, and take-up rates, 78–84,
        79*t*
    extending period of qualification, 94
    groups responding to, 77–78
    higher amounts and insured
        unemployment duration, 81
    in Illinois, 71*n*10
    impact on receipt of unemployment
        insurance, 105–106
    implementing program, 175–206
    larger offers and larger take-up rates,
        93
    levels tested, 111
    qualification for, 205*n*8
    qualification period lengths tested,
        111
    reasons for unemployment reduced
        by, 7
    setting take-up rate, 193

286

About the Institute

The W.E. Upjohn Institute for Employment Research is a nonprofit research organization devoted to finding and promoting solutions to employment-related problems at the national, state, and local levels. It is an activity of the W.E. Upjohn Unemployment Trustee Corporation, which was established in 1932 to administer a fund set aside by the late Dr. W.E. Upjohn, founder of The Upjohn Company, to seek ways to counteract the loss of employment income during economic downturns.

The Institute is funded largely by income from the W.E. Upjohn Unemployment Trust, supplemented by outside grants, contracts, and sales of publications. Activities of the Institute comprise the following elements: 1) a research program conducted by a resident staff of professional social scientists; 2) a competitive grant program, which expands and complements the internal research program by providing financial support to researchers outside the Institute; 3) a publications program, which provides the major vehicle for disseminating the research of staff and grantees, as well as other selected works in the field; and 4) an Employment Management Services division, which manages most of the publicly funded employment and training programs in the local area.

The broad objectives of the Institute's research, grant, and publication programs are to 1) promote scholarship and experimentation on issues of public and private employment and unemployment policy, and 2) make knowledge and scholarship relevant and useful to policymakers in their pursuit of solutions to employment and unemployment problems.

Current areas of concentration for these programs include causes, consequences, and measures to alleviate unemployment; social insurance and income maintenance programs; compensation; workforce quality; work arrangements; family labor issues; labor-management relations; and regional economic development and local labor markets.